TABLE OF CONTENTS

Top 20 Test Taking Tips

1. Carefully follow all the test registration procedures
2. Know the test directions, duration, topics, question types, how many questions
3. Setup a flexible study schedule at least 3-4 weeks before test day
4. Study during the time of day you are most alert, relaxed, and stress free
5. Maximize your learning style; visual learner use visual study aids, auditory learner use auditory study aids
6. Focus on your weakest knowledge base
7. Find a study partner to review with and help clarify questions
8. Practice, practice, practice
9. Get a good night's sleep; don't try to cram the night before the test
10. Eat a well balanced meal
11. Know the exact physical location of the testing site; drive the route to the site prior to test day
12. Bring a set of ear plugs; the testing center could be noisy
13. Wear comfortable, loose fitting, layered clothing to the testing center; prepare for it to be either cold or hot during the test
14. Bring at least 2 current forms of ID to the testing center
15. Arrive to the test early; be prepared to wait and be patient
16. Eliminate the obviously wrong answer choices, then guess the first remaining choice
17. Pace yourself; don't rush, but keep working and move on if you get stuck
18. Maintain a positive attitude even if the test is going poorly
19. Keep your first answer unless you are positive it is wrong
20. Check your work, don't make a careless mistake

Biological Science

Cells in living organisms

The functions of plant and animal cells vary greatly, and the functions of different cells within a single organism can also be vastly different. Animal and plant cells are similar in structure in that they are eukaryotic, which means they contain a nucleus. The nucleus is a round structure that controls the activities of the cell and contains chromosomes. Both types of cells have cell membranes, cytoplasm, vacuoles, and other structures. The main difference between the two is that plant cells have a cell wall made of cellulose that can handle high levels of pressure within the cell, which can occur when liquid enters a plant cell. Plant cells have chloroplasts that are used during the process of photosynthesis, which is the conversion of sunlight into food. Plant cells usually have one large vacuole, whereas animal cells can have many smaller ones. Plant cells have a regular shape, while the shapes of animal cell can vary.

Nuclear parts of a cell

Nucleus (pl. nuclei): This is a small structure that contains the chromosomes and regulates the DNA of a cell. The nucleus is the defining structure of eukaryotic cells, and all eukaryotic cells have a nucleus. The nucleus is responsible for the passing on of genetic traits between generations. The nucleus contains a nuclear envelope, nucleoplasm, a nucleolus, nuclear pores, chromatin, and ribosomes.

Chromosomes: These are highly condensed, threadlike rods of DNA. Short for deoxyribonucleic acid, DNA is the genetic material that stores information about the plant or animal.

Chromatin: This consists of the DNA and protein that make up chromosomes.

Nucleolus (nucleole): This structure contained within the nucleus consists of protein. It is small, round, does not have a membrane, is involved in protein synthesis, and synthesizes and stores RNA (ribonucleic acid).

Nuclear envelope: This encloses the structures of the nucleus. It consists of inner and outer membranes made of lipids.

Nuclear pores: These are involved in the exchange of material between the nucleus and the cytoplasm.

Nucleoplasm: This is the liquid within the nucleus, and is similar to cytoplasm.

Cell structure

Ribosomes: Ribosomes are involved in synthesizing proteins from amino acids. They are numerous, making up about one quarter of the cell. Some cells contain thousands of ribosome. Some are mobile and some are embedded in the rough endoplasmic reticulum.

Golgi complex (Golgi apparatus): This is involved in synthesizing materials such as proteins that are transported out of the cell. It is located near the nucleus and consists of layers of membranes.

Vacuoles: These are sacs used for storage, digestion, and waste removal. There is one large vacuole in plant cells. Animal cells have small, sometimes numerous vacuoles.

Vesicle: This is a small organelle within a cell. It has a membrane and performs varying functions, including moving materials within a cell.

Cytoskeleton: This consists of microtubules that help shape and support the cell.

Microtubules: These are part of the cytoskeleton and help support the cell. They are made of protein.

Cytosol: This is the liquid material in the cell. It is mostly water, but also contains some floating molecules.

Cytoplasm: This is a general term that refers to cytosol and the substructures (organelles) found within the plasma membrane, but not within the nucleus.

Cell membrane (plasma membrane): This defines the cell by acting as a barrier. It helps keeps cytoplasm in and substances located outside the cell out. It also determines what is allowed to enter and exit the cell.

Endoplasmic reticulum: The two types of endoplasmic reticulum are rough (has ribosomes on the surface) and smooth (does not have ribosomes on the surface). It is a tubular network that comprises the transport system of a cell. It is fused to the nuclear membrane and extends through the cytoplasm to the cell membrane.

Mitochondrion (pl. mitochondria): These cell structures vary in terms of size and quantity. Some cells may have one mitochondrion, while others have thousands. This structure performs various functions such as generating ATP, and is also involved in cell growth and death. Mitochondria contain their own DNA that is separate from that contained in the nucleus.

Plant cell structure

Cell wall: Made of cellulose and composed of numerous layers, the cell wall provides plants with a sturdy barrier that can hold fluid within the cell. The cell wall surrounds the cell membrane.

Chloroplast: This is a specialized organelle that plant cells use for photosynthesis, which is the process plants use to create food energy from sunlight. Chloroplasts contain chlorophyll, which has a green color.

Plastid: This is a membrane-bound organelle found in plant cells that is used to make chemical compounds and store food. It can also contain pigments used during photosynthesis. Plastids can develop into more specialized structures such as chloroplasts, chromoplasts (make and hold yellow and orange pigments), amyloplasts (store starch), and leucoplasts (lack pigments, but can become differentiated).

Plasmodesmata (sing. plasmodesma): These are channels between the cell walls of plant cells that allow for transport between cells.

Animal cell structure

Centrosome: This is comprised of the pair of centrioles located at right angles to each other and surrounded by protein. The centrosome is involved in mitosis and the cell cycle.

Centriole: These are cylinder-shaped structures near the nucleus that are involved in cellular division. Each cylinder consists of nine groups of three microtubules. Centrioles occur in pairs.

Lysosome: This digests proteins, lipids, and carbohydrates, and also transports undigested substances to the cell membrane so they can be removed. The shape of a lysosome depends on the material being transported.

Cilia (singular: cilium): These are appendages extending from the surface of the cell, the movement of which causes the cell to move. They can also result in fluid being moved by the cell.

Flagella: These are tail-like structures on cells that use whip-like movements to help the cell move. They are similar to cilia, but are usually longer and not as numerous. A cell usually only has one or a few flagella.

Lipid, organelle, RNA, polymer, monomer, nucleotides, and nucleoid

Lipids take many forms and have varying functions, such as storing energy and acting as a building block of cell membranes. Lipids are produced by anabolysis.

Organelle: This is a general term that refers to an organ or smaller structure within a cell. Membrane-bound organelles are found in eukaryotic cells.

RNA: RNA is short for ribonucleic acid, which is a type of molecule that consists of a long chain (polymer) of nucleotide units.

Polymer: This is a compound of large molecules formed by repeating monomers.

Monomer: A monomer is a small molecule. It is a single compound that forms chemical bonds with other monomers to make a polymer.

Nucleotides: These are molecules that combine to form DNA and RNA. They can be easily stained to make them more visible.

Nucleoid: This is the nucleus-like, irregularly-shaped mass of DNA that contains the chromatin in a prokaryotic cell.

Eukaryotic and prokaryotic cells

The main difference between eukaryotic and prokaryotic cells is that eukaryotic cells have a nucleus and prokaryotic cells do not. Eukaryotic cells are considered more complex, while prokaryotic cells are smaller and simpler. Eukaryotic cells have membrane-bound organelles that perform various functions and contribute to the complexity of these types of cells. Prokaryotic cells do not contain membrane-bound organelles. In prokaryotic cells, the genetic material (DNA) is not contained within a membrane-bound nucleus. Instead, it aggregates in the cytoplasm in a nucleoid. In eukaryotic cells, DNA is mostly contained in chromosomes in the nucleus, although there is some DNA in mitochondria and chloroplasts. Prokaryotic cells usually divide by binary fission and are haploid. Eukaryotic cells divide by mitosis and are diploid. Prokaryotic structures include plasmids, ribosomes, cytoplasm, a cytoskeleton, granules of nutritional substances, a plasma membrane, flagella, and a few others. They are single-celled organisms. Bacteria are prokaryotic cells.

Plant and animal cell differences

Plant cells can be much larger than animal cells, ranging from 10 to 100 micrometers. Animal cells are 10 to 30 micrometers in size. Plant cells can have much larger vacuoles that occupy a large portion of the cell. They also have cell walls, which are thick barriers consisting of protein and sugars. Animal cells lack cell walls. Chloroplasts in plants that perform photosynthesis absorb sunlight and convert it into energy. Mitochondria produce energy from food in animal cells. Plant and animal cells are both eukaryotic, meaning they contain a nucleus. Both plant and animal cells duplicate genetic material, separate it, and then divide in half to reproduce. Plant cells build a cell plate between the two new cells, while animal cells make a cleavage furrow and pinch in half. Microtubules are components of the cytoskeleton in both plant and animal cells. Microtubule organizing centers (MTOCs) make microtubules in plant cells, while centrioles make microtubules in animal cells.

Mitochondria functions

Four functions of mitochondria are: the production of cell energy, cell signaling (how communications are carried out within a cell, cellular differentiation (the process whereby a non-differentiated cell becomes transformed into a cell with a more specialized purpose), and cell cycle and growth regulation (the process whereby the cell gets ready to reproduce and reproduces). Mitochondria are numerous in eukaryotic cells. There may be hundreds or even thousands of mitochondria in a single cell. Mitochondria can be involved in many functions, their main one being supplying the cell with energy. Mitochondria consist of an inner and outer membrane. The inner membrane encloses the matrix, which contains the mitochondrial DNA (mtDNA) and ribosomes. Between the inner and outer membranes are folds (cristae). Chemical reactions occur here that release energy, control water levels in cells, and recycle and create proteins and fats. Aerobic respiration also occurs in the mitochondria.

Cellular respiration

Cellular respiration refers to a set of metabolic reactions that convert chemical bonds into energy stored in the form of ATP. Respiration includes many oxidation and reduction reactions that occur thanks to the electron transport system within the cell. Oxidation is a loss of electrons and reduction is a gain of electrons. Electrons in C-H (carbon/hydrogen) and C-C (carbon/carbon) bonds are donated to oxygen atoms. Processes involved in cellular respiration include glycolysis, the Krebs cycle, the electron transport chain, and chemiosmosis. The two forms of respiration are aerobic and anaerobic. Aerobic respiration is very common, and oxygen is the final electron acceptor. In anaerobic respiration, the final electron acceptor is not oxygen. Aerobic respiration results in more ATP than anaerobic respiration. Fermentation is another process by which energy is converted.

Photosynthesis

Photosynthesis is the conversion of sunlight into energy in plant cells, and also occurs in some types of bacteria and protists. Carbon dioxide and water are converted into glucose during photosynthesis, and light is required during this process. Cyanobacteria are thought to be the descendants of the first organisms to use photosynthesis about 3.5 billion years ago. Photosynthesis is a form of cellular respiration. It occurs in chloroplasts that use thylakoids, which are structures in the membrane that contain light reaction chemicals. Chlorophyll is a pigment that absorbs light. During the process, water is used and oxygen is released. The equation for the chemical reaction that occurs during photosynthesis is $6H_2O + 6CO_2 \rightarrow C_6H_{12}O_6 + 6O_2$. During photosynthesis, six molecules of water and six molecules of carbon dioxide react to form one molecule of sugar and six molecules of oxygen.

Cell transport mechanisms

Active transport mechanisms include exocytosis and endocytosis. Active transport involves transferring substances from areas of lower concentration to areas of higher concentration. Active transport requires energy in the form of ATP. Endocytosis is the ingestion of large particles into a cell, and can be categorized as phagocytosis (ingestion of a particle), pinocytosis (ingestion of a liquid), or receptor mediated. Endocytosis occurs when a substance is too large to cross a cell membrane. Endocytosis is a process by which eukaryotes ingest food particles. During phagocytosis, cell eating vesicles used during ingestion are quickly formed and unformed. Pinocytosis is also known as cell drinking. Exocytosis is the opposite of endocytosis. It is the expulsion or discharge of substances from a cell. A lysosome digests particles with enzymes, and can be expelled through exocytosis. A vacuole containing the substance to be expelled attaches to the cell membrane and expels the substance.

Passive transport mechanisms

Transport mechanisms allow for the movement of substances through membranes. Passive transport mechanisms include simple and facilitated diffusion and osmosis. They do not require energy from the cell. Diffusion is when particles are transported from areas of higher concentration to areas of lower concentration. When equilibrium is reached, diffusion stops. Examples are gas exchange (carbon dioxide and oxygen) during photosynthesis and the transport of oxygen from air to blood and from blood to tissue. Facilitated diffusion is when specific molecules are transported by a specific carrier protein. Carrier proteins vary in terms of size, shape, and charge. Glucose and amino acids are examples of substances transported by carrier proteins. Osmosis is the diffusion of water through a semi-permeable membrane from an area of higher concentration to one of lower concentration. Examples of osmosis include the absorption of water by plant roots and the alimentary canal. Plants lose and gain water through osmosis. A plant cell that swells because of water retention is said to be turgid.

Cell cycle

The term cell cycle refers to the process by which a cell reproduces, which involves cell growth, the duplication of genetic material, and cell division. Complex organisms with many cells use the cell cycle to replace cells as they lose their functionality and wear out. The entire cell cycle in animal cells can take 24 hours. The time required varies among different cell types. Human skin cells, for example, are constantly reproducing. Some other cells only divide infrequently. Once neurons are mature, they do not grow or divide. The two ways that cells can reproduce are through meiosis and mitosis. When cells replicate through mitosis, the "daughter cell" is an exact replica of the parent cell. When cells divide through meiosis, the daughter cells have different genetic coding than the parent cell. Meiosis only happens in specialized reproductive cells called gametes.

Water and gases

Water molecules are important for many reasons. Most cells are mainly composed of water, water is a great solvent for ionic compounds such as salts, water acts as a transport medium for polar solutes, metabolic reactions happen in solutions that contain water, water can act as a temperature buffer for enzyme-catalyzed reactions, water is used in photosynthesis, and water molecules are used or formed in oxidation and reduction reactions. Carbon dioxide is used by plants during photosynthesis, which produces oxygen. Oxygen is used by organisms during respiration. Nitrogen is also used by organisms. Nitrogen is a nutrient for plants, and is also used in the formation of amino and nucleic acids after it is reduced (nitrogen fixation), which is important for cell growth and reproduction. Gases are also used during the formation and break down of biologically important molecules, including proteins, nucleic acids, carbohydrates, and lipids. Carbohydrates, for example, are made of carbon, hydrogen, and oxygen.

Cell division

Cell division is performed in organisms so they can grow and replace cells that are old, worn out, or damaged.

Chromatids: During cell division, the DNA is replicated, and chromatids are the two identical replicated pieces of chromosome that are joined at the centromere to form an "X."

Gametes: These are cells used by organisms to reproduce sexually. Gametes in humans are haploid, meaning they contain only half of the organism's genetic information (23 chromosomes). Other human cells contain all 46 chromosomes.

Haploid/diploid: Haploid means there is one set of chromosomes. Diploid means there are two sets of chromosomes (one set from each parent).

Cytokinesis: This is the splitting of a cell (including the cytoplasm) into two cells. Some believe this occurs following telophase. Others say it occurs from anaphase, as the cell begins to furrow, through telophase, when the cell actually splits into two.

Homeostasis, gene expression, transcription, translation, and cellular differentiation

Homeostasis: This describes the ability and tendency of an organism, cell, or body to adjust to environmental changes to maintain equilibrium.

Gene expression: This refers to the use of information in a gene, usually during the processes of transcription and translation, that result in a protein product.

Transcription: This refers to the synthesis of RNA. Information is provided by DNA.

Translation: This is the decoding of mRNA (messenger RNA) used in the fabrication of protein. It occurs after transcription.

Cellular differentiation: This is the process by which a less specialized cell becomes a more specialized cell.

Size: The size of the nucleus in a eukaryotic cell is about 6 micrometers (μm). It occupies about 10 percent of the cell. A chloroplast is about 1 μm. Plant and animal cell sizes range from about 10 μm to 100 μm, while the sizes of bacteria range from about 1 μm to 10 μm. Atoms have a size of about 0.1 μm.

Meiosis

Meiosis has the same phases as mitosis, but they happen twice. In addition, different events occur during some phases of meiosis than mitosis. The events that occur during the first phase of meiosis are interphase (I), prophase (I), metaphase (I), anaphase (I), telophase (I), and cytokinesis (I). During this first phase of meiosis, chromosomes cross over, genetic material is exchanged, and tetrads of four chromatids are formed. The nuclear membrane dissolves. Homologous pairs of chromatids are separated and travel to different poles. At this point, there has been one cell division resulting in two cells. Each cell goes through a second cell division, which consists of prophase (II), metaphase (II), anaphase (II), telophase (II), and cytokinesis (II). The result is four daughter cells with different sets of chromosomes. The daughter cells are haploid, which means they contain half the genetic material of the parent cell. The second phase of meiosis is similar to the process of mitosis. Meiosis encourages genetic diversity.

Mitosis

Interphase: The cell prepares for division by replicating its genetic and cytoplasmic material. Interphase can be further divided into G_1, S, and G_2.

Prophase: The chromatin thickens into chromosomes and the nuclear membrane begins to disintegrate. Pairs of centrioles move to opposite sides of the cell and spindle fibers begin to form. The mitotic spindle, formed from cytoskeleton parts, moves chromosomes around within the cell.

Metaphase: The spindle moves to the center of the cell and chromosome pairs align along the center of the spindle structure.

Anaphase: The pairs of chromosomes, called sisters, begin to pull apart, and may bend. When they are separated, they are called daughter chromosomes. Grooves appear in the cell membrane.

Telophase: The spindle disintegrates, the nuclear membranes reform, and the chromosomes revert to chromatin. In animal cells, the membrane is pinched. In plant cells, a new cell wall begins to form.

Cytokinesis: This is the physical splitting of the cell (including the cytoplasm) into two cells. Some believe this occurs following telophase. Others say it occurs from anaphase, as the cell begins to furrow, through telophase, when the cell actually splits into two.

Cancerous cells

In cancerous cells, the DNA or gene structure is disrupted. Abnormal numbers of chromosomes can develop. Cancer cells can have defective Krebs cycles, and get most of their energy from glycolysis rather than the Krebs cycle. Normal cells get about 70% of their energy from the Krebs cycle and about 20% from glycolysis. In addition, normal cells usually use oxygen during energy production, while cancer cells mainly produce energy without using oxygen. Cancerous cells lack a blood vessel system and use amino acids to construct it, while normal cells have a built-in blood vessel system. Cancer cells over populate and are very active, making more demands on system resources. The enzymes and hormones involved with cancer cells tend to be overactive or underactive, which can lead to other problems.

Cell theory

The basic tenets of cell theory are that all living things are made up of cells and that cell are the basic units of life. Cell theory has evolved over time and is subject to interpretation. The development of cell theory is attributed to Matthias Schleiden and Theodor Schwann, who developed the theory in the early 1800s. Early cell theory was comprised of four statements: all organisms (living things) are made of cells; new cells are formed from pre-existing cells; all cells are similar; and cells are the most basic units of life. Other concepts related to classic and modern cell theory include statements such as: cells provide the basic units of functionality and structure in living things; cells are both distinct stand-alone units and basic building blocks; energy flow occurs within cells; cells contain genetic information in the form of DNA; and all cells consist of mostly the same chemicals.

Enzymes

Enzymes can be divided into six classes: oxidoreductase, transferase, hydrolase, lyase, isomerase, and ligase. These classes end with the suffix "ase," which is true of most enzymes. Each enzyme catalyzes a chemical reaction. Oxidoreductase enzymes catalyze oxidation reduction (redox) reactions, during which hydrogen and oxygen are gained or lost. Examples include cytochrome oxidase, lactate, and dehydrogenase. Transferase enzymes catalyze the transfer of functional groups, such as the amino or phosphate group. Examples include acetate kinase and alanine deaminase. Hydrolase enzymes break chemical bonds by using water. Examples include lipase and sucrase. Lyase enzymes break chemical bonds or remove groups of atoms without using water. Examples include oxalate decarboxylase and isocitrate lyase. Isomerase enzymes catalyze the rearrangement of atoms within a molecule. Examples include glucose-phosphate isomerase and alanine racemase. Ligase enzymes join two molecules by forming a bond between atoms. Examples of ligases are acetyl-CoA synthetase and DNA ligase.

Metabolism, macromolecules, metabolic pathways, anabolic and catabolic reactions

Metabolism is all of the chemical reactions that take place within a living organism. These chemical changes convert nutrients to energy and macromolecules. Macromolecules are large and complex, and play an important role in cell structure and function. Metabolic pathways refer to a series of reactions in which the product of one reaction is the substrate for the next. These pathways are dependent upon enzymes that act as catalysts. An anabolic reaction is one that builds larger and more complex molecules (macromolecules) from smaller ones. Catabolic reactions are the opposite. Larger molecules are broken down into smaller, simpler molecules. Catabolic reactions release energy, while anabolic ones require energy. The four basic organic macromolecules produced by anabolic reactions are carbohydrates (polysaccharides), nucleic acids, proteins, and lipids. The four basic building blocks involved in catabolic reactions are monosaccharides (glucose), amino acids, fatty acids (glycerol), and nucleotides.

Catabolism

Catabolism is the biosynthetic process by which macromolecules are broken down into smaller molecules. During this process, both energy and molecules that are used in anabolic processes are produced. Hydrolysis is a process used in catabolism. The four main groups of molecules produced through catabolism are monosaccharides (glucose), amino acids, fatty acids (glycerol), and nucleotides. Carbohydrates (polysaccharides) are broken down into sugars or glucose. It is the oxidation of carbohydrates that provides the cells with most of their energy. Glucose can be further broken down by respiration or fermentation by glycolysis. The first step of glycolysis breaks down pyruvic acid with the byproducts of NADH and ATP. Pyruvic acid can then be used in the Krebs cycle or in fermentation. Glycolysis occurs in the cytoplasm of eukaryotic cells. Fatty acids are long chains that are oxidized to acetyl-CoA, which provides energy to cells. Nucleic acids consist of nucleotides. Nucleotide triphosphates such as ATP carry energy. They also release energy when their bonds are broken.

Anabolism

Anabolism is a form of biosynthesis. It usually involves a series of steps, or pathways, where the product of one reaction is used in the next. Anabolism uses smaller molecules to build carbohydrates (polysaccharides), nucleic acids, amino acids and proteins, and lipids. Energy is used and stored during this process. Anabolic reactions can form a variety of macromolecules. An example of polysaccharide biosynthesis in animals and bacteria is glycolysis, the formation of glycogen from glucose with covalent bonds. Examples of nucleic acid synthesis include the formation of DNA, RNA, ATP, and other macromolecules. It can be achieved by either the pentose phosphate or Entner Doudoroff pathways. Protein biosynthesis uses amino acids, which are intermediate products of the Krebs cycle. Lipid biosynthesis uses fatty acids, which are formed from acetyl CoA (coenzyme A) during the

Krebs cycle, and glycerol, which is derived from dihydroxyacetone phosphate and glycolysis.

Proteins

Proteins are macromolecules formed from amino acids. They are polypeptides, which consist of many (10 to 100) peptides linked together. The peptide connections are the result of condensation reactions. A condensation reaction results in a loss of water when two molecules are joined together. A hydrolysis reaction is the opposite of a condensation reaction. During hydrolysis, water is added. -H is added to one of the smaller molecules and OH is added to another molecule being formed. A peptide is a compound of two or more amino acids. Amino acids are formed by the partial hydrolysis of protein, which forms an amide bond. This partial hydrolysis involves an amine group and a carboxylic acid. In the carbon chain of amino acids, there is a carboxylic acid group (-COOH), an amine group (-NH_2), a central carbon atom between them with an attached hydrogen, and an attached "R" group (side chain), which is different for different amino acids. It is the "R" group that determines the properties of the protein.

Types of proteins

Alkyl: This is a nonpolar group that forms hydrophobic amino acids. Amino acids include glycine with a single hydrogen atom R group, alanine with a methyl R group, and valine with an isopropyl R group. Leucine and isoleucine also have alkyl side chains.

Hydroxyl: This is a polar group that forms hydrophilic amino acids such as serine and threonine.

Sulfur: Amino acids in this group include cysteine and methionine.

Carboxylic acid: In proteins belonging to this group, a second carboxylic acid group is attached as the R group. This acid group is polar and can be negatively charged when the acidic proton attaches to a water molecule, which leaves a negatively charged carboxylate ion. Proteins that belong to this group include aspartic acid and glutamic acid.
Amide: The formula for amides is -$CONH_2$. Proteins belonging to this group include glutamine and asparagine.

Amino: This group includes lysine, arginine, and histidine. The double-bonded nitrogen atom can take a proton to become positively charged.

Aromatic: This group has a ring structure, and includes the proteins phenylalanine, tyrosine, and tryptophan. Tyrosine is polar, while tryptophan and phenylalanine are nonpolar.

Looped: This group includes praline. Because it is nonpolar, it forms a ring rather than a chain.

Chemiosmosis and enzymes

Chemiosmosis is a process by which energy is made available for ADP to form ATP. When electrons move down the electron transport chain, the energy pumps protons to one side of a membrane. The equilibrium is disrupted at this point because the concentration gradient where the protons have gathered is greater than the concentration gradient on the other side of the membrane. The protons diffuse through the membrane as a result. The energy of this process fuels phosphorylation.

Enzymes act as catalysts by lowering the activation energy necessary for a reaction. They are proteins, have specific functions, are often globular and 3-D in form, and have names that end in "-ase." An enzyme has an active site where a substrate attaches and products are formed and released. Most enzymes also need a non-protein coenzyme that attaches to the enzyme to form the active site.

Nucleic acids

Nucleic acids are macromolecules that are composed of nucleotides. Hydrolysis is a reaction in which water is broken down into hydrogen cations (H or H^+) and hydroxide anions (OH or OH^-). This is part of the process by which nucleic acids are broken down by enzymes to produce shorter strings of RNA and DNA (oligonucleotides). Oligonucleotides are broken down into smaller sugar nitrogenous units called nucleosides. These can be digested by cells since the sugar is divided from the nitrogenous base. This, in turn, leads to the formation of the five types of nitrogenous bases, sugars, and the preliminary substances involved in the synthesis of new RNA and DNA. DNA and RNA have a double helix shape.

Macromolecular nucleic acid polymers, such as RNA and DNA, are formed from nucleotides, which are monomeric units joined by phosphodiester bonds. Cells require energy in the form of ATP to synthesize proteins from amino acids and replicate DNA. Nitrogen fixation is used to synthesize nucleotides for DNA and amino acids for proteins. Nitrogen fixation uses the enzyme nitrogenase in the reduction of dinitrogen gas (N_2) to ammonia (NH_3). Nucleic acids store information and energy and are also important catalysts. It is the RNA that catalyzes the transfer of DNA genetic information into protein coded information. ATP is an RNA nucleotide. Nucleotides are used to form the nucleic acids. Nucleotides are made of a five carbon sugar, such as ribose or deoxyribose, a nitrogenous base, and one or more phosphates. Nucleotides consisting of more than one phosphate can also store energy in their bonds.

Lipids

Carbohydrates, proteins, and nucleic acids are groups of macromolecules that are polymers. Lipids are not long polymers with high molecular weights. They are hydrophobic, meaning they do not bond well with water or mix well with water solutions. Lipids have numerous C-H bonds. In this way, they are similar to hydrocarbons (substances consisting only of carbon and hydrogen).The major roles of lipids include energy storage and structural functions. Examples of lipids include fats, phospholipids, steroids, and waxes. Fats are made of long chains of fatty acids (three fatty acids bound to a glycerol). Fatty acids are chains with reduced carbon at one end and a carboxylic acid group at the other. An example is soap, which contains the sodium salts of free fatty acids. Phospholipids are lipids that have a

- 15 -

phosphate group rather than a fatty acid. Glycerides are another type of lipid. Examples of glycerides are fat and oil. Glycerides are formed from fatty acids and glycerol (a type of alcohol).

Catabolization of macromolecules

Amino acids are catabolized either during glycolysis or during the Krebs cycle. First, they are broken down into substances that can be catabolized. Processes used to break down amino acids include transamination, which is the transfer of NH_2 (amine), decarboxylation, which is the loss of -COOH groups, and dehydrogenation of H_2. While sugars like glucose from carbohydrates usually begin to be broken down by glycolysis at the beginning of the cycle, eventually going through the Krebs cycle and then the electron transport chain, proteins get broken down into amino acids and have many different entry points into the cycles. Carbohydrates are responsible for providing energy. They are involved in the metabolic energy cycles of photosynthesis and respiration. Structurally, carbohydrates usually take the form of some variation of CH_2O. In respiration, glucose is completely dismantled, but is only partially broken up during fermentation. Lipids get broken down into glycerol for glycolysis and fatty acids enter at the Krebs cycle.

Glycolysis

In glycolysis, glucose is converted into pyruvate and energy stored in ATP bonds is released. Glycolysis can involve various pathways. Various intermediates are produced that are used in other processes, and the pyruvic acid produced by glycolysis can be further used for respiration by the Krebs cycle or in fermentation. Glycolysis occurs in both aerobic and anaerobic organisms. Oxidation of molecules produces reduced coenzymes, such as NADH. The coenzymes relocate hydrogens to the electron transport chain. The proton is transported through the cell membrane and the electron is transported down the chain by proteins. At the end of the chain, water is formed when the final acceptor releases two electrons that combine with oxygen. The protons are pumped back into the cell or organelle by the ATP synthase enzyme, which uses energy produced to add a phosphate to ADP to form ATP. The proton motive force is produced by the protons being moved across the membrane.

Intermediaries of glycolysis

Glycolysis can involve different metabolic pathways. The following 10 steps are based on the Embden-Meyerhof pathway, in which glucose is the starting product and pyruvic acid is the final product. Two molecules of ATP and two of NADH are the products of this process. To start, enzymes utilize ATP to form glucose-6-phosphate. The glucose-6 is converted to fructose-6-phosphate. Another ATP molecule and an enzyme are used to convert fructose-6-phosphate to fructose-1,6-disphosphate. Both dihydroxyacetone phosphate (DHAP) and glyceraldehyde-3-phosphate are formed from fructose-1,6-disphosphate. It is during the preceding reactions that energy is conserved or gained. NAD conversions to NADH molecules and phosphate influx result in 1,3-diphosphoglceric acid. Then, two ADP molecules are phosphorized into ATP molecules, resulting in 3-phosphoglyceric acid, which reforms into 2-phosphoglyceric acid. At this point, water is produced as a product and phosphoenolpyruvic acid is formed. Another set of ADP molecules are phosphorized into ATP molecules. Pyruvic acid is the end result.

Glycolic pathways

Glycolysis is a general term for the conversion of glucose into pyruvate.

Embden-Meyerhof pathway: This is a type of glycolysis in which one molecule of glucose becomes two ATP and two NADH molecules. Pyruvic acid (two pyruvate molecules) is the end product.

Entner-Doudoroff pathway: This is a type of glycolysis in which one glucose molecule forms into one molecule of ATP and two of NADPH, which are used for other reactions. The end product is two pyruvate molecules.

Pentose Phosphate pathway: Also known as the hexose monophosphate shunt, this is a type of glycolysis in which one glucose molecule produces one ATP and two NADPH molecules. Five carbon sugars are metabolized during this reaction. Glucose is broken down into ribose, ribulose, and xylose, which are used during glycolysis and during the Calvin (or Calvin-Benson) cycle to create nucleotides, nucleic acids, and amino acids.

Monosaccharides, disaccharides, starches

The simple sugars can be grouped into monosaccharides (glucose, fructose, and sucrose) and disaccharides. These are both types of carbohydrates. Monosaccharides have one monomer of sugar and disaccharides have two. Monosaccharides (CH_2O) have one carbon for every water molecule. Aldose and ketose are monosaccharides with a carbonyl (=O, double bonded oxygen to carbon) functional group. The difference between aldose and ketose is that the carbonyl group in aldose is connected at an end carbon and the carbonyl group in ketose is connected at a middle carbon. Glucose is a monosaccharide containing six carbons, making it a hexose and an aldose. A disaccharide is formed from two monosaccharides with a glycosidic link. Examples include two glucoses forming a maltose, a glucose and a galactose forming a lactose, and a glucose and a fructose forming a sucrose. A starch is a polysaccharide consisting only of glucose monomers. Examples are amylose, amylopectin, and glycogen.

Krebs cycle

The Krebs cycle is also called the citric acid cycle or the tricarboxylic acid cycle (TCA). It is a catabolic pathway in which the bonds of glucose and occasionally fats or lipids are broken down and reformed into ATP. It is a respiration process that uses oxygen and produces carbon dioxide, water, and ATP. Cells require energy from ATP to synthesize proteins from amino acids and replicate DNA. The cycle is acetyl CoA, citric acid, isocitric acid, ketoglutaric acid (products are amino acids and CO_2), succinyl CoA, succinic acid, fumaric acid, malic acid, and oxaloacetic acid. One of the products of the Krebs cycle is NADH, which is then used in the electron chain transport system to manufacture ATP. From glycolysis, pyruvate is oxidized in a step linking to the Krebs cycle. After the Krebs cycle, NADH and succinate are oxidized in the electron transport chain.

Fermentation

Fermentation is an anaerobic reaction in which glucose is only partially broken down. It releases energy through the oxidation of sugars or other types of organic molecules. Oxygen is sometimes involved, but not always. It is different from respiration in that it uses neither the Krebs cycle nor the electron transport chain and the final electron acceptor is an organic molecule. It uses substrate-level phosphorylation to form ATP. NAD^+ is reduced to NADH and NADH further reduces pyruvic acid to various end products. Fermentation can lead to excess waste products and is less efficient than aerobic respiration. Homolactic fermentation refers to lactic acid fermentation in which the sugars are converted to lactic acid only (there is one end product). In heterolactic fermentation, the sugars are converted to a range of products.

Electron transport chain

The electron transport chain is part of phosphorylation, whereby electrons are transported from enzyme to enzyme until they reach a final acceptor. The electron transport chain includes a series of oxidizing and reducing molecules involved in the release of energy. In redox reactions, electrons are removed from a substrate (oxidative) and H^+ (protons) can also be simultaneously removed. A substrate gains electrons during reduction. For example, when glucose is oxidated, electrons are lost and energy is released. There are enzymes in the membranes of mitochondria. The electrons are carried from one enzyme to another by a co-enzyme. Protons are also released to the other side of the membrane. For example, FAD and $FADH_2$ are used in oxidative phosphorylation. FAD is reduced to $FADH_2$. Electrons are stored there and then sent onward, and the $FADH_2$ becomes FAD again. In aerobic respiration, the final electron acceptor is O_2. In anaerobic respiration, it is something other than O_2.

Homeostasis and feedback loops

Homeostasis is the ability and tendency of an organism, cell, or body to adjust to environmental changes to maintain equilibrium. One way an organism, such as a human body, can maintain homeostasis is through the release of hormones. Some hormones work in pairs. When a condition reaches an upper limit, a hormone is released to correct the condition. When a condition reaches the other end of the spectrum, another hormone is released. Hormones that work in this way are termed antagonistic. Insulin and glucagon are a pair of antagonistic hormones that help regulate the level of glucagon in the blood. Positive feedback loops actually tend to destabilize systems by increasing changes. A negative feedback loop acts to make a system more stable by buffering changes.

Examples of fermentation

Examples of organisms (fermentors) and their products include lactic acid fermentation, whereby streptococcus and lactobacillus bacteria form an end product of lactic acid. Lactic acid can be broken down by propionibacterium freudenreichii into propionic acid and carbon dioxide. This process is involved in making Swiss cheese. Yeast (saccharomyces) and some bacteria produce ethanol during alcohol fermentation, which is commonly used in baking bread and brewing alcohol. Carbon dioxide is also a product of alcohol fermentation. Alcohol fermentation is also involved in making beer. The starter is a malt extract, the fermentor is Saccharomyces cerevisiae, and the end product is ethanol. Citric acid is used as a flavoring. It starts as molasses, which is fermented by aspergillus (a fungus). Lactic acid is found as an end product of fermentation in cheese, yogurt, rye bread, and other foods.

Examples of homeostasis

The hormones insulin and glucagon (an antagonistic pair of hormones) are involved in negative feedback loops in the liver's control of blood sugar levels. Alpha cells secrete glucagon when the concentration of blood glucose decreases. Glucagon is broken down and fatty acids and amino acids are converted to glucose. Once there is more glucose, glucagon secretion is reduced. Beta cells secrete insulin when the concentration of blood glucose increases. This leads to the liver absorbing glucose. Glucose is converted to glycogen, and fat and the concentration of glucose decrease. Insulin production is then reduced. Hormones work in other ways aside from antagonistically. For example, follicle stimulating hormone (FSH) increases the production of estrogen. Once estrogen reaches a certain level, it suppresses FSH production. In some cases, a single hormone can increase or decrease the level of a substance.

DNA

Chromosomes consist of genes, which are single units of genetic information. Genes are made up of deoxyribonucleic acid (DNA). DNA is a nucleic acid located in the cell nucleus. There is also DNA in the mitochondria. DNA replicates to pass on genetic information. The DNA in almost all cells is the same. It is also involved in the biosynthesis of proteins. The model or structure of DNA is described as a double helix. A helix is a curve, and a double helix is two congruent curves connected by horizontal members. The model can be likened to a spiral staircase. It is right-handed. The British scientist Rosalind Elsie Franklin is credited with taking the x-ray diffraction image in 1952 that was used by Francis Crick and James Watson to formulate the double-helix model of DNA and speculate about its important role in carrying and transferring genetic information.

DNA structure

DNA has a double helix shape, resembles a twisted ladder, and is compact. It consists of nucleotides. Nucleotides consist of a five-carbon sugar (pentose), a phosphate group, and a nitrogenous base. Two bases pair up to form the rungs of the ladder. The "side rails" or backbone consists of the covalently bonded sugar and phosphate. The bases are attached to each other with hydrogen bonds, which are easily dismantled so replication can occur. Each base is attached to a phosphate and to a sugar. There are four types of nitrogenous bases: adenine (A), guanine (G), cytosine (C), and thymine (T). There are about 3 billion bases in human DNA. The bases are mostly the same in everybody, but their order is different. It is the order of these bases that creates diversity in people. Adenine (A) pairs with thymine (T), and cytosine (C) pairs with guanine (G).

DNA replication

Pairs of chromosomes are composed of DNA, which is tightly wound to conserve space. When replication starts, it unwinds. The steps in DNA replication are controlled by enzymes. The enzyme helicase instigates the deforming of hydrogen bonds between the bases to split the two strands. The splitting starts at the A-T bases (adenine and thymine) as there are only two hydrogen bonds. The cytosine-guanine base pair has three bonds. The term "origin of replication" is used to refer to where the splitting starts. The portion of the DNA that is unwound to be replicated is called the replication fork. Each strand of DNA is transcribed by an mRNA. It copies the DNA onto itself, base by base, in a complementary manner. The exception is that uracil replaces thymine.

Types of DNA replication

Semiconservative: DNA replication is considered semiconservative because the two replicated copies of DNA each have one strand of the original parent DNA, or half of the original genetic material.

Antiparallel replication: This refers to the fact that during DNA replication, the nucleotides (A, C, G, T, and U) on leading and lagging strands run in opposite directions. RNA synthesis is said to occur in a $5' \rightarrow 3'$ (five prime to three prime) direction. That means that the phosphate group of the nucleotide that is being added to the chain, which is $5'$, is attached to the end of the chain at the end of a hydroxyl group, which is $3'$.

Base pairing: This explains how RNA transcribes DNA in an inverted fashion. C on DNA is inserted as a G on RNA, and A on DNA becomes U on RNA.

Functions of proteins in DNA replication

Many proteins are involved in the replication of DNA, and each has a specific function. Helicase is a protein that facilitates the unwinding of the double helix structure of DNA. Single strand binding (SSB) proteins attach themselves to each strand to prevent the DNA strands from joining back together. After DNA is unwound, there are leading and lagging strands. The leading strand is synthesized continuously and the lagging strand is synthesized in Okazaki fragments. Primase, an RNA polymerase (catalyzing enzyme), acts as a starting point for replication by forming short strands, or primers, of RNA. The DNA clamp, or sliding clamp, helps prevent DNA polymerase from coming apart from the strand. DNA polymerase helps form the DNA strand by linking nucleotides. As the process progresses, RNase H removes the primers. DNA ligase then links the existing shorter strands into a longer strand.

Types of RNA

RNA acts as a helper to DNA and carries out a number of other functions. Types of RNA include ribosomal RNA (rRNA), transfer RNA (tRNA), and messenger RNA (mRNA). Viruses can use RNA to carry their genetic material to DNA. Ribosomal RNA is not believed to have changed much over time. For this reason, it can be used to study relationships in organisms. Messenger RNA carries a copy of a strand of DNA and transports it from the nucleus to the cytoplasm. Transcription is the process whereby DNA uses RNA in transcription. DNA unwinds itself and serves as a template while RNA is being assembled. The DNA molecules are copied to RNA. Translation is the process whereby ribosomes use transcribed RNA to put together the needed protein. Transfer RNA is a molecule that helps in the translation process, and is found in the cytoplasm. Ribosomal RNA is in the ribosomes.

Differences between RNA and DNA

RNA and DNA differ in terms of structure and function. RNA has a different sugar than DNA. It has ribose rather than deoxyribose sugar. The RNA nitrogenous bases are adenine (A), guanine (G), cytosine (C), and uracil (U). Uracil is found only in RNA and thymine in found only in DNA. RNA consists of a single strand and DNA has two strands. If straightened out, DNA has two side rails. RNA only has one "backbone," or strand of sugar and phosphate group components. RNA uses the fully hydroxylated sugar pentose, which includes an extra oxygen compared to deoxyribose, which is the sugar used by DNA. RNA supports the functions carried out by DNA. It aids in gene expression, replication, and transportation.

Nucleotides and ester bonds

RNA

The five bases in DNA and RNA can be categorized as either pyrimidine or purine according to their structure. The pyrimidine bases include cytosine, thymine, and uracil. They are six-sided and have a single ring shape. The purine bases are adenine and guanine, which consist of two attached rings. One ring has five sides and the other has six. When combined with a sugar, any of the five bases become nucleosides. Nucleosides formed from purine bases end in "osine" and those formed from pyrimidine bases end in "idine." Adenosine and thymidine are examples of nucleosides. Bases are the most basic components, followed by nucleosides, nucleotides, and then DNA or RNA.

Ester bonds are bonds in organic compounds that are formed by alcohol and organic acids. Water is typically a product when ester bonds are formed. Fats have ester bonds formed by fatty acids and glycerol (an alcohol).

Codons

Codons are groups of three nucleotides on the messenger RNA, and can be visualized as three rungs of a ladder. A codon has the code for a single amino acid. There are 64 codons but 20 amino acids. More than one combination, or triplet, can be used to synthesize the necessary amino acids. For example, AAA (adenine-adenine-adenine) or AAG (adenine-adenine-guanine) can serve as codons for lysine. These groups of three occur in strings, and might be thought of as frames. For example, AAAUCUUCGU, if read in groups of three from the beginning, would be AAA, UCU, UCG, which are codons for lysine, serine, and serine, respectively. If the same sequence was read in groups of three starting from the second position, the groups would be AAU (asparagine), CUU (proline), and so on. The resulting amino acids would be completely different. For this reason, there are start and stop codons that indicate the beginning and ending of a sequence (or frame). AUG (methionine) is the start codon. UAA, UGA, and UAG, also known as ocher, opal, and amber, respectively, are stop codons

Mutations

RNA

Gene disorders are the result of DNA mutations. DNA mutations lead to unfavorable gene disorders, but also provide genetic variability. This diversity can lead to increased survivability of a species. Mutations can be neutral, beneficial, or harmful. Mutations can be hereditary, meaning they are passed from parent to child. Polymorphism refers to differences in humans, such as eye and hair color, that may have originally been the result of gene mutations, but are now part of the normal variation of the species. Mutations can be de novo, meaning they happen either only in sex cells or shortly after fertilization. They can also be acquired, or somatic. These are the kinds that happen as a result of DNA changes due to environmental factors or replication errors. Mosaicism is when a mutation happens in a cell during an early embryonic stage. The result is that some cells will have the mutation andsome will not.

DNA level mutation

A DNA mutation occurs when the normal gene sequence is altered. Mutations can happen when DNA is damaged as a result of environmental factors, such as chemicals, radiation, or ultraviolet rays from the sun. It can also happen when errors are made during DNA replication. The phosphate-sugar side rail of DNA can be damaged if the bonds between oxygen and phosphate groups are disassociated. Translocation happens when the broken bonds attempt to bond with other DNA. This repair can cause a mutation. The nucleotide itself can be altered. A C, for example, might look like a T. During replication, the damaged C is replicated as a T and paired with a G, which is incorrect base pairing. Another way mutations can occur is if an error is made by the DNA polymerase while replicating a base. This happens about once for every 100,000,000 bases. A repair protein proofreads the code, however, so the mistake is usually repaired.

Ribosomes and tRNA anticodons

When the DNA is unwound during transcription, the mRNA makes a complimentary copy of codons, during which T becomes A, C becomes G, etc. During translation, the rRNA interprets the code again in a complementary fashion. A becomes U (there is no T), G becomes C, etc. Ribosomes make proteins from amino acids by using the information on mRNA as a template for sequencing amino acids in a protein. Transfer RNA (tRNA) carries amino acids that have attached to it to the ribosome. The anticodons on the tRNA are a string of triplet bases that are complementary to the mRNA. For example, a codon that is AAA on the mRNA would be associated with the anticodon UUU on the tRNA. Another example is that GGG on mRNA would be associated with the anticodon CCC on tRNA.

Translocation

Translocation is a genetic mutation in which one piece of a chromosome is transferred to another chromosome. Burkitt's lymphoma, chronic myelogenous leukemia, and Down syndrome are all examples. Trisomy 21, or Down syndrome, occurs when a copy of chromosome 21 attaches to chromosome 14. Most Down syndrome cases are caused by a pair of chromosomes (the 21st) that does not split during meiosis. Both divided cells will have an abnormal number of chromosomes. One will have 22 and the other will have 24. When this egg gets fertilized, it will have three copies of chromosome 21 instead of two. Down syndrome can also be caused by translocation between the 14th and 21st chromosomes. In these instances, genetic material is swapped. There are 200 to 250 genes on the 21st chromosome. The overexpression of the gene results in the following Down syndrome traits: premature aging, decreased immune system function, heart defects, skeletal abnormalities, disruption of DNA synthesis and repair, mental retardation, and cataracts.

Mendel's laws

Mendel's laws are the law of segregation (the first law) and the law of independent assortment (the second law). The law of segregation states that there are two alleles and that half of the total number of alleles are contributed by each parent organism. The law of independent assortment states that traits are passed on randomly and are not influenced by other traits. The exception to this is linked traits. A Punnett square can illustrate how alleles combine from the contributing genes to form various phenotypes. One set of a parent's genes are put in columns, while the genes from the other parent are placed in rows. The allele combinations are shown in each cell. When two different alleles are present in a pair, the dominant one is expressed. A Punnett square can be used to predict the outcome of crosses.

Gene, genotype, phenotype, and allele

A gene is a portion of DNA that identifies how traits are expressed and passed on in an organism. A gene is part of the genetic code. Collectively, all genes form the genotype of an individual. The genotype includes genes that may not be expressed, such as recessive genes. The phenotype is the physical, visual manifestation of genes. It is determined by the basic genetic information and how genes have been affected by their environment. An allele is a variation of a gene. Also known as a trait, it determines the manifestation of a gene. This manifestation results in a specific physical appearance of some facet of an organism, such as eye color or height. For example the genetic information for eye color is a gene. The gene variations responsible for blue, green, brown, or black eyes are called alleles. Locus (pl. loci) refers to the location of a gene or alleles.

Monohybrid and hybrid crosses

Genetic crosses are the possible combinations of alleles, and can be represented using Punnett squares. A monohybrid cross refers to a cross involving only one trait. Typically, the ratio is 3:1 (DD, Dd, Dd, dd), which is the ratio of dominant gene manifestation to recessive gene manifestation. This ratio occurs when both parents have a pair of dominant and recessive genes. If one parent has a pair of dominant genes (DD) and the other has a pair of recessive (dd) genes, the recessive trait can not be expressed in the next generation because the resulting crosses all have the Dd genotype. A dihybrid cross refers to one involving more than one trait, which means more combinations are possible. The ratio of genotypes for a dihybrid cross is 9:3:3:1 when the traits are not linked. The ratio for incomplete dominance is 1:3:1:, which corresponds to dominant, mixed, and recessive phenotypes.

Dominant and recessive genes

Gene traits are represented in pairs with an upper case letter for the dominant trait (A) and a lower case letter for the recessive trait (a). Genes occur in pairs (AA, Aa, or aa). There is one gene on each chromosome half supplied by each parent organism. Since half the genetic material is from each parent, the offspring's traits are represented as a combination of these. A dominant trait only requires one gene of a gene pair for it to be expressed in a phenotype, whereas a recessive requires both genes in order to be manifested. For example, if the mother's genotype is Dd and the father's is dd, the possible combinations are Dd and dd. The dominant trait will be manifested if the genotype is DD or Dd. The recessive trait will be manifested if the genotype is dd. Both DD and dd are homozygous pairs. Dd is heterozygous.

Crossing over, gametes, pedigree analysis, and probability analysis

Crossing over: This refers to the swapping of genetic material between homologous chromosomes. This leads to different combinations of genes showing up in a phenotype. This is part of gene recombination, which is when DNA breaks down and is then reassembled.

Gametes: These are the sex cells in organisms that reproduce sexually. Each gamete contains half the genetic information of the parent. They are haploid (having 23 chromosome pairs in humans). The resulting zygote, which is formed when the two gametes become one cell, is diploid (46 chromosome pairs in humans).

Pedigree analysis: This involves isolating a trait in an organism and tracing its manifestation. Pedigree charts are often used for this type of analysis. A family pedigree shows how a trait can be seen throughout generations.

Probability analysis: This calculates the chances of a particular trait or combination of traits being expressed in an organism.

Co-dominance and incomplete dominance

Co-dominance refers to the expression of both alleles so that both traits are shown. Cows, for example, can have hair colors of red, white, or red and white (not pink). In the latter color, both traits are fully expressed. The ABO human blood typing system is also co-dominant. Incomplete dominance is when both the dominant and recessive genes are expressed, resulting in a phenotype that is a mixture of the two. The fact that snapdragons can be red, white, or pink is a good example. The dominant red gene (RR) results in a red flower because of large amounts of red pigment. White (rr) occurs because both genes call for no pigment. Pink (Rr) occurs because one gene is for red and one is for no pigment. The colors blend to produce pink flowers. A cross of pink flowers (Rr) can result in red (RR), white (rr), or pink (Rr) flowers.

Non-Mendelian terms

Polygenic inheritance: This goes beyond the simplistic Mendelian concept that one gene influences one trait. It refers to traits that are influenced by more than one gene, and takes into account environmental influences on development.

Multiple alleles: Only two alleles make up a gene, but when there are three or more possible alleles, it is known as a multiple allele. A gene where only two alleles are possible is termed polymorphic.

Complete dominance: This refers the situation in which a homozygous pair of dominant alleles (AA) and a heterozygous pair of alleles (Aa) result in the same phenotype. Dominate genes have the following characteristics: they are expressed in each generation; they are passed on to roughly half the offspring; and a parent that does not express the trait can not pass it on to offspring. The Mendelian complete dominance concept states that one gene consisting of two alleles is the only factor involved in the creation of a phenotype. Most traits, however, are more complex.

Linkage

Linkage involves characteristics that are on the same chromosome. This leads to two different traits being seen together more often than not. Linkage is the exception to independent assortment. Sex-linked traits are those that occur on a sex chromosome. Autosomal refers to non-sex chromosomes. In humans, there are 22 autosomal pairs of chromosomes and a pair of sex chromosomes. Depending on the sex, pairs are either XX (female) or XY (male). Since females don't have Y chromosomes, alleles on this gene are only manifested in males. Males can only pass on sex-linked traits on the X chromosome to their daughters since sons would not receive an X from them. Hemizygous means there is only one copy of a gene. Color blindness occurs more in males than females because it is a sex-linked trait on the X chromosome. Since it is recessive, females have a better chance of expressing the dominant characteristic of non-color blindness.

ABO blood system

Human blood typing, which uses the ABO system, is an example of co-dominance and multiple alleles. Multiple alleles means there are more than two possible alleles and therefore more than just four possible gene combinations. The types of alleles are A, B, and O. A and B are co-dominant. In co-dominance, both alleles are completely expressed. A and B both produce enzymes that produce antigens. A produces type A antigens and B produces type B antigens. Antigen molecules are located on the surfaces of red blood cells. Type O does not produce enzymes, nor does it have antigens on its surface. The antigens trigger a response in the immune system to help repel foreign substances. Matching blood types during medical procedures is important since the human immune system can detect and attack blood that is a different type. Specific blood types are used in transfusions, and blood types are determined based on the proteins (or lack of proteins) contained in the blood.

Lethal allele, pleiotropy, epistasis, and karyotype

Lethal allele: This is when a mutation in an essential gene results in the death of the organism. Cystic fibrosis and Tay-Sachs disease are examples of lethal recessive alleles.

Pleiotropy: This refers to a gene that affects more than one trait.

Epistasis: This refers to the situation in which two or more genes determine a single phenotype.

Karyotype: This is a picture of genes based on a sample of blood or skin.

The non-Mendelian concept of polygenetic inheritance takes into account environmental factors on phenotypes. For example, an individual inherits genes that help determine height, but a diet lacking in certain nutrients could limit that individual's ability to reach that height. Another example is the concept of genetic disposition, which is a propensity for a certain disease that is genetically inherited, but not necessarily manifested. For example, individuals with certain skin types are more likely to develop skin cancer. If they limit their exposure to solar radiation, however, this will not necessarily occur.

Genetic engineering, cloning, restriction enzymes, and vectors

Genetic engineering: This refers to changing or manipulating an organism's genes. Other terms that may be used to refer to genetic engineering are recombinant DNA, gene splicing, cloning, and genetic modification or manipulation. Genetic engineering is different from indirect gene manipulation, in which breeding is controlled based on observable phenotypes. Genetic engineering refers to altering the genes themselves.

Cloning: There are two definitions for cloning. The first refers to the natural cloning that occurs in nature when organisms reproduce asexually and make exact copies of them. This can happen in bacteria, plants, birds, and other organisms. The definition heard more in popular culture refers to cloning as the genetic engineering of portions of DNA, cells, or entire organisms.

Blood types

There are four possible blood types: A, B, AB, and O. These types are produced by combinations of the three alleles. AA and AO lead to type A blood. BB and BO lead to type B blood. AB leads to type AB blood because the alleles are co-dominant. AB has both A protein and antigens and B protein and antigens. The O allele is recessive. OO leads to blood type O, which lacks proteins and blood-surface antigens. Blood donors with an O blood type are known as universal donors because they do not have the type of antigens that can trigger immune system responses. Blood donors with type AB blood are known as universal recipients because they do not have the antibodies that will attack A and B antigen molecules. If parents have AB and O blood, offspring have a 50% chance of having type A blood and a 0% chance of having type O blood.

Applications of genetic engineering

Diagnostic and medical applications include treating diabetes with insulin, producing human proteins, treating hemophilia, anemia, and blood clots, and manufacturing hepatitis B vaccine. Gene therapy has been used to replace defective alleles with normal alleles. For example, if a patient has a condition caused by an enzyme deficiency, replacing the defective allele enables the person to produce that enzyme. Medical forensic applications involving DNA analysis include using it to identify individuals and solve criminal cases. Agricultural applications include crop modification to develop types of wheat, cotton, and soybeans that resist weed controlling herbicides. Plants can be altered to make them grow bigger or vaccinated to make them resistant to plant viruses and insects.

Restriction enzymes: These are proteins that can recognize portions of DNA strands and cleave them at certain points.

Vectors: Vectors deliver DNA to a cell, and can include viruses and bacterial plasmids.

Recombinant DNA and gene splicing

Recombinant DNA (rDNA) refers to manipulating sequences of DNA. One portion of DNA is removed and replaced with another. Gene splicing is a way to recombine DNA. In gene splicing, base pairs of DNA are chemically cleaved. Restriction enzymes are used to perform the cutting part of gene splicing. Once base pairs are separated, different additional genetic information can be added by a vector. DNA ligase (an enzyme) is used to put the pieces back together. The process of DNA recombination happens naturally and incrementally as a result of evolution. Use of recombinant DNA produced through genetic engineering has been used in the laboratory in diagnostic, medical forensic and agricultural applications.

Human genome project

The human genome project was an international effort by scientists in 18 countries that was undertaken to gain information about human DNA. The project set out to identify all of the genes in human DNA, which number about 20,000-25,000. Other goals included: determining the sequences of the three billion base pairs comprising human DNA, inputting information collected into databases, producing tools for data analysis and making them available, and opening a discussion about the ethical, legal, and social implications of obtaining such in-depth knowledge about the genetic makeup of humans. The completed mapping and sequencing is expected to lead to further research in the fields of molecular medicine and DNA forensics. It's also expected to spur on research in related fields, such as energy source development, bioarchaeology, human migration and evolution, agriculture improvement and production, livestock breeding, and bioprocessing.

Natural selection, gradualism, and punctuated equilibrium

Natural selection: This theory developed by Darwin states that traits that help give a species a survival advantage are passed on to subsequent generations. Members of a species that do not have the advantageous trait die before they reproduce. Darwin's four principles are: from generation to generation, there are various individuals within a species; genes determine variations; more individuals are born than survive to maturation; and specific genes enable an organism to better survive.

Gradualism: This can be contrasted with punctuationism. It is the idea that evolution proceeds at a steady pace and does not include sudden developments of new species or features from one generation to the next.

Punctuated equilibrium: This can be contrasted with gradualism. It is an idea in evolutionary biology that states that evolution involves long time periods of no change (stasis) accompanied by relatively brief periods (hundreds of thousands of years) of rapid change.

Evidence supporting theory of evolution

Scientific evidence supporting the theory of evolution can be found in biogeography, comparative anatomy and embryology, the fossil record, and molecular evidence. Biogeography studies the geographical distribution of animals and plants. Evidence of evolution related to the area of biogeography includes species that are well suited for extreme environments. The fossil record shows that species lived only for a short time period before becoming extinct. The fossil record can also show the succession of plants and animals. Living fossils are existing species that have not changed much morphologically and are very similar to ancient examples in the fossil record. Examples include the horseshoe crab and ginko. Comparative embryology studies how species are similar in the embryonic stage, but become increasingly specialized and diverse as they age. Vestigial organs are those that still exist, but become nonfunctional. Examples include the hind limbs of whales and the wings of birds that can no longer fly, such as ostriches.

Rate of evolution

The rate of evolution is affected by the variability of a population. Variability increases the likelihood of evolution. Variability in a population can be increased by mutations, immigration, sexual reproduction (as opposed to asexual reproduction), and size. Natural selection, emigration, and smaller populations can lead to decreased variability. Sexual selection affects evolution. If fewer genes are available, it will limit the number of genes passed on to subsequent generations. Some animal mating behaviors are not as successful as others. A male that does not attract a female because of a weak mating call or dull feathers, for example, will not pass on its genes. Mechanical isolation, which refers to sex organs that do not fit together very well, can also decrease successful mating.

Three types of evolution

Three types of evolution are divergent, convergent, and parallel. Divergent evolution refers to two species that become different over time. This can be caused by one of the species adapting to a different environment. Convergent evolution refers to two species that start out fairly different, but evolve to share many similar traits. Parallel evolution refers to species that are not similar and do not become more or less similar over time. Mechanisms of evolution include descent (the passing on of genetic information), mutation, migration, natural selection, and genetic variation and drift. The biological definition of species refers to a group of individuals that can mate and reproduce. Speciation refers to the evolution of a new biological species. The biological species concept (BSC) basically states that a species is a community of individuals that can reproduce and have a niche in nature.

Prezygotic barriers to reproduction

Spatial: This refers to species that are separated by a distance that prevents them from mating.

Geographical: This is when species are physically separated by a barrier. A barrier can divide a population, which is known as vicariance. If a population crosses a barrier to create two species, it is known as dispersal.

Habitat: This refers to species that live in different habitats in the same area.

Temporal: This refers to the fact that species reach sexual maturity at different times. An example is plants that flower at different times of the year.

Behavioral: This refers to the fact that mating rituals distinguish interaction between sexes. For example, many species of crickets are morphologically (structurally) the same, yet a female of one species will only respond to the mating rituals of males within her species.

Mechanical: This refers to physiological structural differences that prevent mating or the transfer of gametes.

Gametic isolation: This refers to the fact that fertilization may not occur when gametes of different species are not compatible.

Allele frequency

The gene pool refers to all alleles of a gene and their combinations. The Hardy-Weinberg principle (or Castle-Hardy Weinberg principle) postulates that the allele frequency for dominant and recessive alleles will remain the same in a population through successive generations if certain conditions exist. These conditions are: no mutations, large populations, random mating, no migration, and equal genotypes. This is an ideal and not how most population's function. Changes in the frequency and types of alleles in a gene pool can be caused by gene flow, random mutation, nonrandom mating, and genetic drift. In organisms that reproduce by sexual reproduction, reproduction isolation is defined as something that acts as a barrier to two species reproducing. These barriers are classified as prezygotic and postzygotic.

Random mutations, nonrandom mating, and gene migration

Random mutations: These are genetic changes caused by DNA errors or environmental factors such as chemicals and radiation. Mutations can be beneficial or harmful.

Nonrandom mating: This refers to the fact that the probability of two individuals mating in a population is not the same for all pairs. Nonrandom mating can be caused by geographical isolation, small populations, and other factors. Nonrandom mating can lead to inbreeding (mating with a relative), which can lead to a decline in physical fitness as seen in a phenotype and the reduction of allele frequency and occurrence.

Gene migration: Also known as gene flow, gene migration is the movement of alleles to another population. This can occur through immigration, when individuals of a species move into an area, or through emigration, when individuals of a species move out of an area.

Postzygotic barriers to reproduction

Hybrid viability: This is when a hybrid zygote does not reach maturity.

Hybrid sterility: This is also known as hybrid infertility. It occurs when two species produce a hybrid offspring that reaches maturity, but is sterile. An example of this is the mule. Mules are the result of a horse and a donkey mating. Mules, however, can not reproduce.

Hybrid breakdown: This is when the first generation is not only viable, but also reaches maturity and can reproduce. Subsequent generations, however, are neither viable nor fertile.

Hybrid zygote abnormality: This is when two species produce a zygote that does not survive to birth or germination, does not develop normally or reach sexual maturity, and cannot reproduce.

Allopatric speciation: This refers to speciation that occurs because of geographical factors, such as physical barriers or dispersal.

Sympatric speciation: This refers to speciation that happens within parent populations.

Parapatric speciation: This refers to speciation that occurs because of an extreme change in habitat.

Bottleneck and adaptive radiation

Bottleneck: This occurs when a small percentage of a population survives a disaster or when the size of a population is greatly reduced for at least one generation. It results in reduced allele diversity, and can even lead to entire alleles being eliminated in a species. This can lead to an increased inability to adapt to certain environmental factors. An example of a bottleneck is that hunting by humans reduced the northern elephant seal population to 20 individuals. Their population is now about 30,000, but the population's genes are much less varied than the genes of the southern elephant seal population. Another example is that a typhoon killed all but 30 people on an island in the South Pacific. One of the survivors had the recessive gene for color blindness. Currently, about 10% of the current population of 2,000 is color blind.

Adaptive radiation: This refers to the fact that speciation occurs through adapting to an environment through natural selection. It also refers to the fact that a species has a common ancestor.

Genetic drift and the founder's effect

Genetic drift: Easily observable in small populations, genetic drift is a change in the frequency of an allele.

Founder's effect: This occurs when a small population breaks away from a larger population and forms a smaller and isolated population. The resulting reduction in allele diversity leads to a greater expression of certain genetic traits than would be observed in a larger population. An example is the Amish in America, who are the descendants of 30 Swiss founders. The Amish are isolated by culture and breed within their population. One of the founders had Ellis-van Creveld syndrome. It is rare in larger populations, but is found at a rate of about 1 in 200 in the Amish community. It results in short stature, extra fingers and toes, and heart defects.

Earth's age, abiotic synthesis and endosymbiotic theory

Earth's age is estimated to be 4.5 billion years.

Abiotic synthesis: This is related to the commonly accepted theory that life originated from inorganic matter. It refers to the making of organic molecules outside of a living body, and is believed to have been the first step in the development of life on Earth. The theory was tested in an experiment performed by a graduate student at Stanford University in 1953. He combined the inorganic molecules water, hydrogen, methane, and ammonia in a closed, sterile flask and applied heat. To recreate the effect of lightning, he used an electric charge. His ingredients started as a clear mixture. After a week, he had a cloudy soup that contained amino acids and organic compounds.

Endosymbiotic theory: This is the belief that eukaryotes (cells with nuclei) developed from prokaryotic cells (those without nuclei). The theory is that chloroplasts in plant cells and mitochondria in animal cells evolved from smaller prokaryotes living within larger prokaryotes.

Origin of life on Earth

One theory of how life originated on Earth is that life developed from nonliving materials. The first stage of this transformation happened when abiotic (nonliving) synthesis took place, which is the formation of monomers like amino acids and nucleotides. Next, monomers joined together to create polymers such as proteins and nucleic acids. These polymers are then believed to have formed into protobionts. The last stage was the development of the process of heredity. Supporters of this theory believe that RNA was the first genetic material. Another theory postulates that hereditary systems came about before the origination of nucleic acids. Another theory is that life, or the precursors for it, were transported to Earth from a meteorite or other object from space. There is no real evidence to support this theory.

Five kingdom classification system

The groupings in the five kingdom classification system are kingdom, phylum/division, class, order, family, genus, and species. A memory aid for this is: King Phillip Came Over For Good Soup. The five kingdoms are Monera, Protista, Fungi, Plantae, and Animalia. The kingdom is the top level classification in this system. Below that are the following groupings: phylum, class, order, family, genus, and species. The Monera kingdom includes about 10,000 known species of prokaryotes, such as bacteria and cyanobacteria. Members of this kingdom can be unicellular organisms or colonies. The next four kingdoms consist of eukaryotes. The Protista kingdom includes about 250,000 species of unicellular protozoans and unicellular and multicellular algae. The Fungi kingdom includes about 100,000 species. A recently introduced system of classification includes a three domain grouping above kingdom. The domain groupings are Archaea, Bacteria (which both consist of prokaryotes), and Eukarya, which include eukaryotes. According to the five kingdom classification system, humans are: kingdom Animalia, phylum Chordata, subphylum Vertebrata, class Mammalia, order Primate, family Hominidae, genus Homo, and species Sapiens.

Protista kingdom

Organisms in the Protista kingdom are classified according to their methods of locomotion, their methods of reproduction, and how they get their nutrients. Protists can move by the use of a flagellum, cilia, or pseudopod. Flagellates have flagellum, which are long tails or whip-like structures that are rotated to help the protist move. Ciliates use cilia, which are smaller hair-like structures on the exterior of a cell that wiggle to help move the surrounding matter. Amoeboids use pseudopodia to move. Bacteria reproduce either sexually or asexually. Binary fission is a form of asexual reproduction whereby bacteria divide in half to produce two new organisms that are clones of the parent. In sexual reproduction, genetic material is exchanged. When kingdom members are categorized according to how they obtain nutrients, the three types of protists are photosynthetic, consumers, and saprophytes. Photosynthetic protists convert sunlight into energy. Organisms that use photosynthesis are considered producers. Consumers, also known as heterotrophs, eat or consume other organisms. Saprophytes consume dead or decaying substances.

Fungi kingdom

Mycology is the study of fungi. The Fungi kingdom includes about 100,000 species. They are further delineated as mushrooms, yeasts, molds, rusts, mildews, stinkhorns, puffballs, and truffles. Fungi are characterized by cell walls that have chitin, a long chain polymer carbohydrate. Fungi are different from species in the Plant kingdom, which have cell walls consisting of cellulose. Fungi are thought to have evolved from a single ancestor. Although they are often thought of as a type of plant, they are more similar to animals than plants. Fungi are typically small and numerous, and have a diverse morphology among species. They can have bright red cups and be orange jellylike masses, and their shapes can resemble golf balls, bird nests with eggs, starfish, parasols, and male genitalia. Some members of the stinkhorn family emit odors similar to dog scat to attract flies that help transport spores that are involved in reproduction. Fungi of this family are also consumed by humans.

Molecular oxygen

When the Earth was formed, the atmosphere did not contain oxygen. It is thought to have appeared in the Paleoproterozoic era about 2.5 to 1.6 billion years ago. First, oxygen combined with iron in oceans to form banded iron formations (thin layers of iron oxides and layers of iron poor rock). After that, oxygen began to "gas out" of the oceans slowly. One of the major events in Earth's geologic history is the great oxygen event, or oxygen catastrophe, during which large amounts of oxygen led to the extinction of anaerobic organisms. This, in turn, led to an increased number of aerobic organisms. Eventually, it also resulted in the development of eukaryotic cells and more complex life forms.

Organism and microbe

An organism is a living thing. A unicellular organism is an organism that has only one cell. Examples of unicellular organisms are bacteria and paramecium. A multicellular organism is one that consists of many cells. Humans are a good example. By some estimates, the human body is made up of billions of cells. Others think the human body has more than 75 trillion cells.

The term microbe refers to small organisms that are only visible through a microscope. Examples include viruses, bacteria, fungi, and protozoa. Microbes are also referred to as microorganisms, and it is these that are studied by microbiologists. Bacteria can be rod shaped, round (cocci), or spiral (spirilla). These shapes are used to differentiate among types of bacteria. Bacteria can be identified by staining them. This particular type of stain is called a gram stain. If bacteria are gram-positive, they absorb the stain and become purple. If bacteria are gram-negative, they do not absorb the stain and become a pinkish color.

Viruses

Some scientists do not consider viruses to belong to any of the five kingdoms or to be living organisms for many reasons. Viruses do not meet the definition of a cell. They cannot be classified as eukaryotic or prokaryotic. They are generally smaller than and not as complex as living cells, which are the basic units of life. Viruses do not have nuclei. They are macromolecules consisting of long chains of genetic material (either RNA or DNA) encased in protein. Viruses also lack membrane-bound organelles, ribosomes, and cytoplasm, all of which are usually found in cells. Viruses do not perform the basic cell processes involved in the ADP/ATP cycle, and they are not capable of cellular respiration or gas exchange. They reproduce by gaining control of a host cell and making it replicate the viral DNA instead of its own.

Characteristics of viruses

Viruses are microorganisms that replicate in the cells of other organisms, including plants, animals, bacteria, and other microorganisms. All viruses have a head. Some also have a tail consisting of protein. The tail is used to attach to a host cell and enter it. This is one way in which viruses introduce their genetic material to the host. The head of a virus, also called a protein capsid, contains genetic material in the form of DNA, RNA, or enzymes. The adenovirus and the herpes virus are both DNA viruses. The HIV retrovirus, influenza, and the rotavirus are RNA viruses. The number of virus types is thought to be in the millions. Virology is a branch of microbiology that is devoted to the study of viruses. Viruses can be transmitted to other organisms in a number of ways, such as by insects, by air, and through direct contact.

Vascular and nonvascular plants

Vascular plants have vascular tissue in the form of xylem and phloem. These make up the parts of the plants, such as the roots, stems, and leaves that are involved in transporting minerals and water throughout the plant. This capability enables vascular plants to grow tall. Food/energy that is converted by photosynthesis in the leaves is brought down to the roots, while water is brought to the top of the plant. Nonvascular (or avascular) plants lack true leaves, stems, and roots. Nonvascular plants do not develop vascular tissue, such as xylem and phloem. They tend to be small, and individual cells are adjacent to their environment.

Plant kingdom groupings

Only plants in the division bryophyta (mosses and liverworts) are nonvascular, which means they do not have xylem to transport water. All of the plants in the remaining divisions are vascular, meaning they have true roots, stems, leaves, and xylem. Pteridophytes are plants that use spores and not seeds to reproduce. They include the following divisions: Psilophyta (whisk fern), Lycophyta (club mosses), Sphenophyta (horsetails), and Pterophyta (ferns). Spermatophytes are plants that use seeds to reproduce. Included in this category are gymnosperms, which are flowerless plants that use naked seeds, and angiosperms, which are flowering plants that contain seeds in or on a fruit. Gymnosperms include the following divisions: cycadophyta (cycads), ginkgophyta (maidenhair tree), gnetophyta (ephedra and welwitschia), and coniferophyta (which includes pinophyta conifers). Angiosperms comprise the division anthophyta (flowering plants).

Plant phyla

Chlorophyta are green algae. Bryophyta are nonvascular mosses and liverworts. They have root-like parts called rhizoids. Since they do not have the vascular structures to transport water, they live in moist environments. Lycophyta are club mosses. They are vascular plants. They use spores and need water to reproduce. Equisetopsida (sphenophyta) are horsetails. Like lycophyta, they need water to reproduce with spores. They have rhizoids and needle-like leaves. The pteridophytes (filicopsida) are ferns. They have stems (rhizomes). Spermatopsida are the seed plants. Gymnosperms are a conifer, which means they have cones with seeds that are used in reproduction. Plants with seeds require less water. Cycadophyta are cone-bearing and look like palms. Gnetophyta are plants that live in the desert. Coniferophyta are pine trees, and have both cones and needles. Ginkgophyta are ginkos. Anthophyta is the division with the largest number of plant species, and includes flowering plants with true seeds.

Processes and systems of plants

Plants are autotrophs, which mean they make their own food. In a sense, they are self sufficient. Three major processes used by plants are photosynthesis, transpiration, and respiration. Photosynthesis involves using sunlight to make food for plants. Transpiration evaporates water out of plants. Respiration is the utilization of food that was produced during photosynthesis.

Two major systems in plants are the shoot and the root system. The shoot system includes leaves, buds, and stems. It also includes the flowers and fruits in flowering plants. The shoot system is located above the ground. The root system is the component of the plant that is underground, and includes roots, tubers, and rhizomes. Meristems form plant cells by mitosis. Cells then differentiate into cell types to form the three types of plant tissues, which are dermal, ground, and vascular. Dermal refers to tissues that form the covering or outer layer of a plant. Ground tissues consist of parenchyma, collenchyma, and/or sclerenchyma cells.

Plant transpiration

The rate of transpiration is affected by light, temperature, humidity, wind, and the saturation of the soil. Light encourages stomata to open, and water is lost more quickly than in the dark. Since water evaporates quicker in higher temperatures, the rate of transpiration increases as the temperature increases. If an area is humid, the rate of transpiration is decreased. The opposite is true for areas of lower humidity. This is explained by the principle of diffusion. The greater the difference in humidity or concentrations of substances in two regions, the greater the rate of diffusion between them will be. Water in the soil replaces water that has been lost through transpiration. If water in the soil is not replaced, the rate of transpiration decreases. Photosynthesis also slows, the stomata close, and the plant wilts when it loses turgor as water is lost from cells.

Plant alternation of generations

Alternation of generations refers to the fact that the two processes used during sexual reproduction alternate. These processes are meiosis and fertilization. In meiosis, sex cells divide and genetic material is reduced by half, which results in a gamete. Two gametes are joined during fertilization, and the resulting cell is diploid. This occurs in both plants and animals. Plants have a gametophyte and a sporophyte generation. The gametophyte generation starts with the production of a haploid spore. More haploid spores are produced through mitosis. Sexual reproduction occurs during this stage, which results in a zygote. This is the start of the second generation, which is known as the sporophyte generation. A primary difference between plant and animal sexual reproduction is that plants can undergo mitosis with haploid cells. Cells can be controlled with this single set of chromosomes.

Plant root system

Plant roots include zones where cell differentiation, elongation and division, and meristem formation occur. Primary meristems include protoderms, ground meristems, procambiums, and apical meristems. There is also a root cap. A tuber is an underground stem that is enlarged and used for food storage. A rhizome is an underground stem of sorts that sends out roots and shoots from its nodes (bulging or swelling points). Vascular tissues include xylem and phloem. Xylem can be scattered throughout a pith or formed into rings. Phloem allows for food transport down a plant. The food travels from where it was produced through photosynthesis to other structures, such as roots, that require the food. Phloem can be made up of bundles of sieve tubes. It is usually located outside the xylem.

Meristems in vegetative growth

The meristems of plants are where new cells are formed through mitosis. These cells then differentiate into specific tissue types, which may form part of the root system or increase a plant's girth, height, or length. Cambiums are meristems that are responsible for secondary growth, which increases girth. Flowering plants go through cycles of vegetative growth, or propagation. They use flowers to reproduce sexually. Vegetative propagation occurs at the apical meristems located on the tip of the stem. These start as undifferentiated cells that can form into more stems, leaves, and secondary meristems (or lateral buds), which form branches. Nodes are areas where leaves can develop. The area between nodes is termed internodal. On a stem, the apical meristem on the end is the terminal bud. Sometimes, this can become a flower bud. Lenticels allow for the diffusion of oxygen and carbon dioxide gas.

Transpiration, respiration, and phylogenetic

Transpiration is the movement of water through a vascular plant. It is also the method by which water is evaporated out of plants. Transpiration mainly happens during the process of photosynthesis, when water and minerals travel up through the xylem and are used and water is released through stomata (flattened oval-shaped openings). During transpiration, water is drawn up a plant. This process also helps cool leaves.

Respiration: This refers to the process of metabolizing sugars to provide plants with the energy they need for growth and reproduction. The chemical equation is $C_6H_{12}O_6 + 6O_2 \rightarrow 6CO_2 + 6H_2O$ + energy. During the process of respiration, sugars are burned, energy is released, oxygen is used, and water and carbon dioxide are produced. Respiration can occur as a light or dark reaction.

Phylogenetic: This refers to organisms that are related because of their evolutionary history.

Reproduction in flowering plants

There are at least 230,000 species of flowering plants. They represent about 90 percent of all plants. Angiosperms have a sexual reproduction phase that includes flowering. When growing plants, one may think they develop in the following order: seeds, growth, flowers, and fruit. The reproductive cycle has the following order: flowers, fruit, and seeds. In other words, seeds are the products of successful reproduction. The colors and scents of flowers serve to attract pollinators. Flowers and other plants can also be pollinated by wind. When a pollen grain meets the ovule and is successfully fertilized, the ovule develops into a seed. A seed consists of three parts: the embryo, the endosperm, and a seed coat. The embryo is a small plant that has started to develop, but this development is paused. Germination is when the embryo starts to grow again. The endosperm consists of proteins, carbohydrates, or fats. It typically serves as a food source for the embryo. The seed coat provides protection from disease, insects, and water.

Reproduction methods

Bryophytes are seedless plants. They include liverworts, hornworts, and mosses. They use spores that form into gametophytes to reproduce. Sperm are flagellated, meaning they require at least some water to swim to the egg. Some bryophytes are plants that are one sex or the other, but other bryophytes have both sexes on the same plant. Ferns also have flagellated sperm and require water for the same reason as bryophytes. Both ferns and bryophytes undergo alternation of generations. These plants spend about half of their reproductive cycles as sporophytes, making haploid spores through meiosis during this stage. The other half of the cycle is spent as a haploid gametophyte. At this point, male and female gametes join to form one zygote. Seed plants use seeds to reproduce. Flowering plants use flowers and seeds.

Pollination in flowering plants

The anthers of the stamens (male parts) have microsporangia that form into a pollen grain, which consists of a small germ cell within a larger cell. The pollen grain is released and lands on a stigma (female) portion of the pistil. It grows a pollen tube the length of the style and ends up at the ovule. The pollen grain releases the sperm and fertilization occurs. In double fertilization, one of the sperm joins with the egg to become a diploid zygote. The other sperm becomes the endosperm nucleus. Seeds are formed. One cotyledon (monocot) or two cotyledons (dicot) also form to store food and surround the embryo. Correspondingly, monocots produce one seed leaf, while dicots produce two. The seed matures and becomes dormant, and fruits typically form.

Sexual parts of flowering plants

Flowering plants can be categorized sexually according to which organs they have. Flowers can be bisexual or unisexual. Species can be dioecious, which means male and female flowers are contained on different individual plants. Monoecious means that both male and female flowers are on one individual. Bisexual flowers are those that have all of the following: sepal, petal, stamen, and pistil. If they have all of these parts, they are considered complete. They have both the male stamen and the female counterpart, the pistil. Unisexual flowers only have a pistil or a stamen, not both. Incomplete flowers do not have all four parts. The flower rests upon a pedicel and is contained with the receptacle. The carpal is made up of the stigma at the tip, a style, and the ovary at the base. The ovary contains the ovules (eggs). Carpels are sometimes formed as a single pistil. The stamen includes the anther and the filament, and produces the male pollen.

Photoperiodism

Photoperiodism refers to the fact that plants are affected by seasons, particularly by the amount of daylight that occurs in each season. The amount of daylight triggers processes such as flowering, growth in roots and stems, and leaves falling off of trees. Long day plants, like the name implies, do not need many night time hours to instigate flowering. Short day plants have an affinity for longer nights and shorter days. Short day plants tend to flower as days get shorter. Long day plants tend to flower when days get longer. Other plants are considered to be day neutral. Examples of long day obligate (meaning long days are essential) plants are oats, clover, and carnations. Examples of long day facultative (meaning long days are desirable, but not essential) plants are turnip, lettuce, wheat, and barley. Examples of short day obligate plants are tobacco, strawberries, and coffee. Examples of short day facultative plants are cotton, sugar cane, and rice.

Fruits in flowering plants

The fruit can encase the mature seed, such as in tomatoes, cherries, and apples. The seed can also be on the outside of the fruit, such as in corn and strawberries. These are called simple fruits, and are produced by one ovary. Another classification of simple fruits is botanical fruits, which are fruits that develop out of a flower. Examples of these are tomatoes, squash, and eggplant. Simple fruits can also have fruits that are dry. Examples of this are poppies, peanuts, and walnuts. Many nuts are simple fruits formed when the ovary wall hardens. One of the seeds produced remains attached. Aggregate fruits are produced by many ovaries in one flower. Each ovary is separately fertilized and forms the aggregate fruit. Examples of these are raspberries, blackberries, and strawberries. Multiple fruits refer to many flowers on a single structure. Examples are pineapples and figs.

Monocot and dicot structures

The diversity of plants leads to an abundance of plant structures. Not all structures are found in all plants, and many plants have different structures that perform similar functions. Monocots and dicots are both flowering plants. The bark of a woody dicot (tree) is structurally very different than the exterior rind of a monocot corn stem, even though both serve as the outermost layer. Within both are the vascular tissues phloem and xylem. In a woody dicot, the tree trunk is made of xylem. When water is abundant, such as during the spring, the xylem vessels that are made are large. Those made later in the summer are narrower since there is less water. When viewed in cross section, these two layers form the ring of a tree's trunk, which is why they can be used to calculate a tree's age.

Tropism, geotropic, plagiotropic, phototropism, and thigmotropism

Tropism refers to the fact that plants grow in response to specific stimuli. Seeds are geotropic (or gravitropic), meaning they grow as a response to gravity. Roots are positively geotropic and grow towards gravity. Stems are negatively geotropic and grow away from the force of gravity. A seed planted upside down will still grow roots and stems in the right direction. Plagiotropic refers to the fact that secondary branches and roots grow at right angles to gravity. Phototropism refers to the fact that a plant bends or grows toward a light source. Thigmotropism refers to how plants respond to contact. Plant hormones are organic compounds that usually influence changes in plants. They can cause fruit to ripen or instigate plant growth. Five major groups of hormones are auxins, gibberellins, ethylenes, cytokinins, and abscisic acids. Auxins occur naturally and can be synthesized. They affect plant cell elongation, apical dominance, and rooting. Gibberellins affect plant height. Ethylenes help fruit ripen. Cytokinins are involved in cell division. Abscisic acids inhibit other hormones.

Animal kingdom subdivisions

The animal kingdom includes about one million species. Metazoans are multicellular animals. Food is ingested and enters a mesoderm-lined coelom (body cavity). Phylum porifera and coelenterate are exceptions. The taxonomy of animals involves grouping them into phyla according to body symmetry and plan, as well as the presence of or lack of segmentation. The more complex phyla that have a coelom and a digestive system are further classified as protostomes or deuterostomes according to blastula development. In protostomes, the blastula's blastopore (opening) forms a mouth. In deuterostomes, the blastopore forms an anus. Taxonomy schemes vary, but there are about 36 phyla of animals. The corresponding term for plants at this level is division. The most notable phyla include chordata, mollusca, porifera, cnidaria, platyhelminthes, nematoda, annelida, arthropoda, and echinodermata, which account for about 96 percent of all animal species.

Animal kingdom facts

The animal kingdom is comprised of more than one million species in about 30 divisions (the plant kingdom uses the term phyla). There about 800,000 species of insects alone, representing half of all animal species. The characteristics that distinguish members of the animal kingdom from members of other kingdoms are that they are multicellular, are heterotrophic, reproduce sexually (there are some exceptions), have cells that do not contain cell walls or photosynthetic pigments, can move at some stage of life, and can rapidly respond to the environment as a result of specialized tissues like nerve and muscle. Heterotrophic refers to the method of getting energy by eating food that has energy releasing substances. Plants, on the other hand, are autotrophs, which mean they make their own energy. During reproduction, animals have a diploid embryo in the blastula stage. This structure is unique to animals. The blastula resembles a fluid-filled ball.

Animal protostomic

Members of the protostomic phyla have mouths that are formed from blastopores.

Mollusca: Classes include bivalvia (organisms with two shells, such as clams, mussels, and oysters), gastropoda (snails and slugs), cephalopoda (octopus, squid, and chambered nautilus), scaphopoda, amphineura (chitons), and monoplacophora.

Annelida: This phylum includes the classes oligochaeta (earthworms), polychaeta (clam worms), and hirudinea (leeches). The have true coeloms enclosed within the mesoderm. They are segmented, have repeating units, and have a nerve trunk.

Arthropoda: The phylum is diverse and populous. Members can be found in all types of environments. They have external skeletons, jointed appendages, bilateral symmetry, and nerve cords. They also have open circulatory systems and sense organs. Subphyla include crustacea (lobster, barnacles, pill bugs, and daphnia), hexapoda (all insects, which have three body segments, six legs, and usual wings), myriapoda (centipedes and millipedes), and chelicerata (the horseshoe crab and arachnids). Pill bugs have gills. Bees, ants, and wasps belong to the order hymenoptera. Like several other insect orders, they undergo complete metamorphosis.

Animal phyla

These four animal phyla lack a coelom or have a pseudocoelom.

Porifera: These are sponges. They lack a coelom and get food as water flows through them. They are usually found in marine and sometimes in freshwater environments. They are perforated and diploblastic, meaning there are two layers of cells.

Cnidaria: Members of this phylum are hydrozoa, jellyfish, and obelia. They have radial symmetry, sac-like bodies, and a polyp or medusa (jellyfish) body plan. They are diploblastic, possessing both an ectoderm and an endoderm. Food can get in through a cavity, but members of this phylum do not have an anus.

Platyhelminthes: These are also known as flatworms. Classes include turbellaria (planarian) and trematoda (which include lung, liver, and blood fluke parasites). They have organs and bilateral symmetry. They have three layers of tissue: an ectoderm, a mesoderm, and an endoderm.

Nematoda: These are roundworms. Hookworms and many other parasites are members of this phylum. They have a pseudocoelom, which means the coelom is not completely enclosed within the mesoderm. They also have a digestive tract that runs directly from the mouth to the anus. They are nonsegmented.

Extrinsic

Extrinsic refers to homeostatic systems that are controlled from outside the body. In higher animals, the nervous system and endocrine system help regulate body functions by responding to stimuli. Hormones in animals regulate many processes, including growth, metabolism, reproduction, and fluid balance. The names of hormones tend to end in "-one." Endocrine hormones are proteins or steroids. Steroid hormones (anabolic steroids) help control the manufacture of protein in muscles and bones.

Invertebrates do not have a backbone, whereas vertebrates do. The great majority of animal species (an estimated 98 percent) are invertebrates, including worms, jellyfish, mollusks, slugs, insects, and spiders. They comprise 30 phyla in all. Vertebrates belong to the phylum chordata. The vertebrate body has two cavities. The thoracic cavity holds the heart and lungs and the abdominal cavity holds the digestive organs. Animals with exoskeletons have skeletons on the outside. Examples are crabs and turtles. Animals with endoskeletons have skeletons on the inside. Examples are humans, tigers, birds, and reptiles.

Animal deuterostomic phyla

Members of the deuterostomic phyla have anuses that are formed from blastopores.

Echinodermata: Members of this phylum have radial symmetry, are marine organisms, and have a water vascular system. Classes include echinoidea (sea urchins and sand dollars), crinoidea (sea lilies), asteroidea (starfish), ophiuroidea (brittle stars), and holothuroidea (sea cucumbers).

Chordata: This phylum includes humans and all other vertebrates, as well as a few invertebrates (urochordata and cephalochordata). Members of this phylum include agnatha (lampreys and hagfish), gnathostomata, chondrichthyes (cartilaginous fish-like sharks, skates, and rays), osteichthyes (bony fishes, including ray-finned fish that humans eat), amphibians (frogs, salamander, and newts), reptiles (lizards, snakes, crocodiles, and dinosaurs), birds, and mammals.

Animal systems and structure

Systems in animals have developed to perform various functions, including providing physical protection and obtaining food. Some animals have internal or external skeletons, shells, or skin that provide protection and support. Skin helps prevent water loss. Muscle systems enable movement. Brains and nervous systems help animals respond to external stimuli by processing incoming and outgoing signals. The main systems in animals are skeletal, muscular, nervous, digestive, respiratory, reproductive, and circulatory. The human stomach, for example, aids in the process of turning consumed food sources into energy. It has many tissue types: smooth muscle tissue, loose connective tissue, nervous tissue, blood, and columnar epithelial tissue. Many animals have a stomach or digestive chamber with two openings. These are known as metazoans.

Animal tissue types

Animals have four main tissues types: epithelial, connective, muscle, and bone. Epithelial tissue is found on body surfaces (like skin) and lining body cavities (like the stomach). Its function is to form and protect various glands. The three types of epithelial tissue are squamous (flattened), cuboidal (cube-shaped), and columnar (elongated). It can be further classified as simple (a single layer) or stratified (more than one layer). Epithelial cells move substances in, around, and out of the body. They can also have protective and secretory functions. Glands comprised of epithelial tissue can be unicellular or multicellular. Connective tissue is used to bind, support, protect, form blood, store fat, and fill space. The two kinds of connective tissue are loose and fibrous. In the human body, cartilage, bone, tendons, ligaments, blood, and protective layers on muscle, nerve, and blood vessels are types of connective tissue. The three types of muscle tissue are skeletal (striated), smooth, and cardiac.

Organ systems

The 11 major organ systems are: skeletal, muscular, nervous, digestive, respiratory, circulatory, skin, excretory, immune, endocrine, and reproductive.

Skeletal: This consists of the bones and joints. The skeletal system provides support for the body through its rigid structure, provides protection for internal organs, and works to make organisms motile. Growth hormone affects the rate of reproduction and the size of body cells, and also helps amino acids move through membranes.

Muscular: This includes the muscles. The muscular system allows the body to move and respond to its environment.

Nervous: This includes the brain, spinal cord, and nerves. The nervous system is a signaling system for intrabody communications among systems, responses to stimuli, and interaction within an environment. Signals are electrochemical. Conscious thoughts and memories and sense interpretation occur in the nervous system. It also controls involuntary muscles and functions, such as breathing and the beating of the heart.

Muscle in mammals

Skeletal muscle is strong, quick, and capable of voluntary contraction. Skeletal muscle fibers are striated and cylinder shaped. They have about 25 nuclei that are located to the side of the cell. Skeletal muscle consists of myofibrils that contain two types of filaments (myofilaments) made of proteins. The two types of filaments are actin and myosin. These filaments are aligned, giving the appearance of striation. During contraction, they slide against each other and become more overlapped. Smooth muscle is weak, slow, and usually contracts involuntarily. Examples in humans can be found in the gastrointestinal tract, blood vessels, bladder, uterus, hair follicles, and parts of the eye. Smooth muscle fibers are not striated, but spindle shaped. They are somewhat long and a little wider in the center. Each cell contains one nucleus that is centrally located. Smooth muscle cells also contain myofibrils, but they are not aligned. Cardiac muscle is strong, quick, and continuously contracts involuntarily. It is found in the myocardium of the heart.

Circulatory and skin systems

Circulatory: This includes the heart, blood, and blood vessels, such as veins, arteries, and capillaries. Blood transports oxygen and nutrients to cells and carbon dioxide to the lungs.

Skin (integumentary): This includes skin, hair, nails, sense receptors, sweat glands, and oil glands. The skin is a sense organ, provides an exterior barrier against disease, regulates body temperature through perspiration, manufactures chemicals and hormones, and provides a place for nerves from the nervous system and parts of the circulation system to travel through. Skin has three layers: epidermis, dermis, and subcutaneous. The epidermis is the thin, outermost, waterproof layer. Basal cells are located in the epidermis. The dermis contains the sweat glands, oil glands, and hair follicles. The subcutaneous layer has connective tissue, and also contains adipose (fat) tissue, nerves, arteries, and veins.

Digestive and respiratory systems

Digestive: This includes the mouth, pharynx, esophagus, stomach, intestines, rectum, anal canal, teeth, salivary glands, tongue, liver, gallbladder, pancreas, and appendix. The system helps change food into a form that the body can process and use for energy and nutrients. Food is eventually eliminated as solid waste. Digestive processes can be mechanical, such as chewing food and churning it in the stomach, and chemical, such as secreting hydrochloric acid to kill bacteria and converting protein to amino acids. The overall system converts large food particles into molecules so the body can use them. The small intestine transports the molecules to the circulatory system. The large intestine absorbs nutrients and prepares the unused portions of food for elimination.

Respiratory: This includes the nose, pharynx, larynx, trachea, bronchi, and lungs. It is involved in gas exchange, which occurs in the alveoli. Fish have gills instead of lungs.

Endocrine system

The endocrine system includes the pituitary gland, pineal gland, hypothalamus, thyroid gland, parathyroids, thymus, adrenals, pancreas, ovaries, and testes. It controls systems and processes by secreting hormones into the blood system. Exocrine glands are those that secrete fluid into ducts. Endocrine glands secrete hormones directly into the blood stream without the use of ducts. Prostaglandin (tissue hormones) diffuses only a short distance from the tissue that created it, and influences nearby cells only. Adrenal glands are located above each kidney. The cortex secretes some sex hormones, as well as mineralocorticoids and glucocorticoids involved in immune suppression and stress response. The medulla secretes epinephrine and norepinephrine. Both elevate blood sugar, increase blood pressure, and accelerate heart rate. Epinephrine also stimulates heart muscle. The islets of Langerhans are clumped within the pancreas and secrete glucagon and insulin, thereby regulating blood sugar levels. The four parathyroid glands at the rear of the thyroid secrete parathyroid hormone.

Excretory, immune, and reproductive systems

Excretory: This includes the kidneys, ureters, bladder, and urethra. The excretory system helps maintain the amount of fluids in the body. Wastes from the blood system and excess water are removed in urine. The system also helps remove solid waste.

Immune: This includes the lymphatic system, lymph nodes, lymph vessels, thymus, and spleen. Lymph fluid is moved throughout the body by lymph vessels that provide protection against disease. This system protects the body from external intrusions, such as microscopic organisms and foreign substances. It can also protect against some cancerous cells.

Reproductive: In the male, this system includes the testes, vas deferens, urethra, prostate, penis, and scrotum. In the female, this system includes the ovaries, fallopian tubes (oviduct and uterine tubes), cervix, uterus, vagina, vulva, and mammary glands. Sexual reproduction helps provide genetic diversity as gametes from each parent contribute half the DNA to the zygote offspring. The system provides a method of transporting the male gametes to the female. It also allows for the growth and development of the embryo. Hormones involved are testosterone, interstitial cell stimulating hormone (ICSH), luteinizing hormone (LH), follicle stimulating hormone (FSH), and estrogen. Estrogens secreted from the ovaries include estradiol, estrone, and estriol. They encourage growth, among other things. Progesterone helps prepare the endometrium for pregnancy.

Reproductive systems in animals

Based on whether or not and when an organism uses meiosis or mitosis, the three possible cycles of reproduction are haplontic, diplontic, and haplodiplontic. Fungi, green algae, and protozoa are haplontic. Animals and some brown algae and fungi are diplontic. Plants and some fungi are haplodiplontic. Diplontic organisms, like multicelled animals, have a dominant diploid life cycle. The haploid generation is simply the egg and sperm. Monoecious species are bisexual (hermaphroditic). In this case, the individual has both male and female organs: sperm-bearing testicles and egg-bearing ovaries. Hermaphroditic species can self fertilize. Some worms are hermaphroditic. Cross fertilization is when individuals exchange genetic information. Most animal species are dioecious, meaning individuals are distinctly male or female.

Hormones

The small cone-like pineal glands located in the brain secrete melatonin, which acts as a biological clock. The dual-lobed pituitary gland in the brain secretes growth hormone (stimulates tissue growth), thyroid stimulating hormone (signals the body to produce thyroxin), adrenocorticotropic hormone (signals the adrenal gland to produce cortisol), follicle-stimulating hormone (signals ovarian follicles to mature in females; helps regulate sperm cell production in males), luteinizing hormone (stimulates the production of estrogens and starts ovulation; stimulates production of testosterone), melanocyte-stimulating hormone (skin tone), and prolactin (stimulates milk let-down). These are all secreted by the anterior lobe. The posterior lobe secretes antidiuretic hormone and oxytocin. The thyroid in the neck secretes thyroxine, triiodothyronine, and calcitonin. These are involved with brain development, reproductive tract functions, and metabolism regulation. The thymus secretes thymosin.

Nutritional requirements

Carbohydrates are the primary source of energy as they can be easily converted to glucose. Fats (oils or lipids) are usually not very water soluble, and vitamins A, D, E, and K are fat soluble. Fats are needed to help process these vitamins and can also store energy. Fats have the highest calorie value per gram (9,000 calories). Dietary fiber, or roughage, helps the excretory system. In humans, fiber can help regulate blood sugar levels, reduce heart disease, help food pass through the digestive system, and add bulk. Dietary minerals are chemical elements that are involved with biochemical functions in the body. Proteins consist of amino acids. Proteins are broken down in the body into amino acids that are used for protein biosynthesis or fuel. Vitamins are compounds that are not made by the body, but obtained through the diet. Water is necessary to prevent dehydration since water is lost through the excretory system and perspiration.

Classifications of animals

As heterotrophs, animals can be further classified as carnivores, herbivores, omnivores, and parasites. Predation refers to a predator that feeds on another organism, which results in its death. Detritivory refers to heterotrophs that consume organic dead matter. Carnivores are animals that are meat eaters. Herbivores are plant eaters, and omnivores eat both meat and plants. A parasite's food source is its host. A parasite lives off of a host, which does not benefit from the interaction. Nutrients can be classified as carbohydrates, fats, fiber, minerals, proteins, vitamins, and water. Each supply a specific substance required for various species to survive, grow, and reproduce. A calorie is a measurement of heat energy. It can be used to represent both how much energy a food can provide and how much energy an organism needs to live.

Vitamins

Humans need dietary vitamins, which can be classified as either water soluble or fat soluble. Vitamins A, D, E, and K are fat soluble. Vitamins C and B are water soluble. Vitamin A (retinol) can be found in milk, eggs, liver, and some vegetables and fruits. It plays a role in immune system function, cell growth, and eye function.

Vitamin C (ascorbic acid) is in berries, peppers, and citrus fruits. It helps promote cell cohesiveness and healthy bones, teeth, and gums. It also improves brain function and aids in the absorption of some minerals. Other vitamins include: D (calciferol), which strengthens bones; vitamin B_2 (riboflavin), which is found in eggs; vitamin E (tocopherol); B_{12} (cyanocobalamin), which plays a role in red blood cell and nerve function; K (phylloquinone), which is found in alfalfa; B_5 (pantothenic acid); B_7 (biotin); B_6 (pyridoxine); B_3 (niacin); B_9 (folic acid); and B_1 (thiamine), which is needed to convert carbohydrates and plays a role in heart, muscle and nervous system function.

Minerals

Dietary minerals that are necessary for humans include potassium, chloride, sodium, calcium, phosphorus, magnesium, zinc, iron, manganese, copper, iodine, selenium, and molybdenum. Potassium is involved with ATP synthesis, and can be found in beans, bananas, and potatoes. Chloride, found in salt, is involved in making hydrochloric acid in the stomach. Substances like potassium and sodium are electrolytes, which mean they are conductive. Calcium is in dairy products, nuts, and green leafy vegetables. It is involved in the functions of the muscle, heart, digestive system, and bones. Magnesium is in nuts and soy beans. It is involved in ATP synthesis. Some enzymes need zinc to function. Iron is in green leafy vegetables, fish, eggs, beans, whole and enriched grains, and red meat. It is used by proteins and enzymes. Manganese and selenium are enzyme co-factors.

Early growth in humans

The zygote has genetic information from both parent organisms. After fertilization, the zygote undergoes many mitotic divisions, also called cleavage, by which the cell divides and grows into a morula and then a blastula. This hollow sphere undergoes rearrangement and differentiation. In sponges, blastula larvae swim to a new location and then form into a new individual. In humans, the blastocyst is implanted by day six or seven. It attaches to the endometrium. The blastula forms a gastrula with a digestive chamber and two germ layers: the external ectoderm and internal endoderm. In most cases, a mesoderm also develops between them. These germ layers then differentiate to form tissues and organs. Roughly two weeks after fertilization, the embryo starts to form a yolk sac that will make blood cells, an embryonic disc, and a chorion (the placenta). By week three, the beginnings of the spinal cord, brain, muscles, bones, and face appear. After that, cardiac cells begin to beat.

Process of reproduction

Individuals of a species have specialized reproductive cells. These cells are responsible for meiosis, which typically results in motile spermatozoa in the male and non-motile, food-containing ova in the female (gametogenesis). Gametogenesis refers to the production of haploid gametes. Spermatogenesis refers to sperm production, which occurs in the testes. Oogenesis refers to egg formation, which takes place in the ovaries. It also produces a polar body. Before fertilization, the oocyte continues to develop in a follicle. In the female, human luteinizing hormone (LH) causes the follicle to break open and the oocyte to slowly move down the fallopian tube. Fertilization occurs when the two gametes fuse to form a zygote, which develops into an individual. Sperm needs to be deposited within five days of ovulation for fertilization to occur. The ovaries secrete estrogen and progesterone. The testes secrete testosterone. The placenta secretes chorionic gonadotropin.

Changes that can lead to disease

Sometimes, the body's immune system attacks its own cells even when they are harmless. Faulty genes can lead to body parts and systems that do not function properly. Viruses, which can get introduced to the body in a variety of ways, can cause gastrointestinal pain and destroy immune system cells, which leave the body vulnerable to secondary bacterial infections and cancer cell growth. Cardiac dysfunction is a response (a compensatory mechanism) to the heart trying to maintain normal heart function. Eventually, this causes the cardiac system to weaken. When the heart muscle contracts to pump blood out, it is referred to as systolic blood flow. When the heart muscle relaxes and blood flows back in, it is referred to as diastolic blood flow. If there are problems related to systolic and/or diastolic blood flow, the amount of blood output can be lessened. The ventricle can become stiffer and will not completely fill. Dysfunction can cause the heart to try to compensate and maintain normalcy by pumping harder.

Asexual reproduction

Asexual reproduction occurs when only one parent is responsible for reproduction. Forms of this include budding, fragmentation, parthenogenesis, and self-fertilization.

Budding: This occurs when the offspring start as a growth on the parent organism's body. Jellyfish and some echinoderms have buds that leave the parent. Other organisms, such as corals, continue to be attached and form colonies.

Fragmentation: This is similar to budding, but after maturity the individual fragments into about eight pieces. Each fragment develops into another mature individual. Some small worms reproduce using this method.

Parthenogenesis: This is also known as virgin birth because the female produces eggs that develop without being fertilized. Specific species of fish, insects, frogs, and lizards reproduce by parthenogenesis.

Self-fertilization: Some species are considered hermaphroditic, meaning individuals have both male and female reproductive parts. Fertilization can be achieved within the individual.

Social behaviors

Territoriality: This refers to members of a species protecting areas from other members of their species and from other species. Species members claim specific areas as their own.

Dominance: This refers to the species in a community that is the most populous.

Altruism: This is when a species or individual in a community exhibits behaviors that benefit another individual at a cost to itself. In biology, altruism does not have to be a conscious sacrifice.

Threat display: This refers to behavior by an organism that is intended to intimidate or frighten away members of its own or another species.

The principle of competitive exclusion (Gause's Law) states that if there are limited or insufficient resources and species are competing for them, these species will not be able to co-exist. The result is that one of the species will become extinct or be forced to undergo a behavioral or evolutionary change. Another way to say this is that "complete competitors cannot coexist."

Population

Population is a measure of how many individuals exist in a specific area. It can be used to measure the size of human, plant, or animal groups. Population growth depends on many factors. Factors that can limit the number of individuals in a population include lack of resources such as food and water, space, habitat destruction, competition, disease, and predators. Exponential growth refers to an unlimited rising growth rate. This kind of growth can be plotted on a chart in the shape of a J. Carrying capacity is the population size that can be sustained. The world's population is about 6.8 billion and growing. The human population has not yet reached its carrying capacity. Population dynamics refers to how a population changes over time and the factors that cause changes. An S-shaped curve shows that population growth has leveled off. Biotic potential refers to the maximum reproductive capacity of a population given ideal environmental conditions.

Interspecific relationships

Predation, parasitism, commensalism, and mutualism are all types of species interactions that affect species populations. Intraspecific relationships are relationships among members of a species. Interspecific relationships are relationships between members of different species.

Predation: This is a relationship in which one individual feeds on another (the prey), causing the prey to die.

Commensalism: This refers to interspecific relationships in which one of the organisms benefits. Mutualism, competition, and parasitism are all types of commensalism.

Mutualism: This is a relationship in which both organisms benefit from an interaction.

Competition: This is a relationship in which both organisms are harmed.

Parasitism: This is a relationship in which one organism benefits and the other is harmed.

Biomass: In ecology, biomass refers to the mass of one or all of the species (species biomass) in an ecosystem or area.

Community

A community is any number of species interacting within a given area. A niche is the role of a species within a community. Species diversity refers to the number of species within a community and their populations.

A biome refers to an area in which species are associated because of climate. The six major biomes in North America are desert, tropical rain forest, grassland, coniferous forest, deciduous forest, and tundra.

Biotic: Biotic factors are the living factors, such as other organisms, that affect a community or population. Abiotic factors are nonliving factors that affect a community or population, such as facets of the environment.

Ecology: Ecology is the study of plants, animals, their environments, and how they interact.

Ecosystem: An ecosystem is a community of species and all of the environment factors that affect them.

Food chains and biomagnifications

A food chain is a linking of organisms in a community that is based on how they use each other as food sources. Each link in the chain consumes the link above it and is consumed by the link below it. The exceptions are the organism at the top of the food chain and the organism at the bottom.

Biomagnification (bioamplification): This refers to an increase in concentration of a substance within a food chain. Examples are pesticides or mercury. Mercury is emitted from coal-fired power plants and gets into the water supply, where it is eaten by a fish. A larger fish eats smaller fish, and humans eat fish. The concentration of mercury in humans has now risen. Biomagnification is affected by the persistence of a chemical, whether it can be broken down and negated, food chain energetics, and whether organisms can reduce or negate the substance.

Ecoystem stability and ecologic succession

Ecosystem stability: This is a concept that states that a stable ecosystem is perfectly efficient. Seasonal changes or expected climate fluctuations are balanced by homeostasis. It also states that interspecies interactions are part of the balance of the system. Four principles of ecosystem stability are that waste disposal and nutrient replenishment by recycling is complete, the system uses sunlight as an energy source, biodiversity remains, and populations are stable in that they do not over consume resources.

Ecologic succession: This is the concept that states that there is an orderly progression of change within a community. An example of primary succession is that over hundreds of years bare rock decomposes to sand, which eventually leads to soil formation, which eventually leads to the growth of grasses and trees. Secondary succession occurs after a disturbance or major event that greatly affects a community, such as a wild fire or construction of a dam.

Biochemical cycles

Biochemical cycles are how chemical elements required by living organisms cycle between living and nonliving organisms. Elements that are frequently required are phosphorus, sulfur, oxygen, carbon, gaseous nitrogen, and water. Elements can go through gas cycles, sedimentary cycles, or both. Elements circulate through the air in a gas cycle and from land to water in a sedimentary one.

Mimicry is an adaptation developed as a response to predation. It refers to an organism that has a similar appearance to another species, which is meant to fool the predator into thinking the organism is more dangerous than it really is. Two examples are the drone fly and the io moth. The fly looks like a bee, but cannot sting. The io moth has markings on its wings that make it look like an owl. The moth can startle predators and gain time to escape. Predators can also use mimicry to lure their prey.

Food webs

A food web consists of interconnected food chains in a community. The organisms can be linked to show the direction of energy flow. Energy flow in this sense is used to refer to the actual caloric flow through a system from trophic level to trophic level. Trophic level refers to a link in a food chain or a level of nutrition. The 10% rule is that from trophic level to level, about 90% of the energy is lost (in the form of heat, for example). The lowest trophic level consists of primary producers (usually plants), then primary consumers, then secondary consumers, and finally tertiary consumers (large carnivores). The final link is decomposers, which break down the consumers at the top. Food chains usually do not contain more than six links. These links may also be referred to as ecological pyramids.

Contributing individuals to the theory of evolution

Cuvier (1744-1829)
Cuvier was a French naturalist who used the fossil record (paleontology) to compare the anatomies of extinct species and existing species to make conclusions about extinction. He believed in the catastrophism theory more strongly than the theory of evolution.

Lamarck (1769-1832)
Lamarck was a French naturalist who believed in the idea of evolution and thought it was a natural occurrence influenced by the environment. He studied medicine and botany. Lamarck put forth a theory of evolution by inheritance of acquired characteristics. He theorized that organisms became more complex by moving up a ladder of progress.

Lyell (1797-1875)
Lyell was a British geologist who believed in geographical uniformitarianism, which can be contrasted with catastrophism.

Charles Robert Darwin (1809-1882)
Darwin was an English naturalist known for his belief that evolution occurred by natural selection. He believed that species descend from common ancestors.

Alfred Russell Wallace (1823-1913)
He was a British naturalist who independently developed a theory of evolution by natural selection. He believed in the transmutation of species (that one species develops into another).

Inquiry

Teaching with the concept of scientific inquiry in mind encourages students to think like scientists rather than merely practice the rote memorization of facts and history. This belief in scientific inquiry puts the burden of learning on students, which is a much different approach than expecting them to simply accept and memorize what they are taught. The standards for science as inquiry are intended to be comprehensive, encompassing a student's K-12 education. More are addressed as students gain knowledge. The National

Science Education Standards state that engaging students in inquiry helps them develop the following five skills:
- Understand scientific concepts.
- Appreciate "how we know" what we know in science.
- Understand the nature of science.
- Develop the skills necessary to become independent inquirers about the natural world.
- Develop the skills necessary to use the skills, abilities, and attitudes associated with science.

Abilities that K-4 students should acquire

The six abilities that grades K-4 students should acquire are as follows:
- They should be able to ask questions about objects, organisms, and events in the environment.
- They should be able to devise a simple investigation to answer a question.
- They should be able to use tools such as magnifying glasses, rulers, and balances to gather data and make observations.
- They should be able to use the gathered data and observations to provide an explanation.
- They should be able to talk about, draw pictures, or use another method to communicate the results of an investigation and what they learned.
- With respect to the nature of scientific inquiry and scientists, students should understand that investigations involve formulating questions and answers, using different methods of discovering and disclosing answers, using basic tools, observing, sharing answers, and looking at and understanding others' work.

Abilities that 5-8 students should acquire

The five abilities that grades 5-8 students should acquire are as follows:
- They should be able to reformulate and clarify questions until they can be answered through scientific investigation.
- They should be able to create and carry out a scientific investigation, interpret the data to provide explanations, and use further data to revise explanations.
- They should be able to identify the tools necessary to gather and analyze data. They should be able to use computer hardware and software to store, organize, and gather data.
- They should be able to provide descriptions and explanations, create models, and make predictions based on the body of knowledge they possess.
- They should be able to explain cause and effect relationships using explanations and data from experiments.

Abilities that 9-12 students should acquire

The six abilities that 9-12 students should acquire are as follows:
- They should be able to identify questions and concepts that guide scientific investigation. In other words, they should be able to create a hypothesis and an appropriate experiment to test that hypothesis.

- They should be able to design and conduct a scientific investigation from start to finish. This includes being able to guide the inquiry by choosing the proper technologies and methods, determining variables, selecting an appropriate method for presenting data, and conducting peer reviews.
- They should be able to use technology and mathematics in investigations.
- They should be able to formulate and revise scientific explanations and models.
- They should be able to recognize and analyze alternative explanations. In other words, they should be able to devise other possibilities based on the current body of knowledge.
- They should be able to communicate and defend a scientific argument in both written and oral form.

Scientific knowledge

The National Science Education Standards suggest that science as a whole and its unifying concepts and processes are a way of thought that is taught throughout a student's K-12 education. There are eight areas of content, and all the concepts, procedures, and underlying principles contained within make up the body of scientific knowledge. The areas of content are: unifying concepts and processes in science, science as inquiry, physical science, life science, earth and space science, science and technology, science in personal and social perspectives, and history and nature of science. Specific unifying concepts and processes included in the standards and repeated throughout the content areas are: systems, order, and organization; evidence, models, and explanation; change, constancy, and measurement; evolution and equilibrium; and form and function.

Evolution of scientific knowledge

When one examines the history of scientific knowledge, it is clear that it is constantly evolving. The body of facts, models, theories, and laws grows and changes over time. In other words, one scientific discovery leads to the next. Some advances in science and technology have important and long-lasting effects on science and society. Some discoveries were so alien to the accepted beliefs of the time that not only were they rejected as wrong, but were also considered outright blasphemy. Today, however, many beliefs once considered incorrect have become an ingrained part of scientific knowledge, and have also been the basis of new advances. Examples of advances include: Copernicus's heliocentric view of the universe, Newton's laws of motion and planetary orbits, relativity, geologic time scale, plate tectonics, atomic theory, nuclear physics, biological evolution, germ theory, industrial revolution, molecular biology, information and communication, quantum theory, galactic universe, and medical and health technology.

Facts, hypotheses, theories, models, and laws

A scientific fact is considered an objective and verifiable observation. A scientific theory is a greater body of accepted knowledge, principles, or relationships that might explain a fact. A hypothesis is an educated guess that is not yet proven. It is used to predict the outcome of an experiment in an attempt to solve a problem or answer a question. A law is an explanation of events that always lead to the same outcome. It is a fact that an object falls. The law of gravity explains why an object falls. The theory of relativity, although generally accepted, has been neither proven nor disproved. A model is used to explain something on a smaller scale or in simpler terms to provide an example. It is a representation of an idea that can be used to explain events or applied to new situations to predict outcomes or determine results.

Scientific method

One could argue that scientific knowledge is the sum of all scientific inquiries for truths about the natural world carried out throughout the history of human kind. More simply put, it is thanks to scientific inquiry that we know what we do about the world. Scientists use a number of generally accepted techniques collectively known as the scientific method. The scientific method generally involves carrying out the following steps:

- Identifying a problem or posing a question
- Formulating a hypothesis or an educated guess
- Conducting experiments or tests that will provide a basis to solve the problem or answer the question
- Observing the results of the test
- Drawing conclusions

An important part of the scientific method is using acceptable experimentation techniques to ensure results are not skewed. Objectivity is also important if valid results are to be obtained. Another important part of the scientific method is peer review. It is essential that experiments be performed and data be recorded in such a way that experiments can be reproduced to verify results.

CGS and MKS

The metric system is the accepted standard of measurement in the scientific community. The International System (SI) of Units is a set of measurements (including the metric system) that is almost globally accepted. The United States, Liberia, and Myanmar have not accepted this system. Standardization is important because it allows the results of experiments to be compared and reproduced without the need to laboriously convert measurements. The SI is based partially on the meter-kilogram-second (MKS) system rather than the centimeter-gram-second (CGS) system. The MKS system considers meters, kilograms, and seconds to be the basic units of measurement, while the CGS system considers centimeters, grams, and seconds to be the basic units of measurement. Under the MKS system, the length of an object would be expressed as 1 meter instead of 100 centimeters, which is how it would be described under the CGS system.

Metric system

Using the metric system is generally accepted as the preferred method for taking measurements. Having a universal standard allows individuals to interpret measurements more easily, regardless of where they are located. The basic units of measurement are: the meter, which measures length; the liter, which measures volume; and the gram, which measures mass. The metric system starts with a base unit and increases or decreases in units of 10. The prefix and the base unit combined are used to indicate an amount. For example, deka is 10 times the base unit. A dekameter is 10 meters; a dekaliter is 10 liters; and a dekagram is 10 grams. The prefix hecto refers to 100 times the base amount; kilo is 1,000 times the base amount. The prefixes that indicate a fraction of the base unit are deci,

- 52 -

which is 1/10 of the base unit; centi, which is 1/100 of the base unit; and milli, which is 1/1000 of the base unit.

Metric prefixes for multiples and subdivisions

The prefixes for multiples are as follows: deka (da), 10^1 (deka is the American spelling, but deca is also used); hecto (h), 10^2; kilo (k), 10^3; mega (M), 10^6; giga (G), 10^9; tera (T), 10^{12}; peta (P), 10^{15}; exa (E), 10^{18}; zetta (Z), 10^{21}; and yotta (Y), 10^{24}. The prefixes for subdivisions are as follows: deci (d), 10^{-1}; centi (c), 10^{-2}; milli (m), 10^{-3}; micro (μ), 10^{-6}; nano (n), 10^{-9}; pico (p), 10^{-12}; femto (f), 10^{-15}; atto (a), 10^{-18}; zepto (z), 10^{-21}; and yocto (y), 10^{-24}. The rule of thumb is that prefixes greater than 10^3 are capitalized. These abbreviations do not need a period after them. A decimeter is a tenth of a meter, a deciliter is a tenth of a liter, and a decigram is a tenth of a gram. Pluralization is understood. For example, when referring to 5 mL of water, no "s" needs to be added to the abbreviation.

SI units of measurement

SI uses second(s) to measure time. Fractions of seconds are usually measured in metric terms using prefixes such as millisecond (1/1,000 of a second) or nanosecond (1/1,000,000,000 of a second). Increments of time larger than a second are measured in minutes and hours, which are multiples of 60 and 24. An example of this is a swimmer's time in the 800-meter freestyle being described as 7:32.67, meaning 7 minutes, 32 seconds, and 67 one-hundreds of a second. One second is equal to 1/60 of a minute, 1/3,600 of an hour, and 1/86,400 of a day. Other SI base units are the ampere (A) (used to measure electric current), the kelvin (K) (used to measure thermodynamic temperature), the candela (cd) (used to measure luminous intensity), and the mole (mol) (used to measure the amount of a substance at a molecular level). Meter (m) is used to measure length and kilogram (kg) is used to measure mass.

Significant figures and estimation

The mathematical concept of significant figures or significant digits is often used to determine the accuracy of measurements or the level of confidence one has in a specific measurement. The significant figures of a measurement include all the digits known with certainty plus one estimated or uncertain digit. There are a number of rules for determining which digits are considered "important" or "interesting." They are: all non-zero digits are significant, zeros between digits are significant, and leading and trailing zeros are not significant unless they appear to the right of the non-zero digits in a decimal. For example, in 0.01230 the significant digits are 1230, and this number would be said to be accurate to the hundred-thousandths place. The zero indicates that the amount has actually been measured as 0. Other zeros are considered place holders, and are not important. A decimal point may be placed after zeros to indicate their importance (in 100. for example).

Convertion from decimal notation to scientific notation

Scientific notation is used because values in science can be very large or very small, which makes them unwieldy. A number in decimal notation is 93,000,000. In scientific notation, it is 9.3×10^7. The first number, 9.3, is the coefficient. It is always greater than or equal to 1 and less than 10. This number is followed by a multiplication sign. The base is always 10 in

- 53 -

scientific notation. If the number is greater than zero, the exponent is a positive number. If it is less than zero, the exponent is negative. The first digit of the number is followed by a decimal point and then the rest of the number. In this case, the number is 9.3. To get that number, the decimal point was moved seven places from the end of the number, 93,000,000. The number of places, seven, is the exponent.

Lab report

A lab report is an item developed after an experiment that is intended to present the results of a lab experiment. Generally, it should be prepared using a word processor, not hand-written or recorded in a notebook. A lab report should be formally presented. It is intended to persuade others with its acceptance or rejection of a hypothesis and become part of the body of scientific knowledge. It should include a brief but descriptive title and an abstract. The abstract is a summary of the report. It should include a purpose that states the problem that was explored or the question that was answered. It should also include a hypothesis that describes the anticipated results of the experiment. The experiment should include a control and one variable to ensure the results can be interpreted correctly. Observations and results can be presented using written narratives, tables, graphs, and illustrations. The report should also include a summation or conclusion explaining whether the results supported the hypothesis.

Lab notebook

A lab notebook is a record of all pre-lab work and lab work. It differs from a lab report, which is prepared after lab work is completed. A lab notebook is a formal record of lab preparations and what was done. Observational recordings should not be altered, erased, or whited-out to make corrections. Drawing a single line through an entry is sufficient to make changes. Pages should be numbered and should not be torn out. Entries should be made neatly, but don't necessarily have to be complete sentences. Entries should provide detailed information and be recorded in such a way that another person could use them to replicate the experiment. Quantitative data may be recorded in tabular form, and may include calculations made during an experiment. Lab book entries can also include references and research performed before the experiment. Entries may also consist of information about a lab experiment, including the objective or purpose, the procedures, data collected, and the results.

Graphs and charts

Graphs and charts are effective ways to present scientific data such as observations, statistical analyses, and comparisons between dependent variables and independent variables. On a line chart, the independent variable (the one that acts as a control or does not change during an experiment) is represented on the horizontal axis (the x-axis). The dependent variables (the ones that are manipulated during an experiment) are represented on the y-axis. The points are charted and a line is drawn to connect the points. An XY or scatter plot is often used to plot many points. A "best fit" line is drawn, which allows outliers to be identified more easily. Charts and their axes should have titles. The x and y interval units should be evenly spaced and labeled. Other types of charts are bar charts and histograms, which can be used to compare differences between the data collected for two variables. A pie chart can graphically show the relation of parts to a whole.

Presentation of data

Data collected during a science lab can be organized and presented in any number of ways. While straight narrative is a suitable method for presenting some lab results, it is not a suitable way to present numbers and quantitative measurements. These types of observations can often be better presented with tables and graphs. Data that is presented in tables and organized in rows and columns may also be used to make graphs quite easily. Other methods of presenting data include illustrations, photographs, video, and even audio formats. In a formal report, tables and figures are labeled and referred to by their labels. For example, a picture of a bubbly solution might be labeled Figure 1, Bubbly Solution. It would be referred to in the text in the following way: "The reaction created bubbles 10 mm in size, as shown in Figure 1, Bubbly Solution." Graphs are also labeled as figures. Tables are labeled in a different way. Examples include: Table 1, Results of Statistical Analysis, or Table 2, Data from Lab 2.

Errors

Errors that occur during an experiment can be classified into two categories: random errors and systematic errors. Random errors can result in collected data that does not seem to fit and may be wildly different from the rest of the data, or they may result in data that is indistinguishable from the rest. Random errors are not consistent across the data set. In large data sets, random errors may contribute to the variability of data, but they will not affect the average. Random errors are sometimes referred to as noise. They may be caused by a student's inability to take the same measurement in exactly the same way or by outside factors that are not considered variables, but influence the data. A systematic error will show up consistently across a sample or data set, and may be the result of a flaw in the experiment design. This type of error affects the average, and is also known as bias.

Accident safety measures

Any spills or accidents should be reported to the teacher so that he can determine the safest clean-up method. The student should start to wash off a chemical spilled on the skin while reporting the incident. Some spills may require removal of contaminated clothing and use of the safety shower. Broken glass should be disposed of in a designated container. If someone's clothing catches fire they should walk to the safety shower and use it to extinguish the flames. A fire blanket may be used to smother a lab fire. A fire extinguisher, phone, spill neutralizers, and a first aid box are other types of safety equipment found in the lab. Students should be familiar with routes out of the room and the building in case of fire. Students should use the eye wash station if a chemical gets in the eyes.

Lab safety measures

Students should wear a lab apron and safety goggles. Loose or dangling clothing and jewelry, necklaces, and earrings should not be worn. Those with long hair should tie it back. Care should always be taken not to splash chemicals. Open-toed shoes such as sandals and flip-flops should not be worn, nor should wrist watches. Glasses are preferable to contact lenses since the latter carries a risk of chemicals getting caught between the lens and the eye. Students should always be supervised. The area where the experiment is taking place and the surrounding floor should be free of clutter. Only the lab book and the items necessary for the experiment should be present. There is no smoking, eating, or chewing gum in the lab. Cords should not be allowed to dangle from work stations. There should be no rough-housing in the lab. Hands should be washed after the lab is complete.

Fume hood

Because of the potential safety hazards associated with chemistry lab experiments, such as fire from vapors and the inhalation of toxic fumes, a fume hood should be used in many instances. It carries away vapors from reagents or reactions. A fume hood can reduce exposure to potentially harmful fumes or vapors. Equipment or reactions are placed as far back in the hood as practical to help enhance the collection of the fumes. The glass safety shield automatically closes to the appropriate height, and should be low enough to protect the face and body. The safety shield should only be raised to move equipment in and out of the hood. One should not climb inside a hood or stick one's head inside. All spills should be wiped up immediately and the glass should be cleaned if a splash occurs.

Possible safety hazards

Some specific safety hazards possible in a chemistry lab include:
- Fire: Fire can be caused by volatile solvents such as ether, acetone, and benzene being kept in an open beaker or Erlenmeyer flask. Vapors can creep along the table and ignite if they reach a flame or spark. Solvents should be heated in a hood with a steam bath, not on a hot plate.
- Explosion: Heating or creating a reaction in a closed system can cause an explosion, resulting in flying glass and chemical splashes. The system should be vented to prevent this.
- Chemical and thermal burns: Many mineral acids and alkalis are corrosive to the skin and eyes. Others like acid halides and phenols are corrosive and often toxic.
- Cuts from broken glass.
- Absorption of toxic chemicals such as dimethyl sulfoxide (DMSO) and nitrobenzene through the skin. Inhalation of toxic fumes: Some compounds, such as acetyl chloride, severely irritate membranes in the eyes, nose, throat, and lungs. Others, such as benzyl chloride, cause eye irritation and tears.
- Ingestion of toxic chemicals.

Safety gloves

There are many types of gloves available to help protect the skin from cuts, burns, and chemical splashes. There are many considerations to take into account when choosing a glove. For example, gloves that are highly protective may limit dexterity. Some gloves may not offer appropriate protection against a specific chemical. Other considerations include degradation rating, which indicates how effective a glove is when exposed to chemicals; breakthrough time, which indicates how quickly a chemical breaks through the surface of the glove; and permeation rate, which indicates how quickly chemicals seep through after the initial breakthrough. Disposable latex, vinyl, or nitrile examination gloves are usually appropriate for most circumstances, and offer protection from incidental splashes and contact. Other types of gloves include butyl, neoprene, PVC, PVA, viton, silver shield, and natural rubber. Each offers its own type of protection, but may have drawbacks as well. Double gloving can improve resistance or dexterity in some instances.

Chemical handling and storage

Students should take care when carrying chemicals from one place to another. They should never be taken from the room, tasted, or touched with bare hands. Safety gloves should be worn when appropriate and glove/chemical interactions and glove deterioration should be considered. Hands should always be washed thoroughly after a lab. Potentially hazardous materials intended for use in chemistry, biology, or other science labs should be secured in a safe area where relevant material safety data sheets (MSDS) can be accessed. Chemicals and solutions should be used as directed and labels should be read before handling solutions and chemicals. Extra chemicals should not be returned to their original containers, but should be disposed of as directed by the school district's rules or local ordinances. Local municipalities often have hazardous waste disposal programs. Acids should be stored separately. Flammable liquids should be stored away from acids, bases, and oxidizers.

Bunsen burners

First, loose clothing should be tucked in, long hair should be tied back, and safety goggles and aprons should be worn. Students should be familiar with other safety precautions as well. They should know where the safety shower and eye wash centers are and how to use them. They should also know what to do in case of a fire or accident. Ensure that the Bunsen burner being lit and burners at nearby work stations are turned off before starting. When lighting the burner, strikers should always be used instead of matches. Do not touch the hot barrel. Tongs (never fingers) should be used to hold the material in the flame. To heat liquid, a flask may be set upon wire gauze on a tripod and secured with an iron ring or clamp on a stand. The flame is extinguished by turning off the gas at the source.

Lab animals and dissections

Animals to be used for dissections in a general science, biology, or physiology class should be obtained from a company that provides animals for this purpose. Road kill or decaying animals that a student brings in should not be used. It is possible that such an animal may have a pathogen or a virus, such as rabies, which can be transmitted via the saliva of even a dead animal. Students should use gloves and should not participate if they have open sores or moral objections. It is generally accepted that biological experiments may be performed on lower-order life forms and invertebrates, but not on mammalian vertebrates and birds. No animals should be harmed physiologically. Experimental animals should be kept, cared for, and handled in a safe manner and with compassion. Pathogenic (anything able to cause a disease) substances should not be used in lab experiments.

Lab glassware: flasks, beakers, and pipettes

Two types of flasks commonly used in lab settings are Erlenmeyer flasks and volumetric flasks, which can also be used to accurately measure liquids. Erlenmeyer flasks and beakers can be used for mixing, transporting, and reacting, but are not appropriate for accurate measurements. A pipette can be used to accurately measure small amounts of liquid. Liquid is drawn into the pipette through the bulb and a finger is then quickly placed at the top of the container. The liquid measurement is read exactly at the meniscus. Liquid can be released from the pipette by lifting the finger. There are also plastic disposal pipettes. A repipette is a hand-operated pump that dispenses solutions.

Lab glassware: graduated cylinders and burettes

Graduated cylinders are used for precise measurements and are considered more accurate than flasks or beakers. They are made of either polypropylene (which is shatter-resistant and resistant to chemicals but can not be heated) or polymethylpentene (which is known for its clarity). They are lighter to ship and less fragile than glass. To read a graduated cylinder, it should be placed on a flat surface and read at eye level. The surface of a liquid in a graduated cylinder forms a lens-shaped curve. The measurement should be taken from the bottom of the curve. A ring may be placed at the top of tall, narrow cylinders to help avoid breakage if they are tipped over. A burette, or buret, is a piece of lab glassware used to accurately dispense liquid. It looks similar to a narrow graduated cylinder, but includes a stopcock and tip. It may be filled with a funnel or pipette.

Light microscopes

There are different kinds of microscopes, but optical or light microscopes are the most commonly used in lab settings. Light and lenses are used to magnify and view samples. A specimen or sample is placed on a slide and the slide is placed on a stage with a hole in it. Light passes through the hole and illuminates the sample. The sample is magnified by lenses and viewed through the eyepiece. A simple microscope has one lens, while a typical compound microscope has three lenses. The light source can be room light redirected by a mirror or the microscope can have its own independent light source that passes through a condenser. In this case, there are diaphragms and filters to allow light intensity to be controlled. Optical microscopes also have coarse and fine adjustment knobs.

Other types of microscopes

Other types of microscopes include digital microscopes, which use a camera and a monitor to allow viewing of the sample. No eyepiece or methods for viewing samples directly exist. Scanning electron microscopes (SEMs) provide greater detail of a sample in terms of the surface topography and can produce magnifications much greater than those possible with optical microscopes. The technology of an SEM is quite different from an optical microscope in that it doesn't rely on lenses to magnify objects, but uses samples placed in a chamber. In one type of SEM, a beam of electrons from an electron gun scans and actually interacts with the sample to produce an image.

Balances

Unlike laboratory glassware that measures volume, balances such as triple-beam balances, spring balances, and electronic balances measure mass and force. An electronic balance is the most accurate, followed by a triple-beam balance and then a spring balance. One part of a triple-beam balance is the plate, which is where the item to be weighed is placed. There are also three beams that have hatch marks indicating amounts and hold the weights that rest in the notches. The front beam measures weights between 0 and 10 grams, the middle beam measures weights in 100 gram increments, and the far beam measures weights in 10 gram increments. The sum of the weight of each beam is the total weight of the object. A triple beam balance also includes a set screw to calibrate the equipment and a mark indicating the object and counterweights are in balance. Analytical balances are accurate to within 0.0001 g.

Slide preparation

Wet mount slides designed for use with a light microscope typically require a thin portion of the specimen to be placed on a standard glass slide. A drop of water is added and a cover slip or cover glass is placed on top. Air bubbles and fingerprints can make viewing difficult. Placing the cover slip on at a 45 degree angle and allowing it to drop into place can help avoid the problem of air bubbles. A cover slip should always be used when viewing wet mount slides. The viewer should start with the objective in its lowest position and then fine focus. The microscope should be carried with two hands and stored with the low-power objective in the down position. Lenses should be cleaned with lens paper only. A graticule slide is marked with a grid line, and is useful only for counting or estimating a quantity.

Chromatography

Chromatography refers to a set of laboratory techniques used to separate or analyze mixtures. Mixtures are dissolved in their mobile phases. In the stationary or bonded phase, the desired component is separated from other molecules in the mixture. In chromatography, the analyte is the substance to be separated. Preparative chromatography refers to the type of chromatography that involves purifying a substance for further use rather than further analysis. Analytical chromatography involves analyzing the isolated substance. Other types of chromatography include column, planar, paper, thin layer, displacement, supercritical fluid, affinity, ion exchange, and site exclusion chromatography. Reversed phase, two-dimensional, simulated moving bed, pyrolysis, fast protein, counter current, and chiral are also types of chromatography. Gas chromatography refers to the separation technique in which the mobile phase of a substance is in gas form.

Preparation of materials for classroom use

A reagent or reactant is a chemical agent for use in chemical reactions. When preparing for a lab, it should be confirmed that glassware and other equipment has been cleaned and/or sterilized. There should be enough materials, reagents, or other solutions needed for the lab for every group of students completing the experiment. Distilled water should be used instead of tap water when performing lab experiments because distilled water has most of its impurities removed. Other needed apparatus such as funnels, filter paper, balances, Bunsen burners, ring stands, and/or microscopes should also be set up. After the lab, it should be confirmed that sinks, workstations, and any equipment used have been cleaned. If chemicals or specimens need to be kept at a certain temperature by refrigerating them or using another storage method, the temperature should be checked periodically to ensure the sample does not spoil.

Centrifugation

A centrifuge is used to perform centrifugation, which is a process that separates a heterogeneous mixture (one consisting of two or more compounds) of a solid and a liquid by spinning it. Centrifugation uses centrifugal force to separate compounds in a mixture. The solid precipitate settles in the bottom of the test tube and the liquid component of the solution, called the centrifugate, is clear. A well-known application of this process is using a centrifuge to separate blood cells and plasma. The heavier cells settle on the bottom of the test tube and the lighter plasma stays on top. An accessible example of this principle is using a salad spinner to help dry lettuce.

Spectrophotometry

Spectrophotometry involves measuring the amount of visible light absorbed by a colored solution. There are analog and digital spectrometers that measure percent absorbency and percent transmittance. A single beam spectrometer measures relative light intensity. A double beam spectrometer compares light intensity between a reference sample and a test sample. Spectrometers measure the wavelength of light. Spectrometry not only involves working with visible light, but also near-ultraviolet and near-infrared light. A spectrophotometer includes an illumination source. An output wavelength is selected and beamed at the sample, the sample absorbs light, and the detector responds to the light and outputs an analog electronic current in a usable form. A spectrophotometer may require calibration. Some types can be used to identify unknown chemicals.

Electrophoresis, calorimetry, and titration

Electrophoresis is the process whereby molecules are separated using electrical charges. This is possible because particles disbursed in a fluid usually carry electric charges on their surfaces. Molecules are pulled through the fluid toward the positive end if the molecules have a negative charge, and are pulled through the fluid toward the negative end if the molecules have a positive charge. Calorimetry is used to determine the heat released or absorbed in a chemical reaction. Titration helps determine the precise endpoint of a reaction. With this information, the precise quantity of reactant in the titration flask can be determined. A burette is used to deliver the second reactant to the flask and an indicator or pH meter is used to detect the endpoint of the reaction.

Field studies

Field studies may facilitate scientific inquiry in a manner similar to indoor lab experiments. Field studies can be interdisciplinary in nature and can help students learn about any number of scientific concepts and apply many scientific processes. Research projects can be conducted at accessible locations, such as school campuses and local parks, or at more remote locations, including local state and national parks, beaches, mountains, and other places with unique geological properties. Students can practice the general techniques of observation, data collection and organization, collaborative planning, and analysis of experiments. Field studies give students the chance to learn through hands-on applications of scientific processes, such as map making in geography, observation of stratification in geology, observation of life cycles of plants and animals in live and changing biological settings, analysis of water quality in chemistry, and quantitative analysis in math and statistics, just to name a few.

Field study safety concerns

Students should watch out for obvious outdoor hazards. These include poisonous flora and fauna such as poison ivy, poison oak, and sumac. Depending on the region of the United States in which the field study is being conducted, hazards may also include rattlesnakes and black widow or brown recluse spiders. Students should also be made aware of potentially hazardous situations specific to geographic locales, such as great tidal changes, incoming waves, and blow holes at the beach; the chance of becoming lost or disoriented in a nature setting; thunderstorms, sudden rain, snow storms, and flash flooding; steep paths or paths with precarious footing; dilapidated foot bridges; and fast moving streams. Students should also be aware of the possibility of coming into contact with pathogens if, for example, they are conducting an on-campus survey of micro-organisms.

Field study techniques

Field studies allow for great flexibility in the use of traditional and technological methods for making observations and collecting data. For example, a nature study could consist of a simple survey of bird species within a given area. Information could be recorded using still photography or a video camera. This type of activity gives students the chance to use technologies other than computers. Computers could still be used to create a slide show of transferred images or a digital lab report. If a quantitative study of birds was being performed, the simple technique of using a pencil and paper to tabulate the number of birds counted in the field could also be used. Other techniques used during field studies could include collecting specimens for lab study, observing coastal ecosystems and tides, and collecting weather data such as temperature, precipitation amounts, and air pressure in a particular locale.

Contributing individuals to scientific methodology

Charles Robert Darwin (d. 1882)
Best known for contributing to the survival of the fittest through natural selection theory of evolution by observing different species of birds, specifically finches, in various geographic locations. Although the species Darwin looked at were different, he speculated they had a common ancestor. He reasoned that specific traits persisted because they gave the birds a greater chance of surviving and reproducing. He also discovered fossils, noted stratification, dissected marine animals, and interacted with indigenous peoples. He contributed to the fields of biology, marine biology, anthropology, paleontology, geography, and zoology.

Anton van Leeuwenhoek (d. 1723)
Used homemade magnifying glasses to become the first person to observe single-celled organisms. He observed bacteria, yeast, plants, and other microscopic organisms. His observations contributed to the field of microbiology.

Carl Linnaeus (d. 1778)
Created a method to classify plants and animals, which became known as the Linnaean taxonomy. This was an important contribution because it offered a way to organize and therefore study large amounts of data.

Barbara McClintock (d. 1992)
Created the first genetic map for maize and was able to demonstrate basic genetic principles, such as how recombination is an exchange of chromosomal information. She also discovered how transposition flips the switch for traits. Her work contributed to the field of genetics, in particular to areas of study concerned with the structure and function of cells and chromosomes.

Gregor Johann Mendel (d. 1884)

Famous for experimenting with pea plants to observe the occurrence of inherited traits. He eventually became known as the father of genetics.

James Watson and Francis Crick (d. 2004)

Co-discoverers of the structure of deoxyribonucleic acid (DNA), which has a double helix shape. DNA contains the code for genetic information. The discovery of the double helix shape was important because it helped to explain how DNA replicates.

Physical Science

Atoms

All matter consists of atoms. Atoms consist of a nucleus and electrons. The nucleus consists of protons and neutrons. The properties of these are measurable; they have mass and an electrical charge. The nucleus is positively charged due to the presence of protons. Electrons are negatively charged and orbit the nucleus. The nucleus has considerably more mass than the surrounding electrons. Atoms can bond together to make molecules. Atoms that have an equal number of protons and electrons are electrically neutral. If the number of protons and electrons in an atom is not equal, the atom has a positive or negative charge and is an ion.

Atoms are extremely small. A hydrogen atom is about 5×10^{-8} mm in diameter. According to some estimates, five trillion hydrogen atoms could fit on the head of a pin. Atomic radius refers to the average distance between the nucleus and the outermost electron. Models of atoms that include the proton, nucleus, and electrons typically show the electrons very close to the nucleus and revolving around it, similar to how the Earth orbits the sun. However, another model relates the Earth as the nucleus and its atmosphere as electrons, which is the basis of the term "electron cloud." Another description is that electrons swarm around the nucleus. It should be noted that these atomic models are not to scale. A more accurate representation would be a nucleus with a diameter of about 2 cm in a stadium. The electrons would be in the bleachers. This model is similar to the not-to-scale solar system model.

Matter refers to substances that have mass and occupy space (or volume). The traditional definition of matter describes it as having three states: solid, liquid, and gas. These different states are caused by differences in the distances and angles between molecules or atoms, which result in differences in the energy that binds them. Solid structures are rigid or nearly rigid and have strong bonds. Molecules or atoms of liquids move around and have weak bonds, although they are not weak enough to readily break. Molecules or atoms of gases move almost independently of each other, are typically far apart, and do not form bonds. The current definition of matter describes it as having four states. The fourth is plasma, which is an ionized gas that has some electrons that are described as free because they are not bound to an atom or molecule.

An atom is one of the most basic units of matter. An atom consists of a central nucleus surrounded by electrons. The nucleus of an atom consists of protons and neutrons. It is positively charged, dense, and heavier than the surrounding electrons. The plural form of nucleus is nuclei. Neutrons are the uncharged atomic particles contained within the nucleus. The number of neutrons in a nucleus can be represented as "N." Along with neutrons, protons make up the nucleus of an atom. The number of protons in the nucleus determines the atomic number of an element. Carbon atoms, for example, have six protons. The atomic number of carbon is 6. Nucleon refers collectively to neutrons and protons. Electrons are atomic particles that are negatively charged and orbit the nucleus of an atom. The number of protons minus the number of electrons indicates the charge of an atom. The atomic number of an element refers to the number of protons in the nucleus of an atom. It is a unique identifier. It can be represented as Z. Atoms with a neutral charge have an atomic number that is equal to the number of electrons. Atomic mass is also known as the mass number. The atomic mass is the total number of protons and neutrons in the nucleus of an atom. It is referred to as "A." The atomic mass (A) is equal to the number of protons (Z) plus the number of neutrons (N). This can be represented by the equation $A = Z + N$. The mass of electrons in an atom is basically insignificant because it is so small. Atomic weight may sometimes be referred to as "relative atomic mass," but should not be confused with atomic mass. Atomic weight is the ratio of the average mass per atom of a sample (which can include various isotopes of an element) to 1/12 of the mass of an atom of carbon-12.

An element is matter with one particular type of atom. It can be identified by its atomic number, or the number of protons in its nucleus. There are approximately 117 elements currently known, 94 of which occur naturally on Earth. Elements from the periodic table include hydrogen, carbon, iron, helium, mercury, and oxygen. Atoms combine to form molecules. For example, two atoms of hydrogen (H) and one atom of oxygen (O) combine to form water (H_2O).

Compounds are substances containing two or more elements. Compounds are formed by chemical reactions and frequently have different properties than the original elements. Compounds are decomposed by a chemical reaction rather than separated by a physical one.

Binary compounds refer to compounds that contain only two elements. They can be ionic or covalent. Binary ionic compounds are formed by cations (metallic positive ions) and anions (nonmetal negative ions). Ionic compounds are not molecules. The suffix "ide" is used if there is one anion, as in the case of cuprous oxide, for example. Another example is that fluorine is an element, while fluoride is the negative ion of fluorine. The binary compound barium fluoride would be written as BaF_2. This is because one barium ion has a charge of +2 and one fluoride ion has a charge of -1, so it would take two fluoride ions to balance out the one barium ion. If there is no charge symbol, it is assumed that the charge is 1. The suffixes "ate" or "ite" are used when there is more than one anion, as in the case of mercurous nitrate, for example. A ternary compound is one formed of three elements.

Hydrogen bonds are weaker than covalent and ionic bonds, and refer to the type of attraction in an electronegative atom such as oxygen, fluorine, or nitrogen. Hydrogen bonds can form within a single molecule or between molecules. A water molecule is polar, meaning it is partially positively charged on one end (the hydrogen end) and partially negatively charged on the other (the oxygen end). This is because the hydrogen atoms are arranged around the oxygen atom in a close tetrahedron. Hydrogen is oxidized (its number of electrons is reduced) when it bonds with oxygen to form water. Hydrogen bonds tend not only to be weak, but also short-lived. They also tend to be numerous. Hydrogen bonds give water many of its important properties, including its high specific heat and high heat of vaporization, its solvent qualities, its adhesiveness and cohesiveness, its hydrophobic qualities, and its ability to float in its solid form. Hydrogen bonds are also an important component of proteins, nucleic acids, and DNA.

Elements are represented in upper case letters. If there is no subscript, it indicates there is only one atom of the element. Otherwise, the subscript indicates the number of atoms. In molecular formulas, elements are organized according to the Hill system. Carbon is first, hydrogen comes next, and the remaining elements are listed in alphabetical order. If there is no carbon, all elements are listed alphabetically. There are a couple of exceptions to these rules. First, oxygen is usually listed last in oxides. Second, in ionic compounds the positive ion is listed first, followed by the negative ion. In CO_2, for example, C indicates 1 atom of carbon and O_2 indicates 2 atoms of oxygen. The compound is carbon dioxide. The formula for ammonia (an ionic compound) is NH_3, which is one atom of nitrogen and three of hydrogen. H_2O is two atoms of hydrogen and one of oxygen. Sugar is $C_6H_{12}O_6$, which is 6 atoms of carbon, 12 of hydrogen, and 6 of oxygen.

Chemical properties are qualities of a substance which can't be determined by simply looking at the substance and must be determined through chemical reactions. Some chemical properties of elements include: atomic number, electron configuration, electrons per shell, electronegativity, atomic radius, and isotopes.

In contrast to chemical properties, physical properties can be observed or measured without chemical reactions. These include properties such as color, elasticity, mass, volume, and temperature. Mass is a measure of the amount of substance in an object. Weight is a measure of the gravitational pull of Earth on an object. Volume is a measure of the amount of space occupied. There are many formulas to determine volume. For example, the volume of a cube is the length of one side cubed (a^3) and the volume of a rectangular prism is length times width times height ($l \cdot w \cdot h$). The volume of an irregular shape can be determined by how much water it displaces. Density is a measure of the amount of mass per unit volume. The formula to find density is mass divided by volume ($D=m/V$). It is expressed in terms of mass per cubic unit, such as grams per cubic centimeter (g/cm^3). Specific gravity is a measure of the ratio of a substance's density compared to the density of water.

Both physical changes and chemical reactions are everyday occurrences. Physical changes do not result in different substances. For example, when water becomes ice it has undergone a physical change, but not a chemical change. It has changed its form, but not its composition. It is still H_2O. Chemical properties are concerned with the constituent particles that make up the physicality of a substance. Chemical properties are apparent when chemical changes occur. The chemical properties of a substance are influenced by its electron configuration, which is determined in part by the number of protons in the nucleus (the atomic number). Carbon, for example, has 6 protons and 6 electrons. It is an element's outermost valence electrons that mainly determine its chemical properties. Chemical reactions may release or consume energy.

Solutions and Mixtures

A solution is a homogeneous mixture. A mixture is two or more different substances that are mixed together, but not combined chemically. Homogeneous mixtures are those that are uniform in their composition. Solutions consist of a solute (the substance that is dissolved) and a solvent (the substance that does the dissolving). An example is sugar water. The solvent is the water and the solute is the sugar. The intermolecular attraction between the solvent and the solute is called solvation. Hydration refers to solutions in which water is the solvent. Solutions are formed when the forces of the molecules of the solute and the solvent are as strong as the individual molecular forces of the solute and the solvent. An example is that salt (NaCl) dissolves in water to create a solution. The Na^+ and the Cl^- ions in salt interact with the molecules of water and vice versa to overcome the individual molecular forces of the solute and the solvent.

The term dilute is used when there is less solute. Adding more solvent is known as diluting a solution, as is removing a portion of the solute. Concentrated is the term used when there is more solute. Adding more solute makes a solution more concentrated, as does removing a portion of the solvent.

For solvation to occur, bonds of similar strength must be broken and formed. Nonpolar substances are usually soluble in nonpolar solvents. Ionic and polar matter is usually soluble in polar solvents. Water is a polar solvent. Oil is nonpolar. Heptane (C_7H_{16}) is another nonpolar liquid that is said to be immiscible in water, meaning it can't combine with water. The hydrogen bonds of the water molecules are stronger than the London dispersion forces of the heptane. Polar molecules such as NH_3 (ammonia), SO_2 (sulfur dioxide), and H_2S (hydrogen sulfide) are termed hydrophilic, meaning they readily combine with water. Nonpolar molecules, including the noble gases and other gases such as He (helium), Ne (neon), and CO_2 (carbon dioxide) are termed hydrophobic, meaning they repel or do not readily combine with water. One way to remember this is that "like dissolves like." Polar solvents dissolve polar solutes, while nonpolar solvents dissolve nonpolar solutes.

Solids tend to dissolve faster when the temperature is increased. Higher temperatures help break bonds through an increase in kinetic energy. Solubility tends to increase for solids being dissolved in water as the temperature approaches 100 °C, but at higher temperatures ionic solutes tend to become less soluble. Gases tend to be less soluble at higher temperatures. When solutions are saturated at high temperatures, the solute will precipitate (return to solid form) and "fall out of the solution" as the solution cools. Melting points can be lowered by using a solvent such as salt on icy roads, which lowers the freezing point of ice. Adding salt to water when making ice cream also lowers the melting point of the water. A solution's melting point is usually lower than the melting point of the solvent alone. Pressure has little effect on the solubility of liquid solutions. In gas solutions, an increase in pressure increases solubility, and vice versa.

The concentration of a solution is measured in terms of molarity. One molar (M) is equal to a quantity of moles of solute per liter of solution. Adding one mole of a substance to one liter of solution would most likely result in a molarity greater than one. The amount of substance should be measured into a small amount of solution, and then more solution should be added to reach a volume of one liter to ensure accuracy. Molality refers to the concentration or ratio of moles of solute per kilogram of solvent. Colligative properties refer to how a solvent acts when it becomes a solution. Colligative properties are determined by the number of solute molecules rather than their exact characteristics. Some examples of colligative properties are that a solution's osmotic pressure and boiling point increase and its melting point decreases when the amount of solute is increased. As the amount of solute is increased, vapor will decrease above the solution when it is composed of a solid, nonvolatile solute dissolved in a liquid.

Atomic Theory

Atomic theory is concerned with the characteristics and properties of atoms that make up matter. It deals with matter on a microscopic level as opposed to a macroscopic level. Atomic theory, for instance, discusses the kinetic motion of atoms in order to explain the properties of macroscopic quantities of matter. John Dalton (1766-1844) is credited with making many contributions to the field of atomic theory that are still considered valid. This includes the notion that all matter consists of atoms and that atoms are indestructible. In other words, atoms can be neither created nor destroyed. This is also the theory behind the conservation of matter, which explains why chemical reactions do not result in any detectable gains or losses in matter. This holds true for chemical reactions and smaller scale processes. When dealing with large amounts of energy, however, atoms can be destroyed by nuclear reactions. This can happen in particle colliders or atom smashers.

There have been many revisions to theories regarding the structure of atoms and their particles. Part of the challenge in developing an understanding of matter is that atoms and their particles are too small to be seen. It is believed that the first conceptualization of the atom was developed by Democritus in 400 B.C. Some of the more notable models are the solid sphere or billiard ball model postulated by John Dalton, the plum pudding or raisin bun model by J.J. Thomson, the planetary or nuclear model by Ernest Rutherford, the Bohr or orbit model by Niels Bohr, and the electron cloud or quantum mechanical model by Louis de Broglie and Erwin Schrodinger. Rutherford directed the alpha scattering experiment that discounted the plum pudding model. The shortcoming of the Bohr model was the belief that electrons orbited in fixed rather than changing ecliptic orbits.

Radioactivity

Radioisotopes, also known as radionuclides or radioactive isotopes, are atoms that have an unstable nucleus. This is a nucleus that has excess energy and the potential to make radiation particles within the nucleus (subatomic particles) or undergo radioactive decay, which can result in the emission of gamma rays. Radionuclides may occur naturally, but can also be artificially produced.

Radioactive decay occurs when an unstable atomic nucleus spontaneously loses energy by emitting ionizing particles and radiation. Decay is a form of energy transfer, as energy is lost. It also results in different products. Before decay there is one type of atom, called the parent nuclide. After decay there are one or more different products, called the daughter nuclide(s). Radioactivity refers to particles that are emitted from nuclei as a result of nuclear instability.

Radioactive half-life is the time it takes for half of the radioactive nuclei in a sample to undergo radioactive decay. Radioactive decay rates are usually expressed in terms of half-lives. The different types of radioactivity lead to different decay paths, which transmute the nuclei into other chemical elements. Decay products (or daughter nuclides) make radioactive dating possible. Decay chains are a series of decays that result in different products. For example, uranium-238 is often found in granite. Its decay chain includes 14 daughter products. It eventually becomes a stable isotope of lead, which is why lead is often found with deposits of uranium ore. Its first half-life is equivalent to the approximate age of the earth, about 4.5 billion years. One of its products is radon, a radioactive gas. Radiation is when energy is emitted by one body and absorbed by another. Nuclear weapons, nuclear reactors, and radioactive substances are all examples of things that involve ionizing radiation. Acoustic and electromagnetic radiation are other types of radiation.

Isotopes that have not been observed to decay are stable, or non-radioactive, isotopes. It is not known whether some stable isotopes may have such long decay times that observing decay is not possible. Currently, 80 elements have one or more stable isotopes. There are

256 known stable isotopes in total. Carbon, for example, has three isotopes. Two (carbon-12 and carbon-13) are stable and one (carbon-14) is radioactive. Radioactive isotopes have unstable nuclei and can undergo spontaneous nuclear reactions, which results in particles or radiation being emitted. It cannot be predicted when a specific nucleus will decay, but large groups of identical nuclei decay at predictable rates. Knowledge about rates of decay can be used to estimate the age of materials that contain radioactive isotopes.

The conservation of mass number is a concept related to nuclear reactions. Two conditions are required to balance a nuclear reaction. They are conservation of mass number and conservation of nuclear charge. In a nuclear equation, the mass numbers should be equal on each side of the arrow. In this type of equation, the mass number is in superscript in front of the element and the atomic number is in subscript. The total number of nucleons is the same even though the product elements are different. For example, when a specific isotope of uranium decays into thorium and helium, the original mass number of uranium is 238. After the reaction, the mass number of thorium is 234 and the mass number of helium is 4 (238 = 234 + 4). The mass number is the same on both sides of the equation.

Ionizing radiation is that which can cause an electron to detach from an atom. It occurs in radioactive reactions and comes in three types: alpha (α), beta (β), and gamma (γ). Alpha rays are positive, beta rays are negative, and gamma rays are neutral. Alpha particles are larger than beta particles and can cause severe damage if ingested. Because of their large mass, however, they can be stopped easily. Even paper can protect against this type of radiation. Beta particles can be beta-minus or beta-plus. Beta-minus particles contain an energetic electron, while beta-plus particles are emitted by positrons and can result in gamma photons. Beta particles can be stopped with thin metal. Gamma rays are a type of high energy electromagnetic radiation consisting of photons. Gamma radiation rids the decaying nucleus of excess energy after it has emitted either alpha or beta radiation. Gamma rays can cause serious damage when absorbed by living tissue, and it takes thick lead to stop them. Alpha, beta, and gamma radiation can also have positive applications.

Nuclear fission and nuclear fusion are similar in that they occur in the nucleus of an atom, can release great amounts of energy, and result in the formation of different elements (known as nuclear transmutation). They are different in that one breaks apart a nucleus and the other joins nuclei. Nuclear fission is the splitting of a large nucleus into smaller pieces. Nuclear fusion is the joining of two nuclei, which occurs under extreme temperatures and pressures. Fusion occurs naturally in stars, and is the process responsible for the release of great amounts of energy. When fusion occurs, many atomic nuclei with like charges are joined together, forming a heavier nucleus. When this occurs, energy can be absorbed and/or released.

Periodic Table

The periodic table groups elements with similar chemical properties together. The grouping of elements is based on atomic structure. It shows periodic trends of physical and chemical properties and identifies families of elements with similar properties. It is a common model for organizing and understanding elements. In the periodic table, each element has its own cell that includes varying amounts of information presented in symbol form about the properties of the element. Cells in the table are arranged in rows (periods) and columns (groups or families). At minimum, a cell includes the symbol for the element and its atomic number. The cell for hydrogen, for example, which appears first in the upper left corner, includes an "H" and a "1" above the letter. Elements are ordered by atomic number, left to right, top to bottom.

In the periodic table, the groups are the columns numbered 1 through 18 that group elements with similar outer electron shell configurations. Since the configuration of the outer electron shell is one of the primary factors affecting an element's chemical properties, elements within the same group have similar chemical properties. Previous naming conventions for groups have included the use of Roman numerals and upper-case letters. Currently, the periodic table groups are: Group 1, alkali metals; Group 2, alkaline earth metals; Groups 3-12, transition metals; Group 13, boron family; Group 14; carbon family; Group 15, pnictogens; Group 16, chalcogens; Group 17, halogens; Group 18, noble gases.

In the periodic table, there are seven periods (rows), and within each period there are blocks that group elements with the same outer electron subshell (more on this in the next section). The number of electrons in that outer shell determines which group an element belongs to within a given block. Each row's number (1, 2, 3, etc.) corresponds to the highest number electron shell that is in use. For example, row 2 uses only electron shells 1 and 2, while row 7 uses all shells from 1-7.

Atomic radii will decrease from left to right across a period (row) on the periodic table. In a group (column), there is an increase in the atomic radii of elements from top to bottom. Ionic radii will be smaller than the atomic radii for metals, but the opposite is true for non-metals. From left to right, electronegativity, or an atom's likeliness of taking another atom's electrons, increases. In a group, electronegativity decreases from top to bottom. Ionization energy or the amount of energy needed to get rid of an atom's outermost electron, increases across a period and decreases down a group. Electron affinity will become more negative across a period but will not change much within a group. The melting point decreases from top to bottom in the metal groups and increases from top to bottom in the non-metal groups.

Electronegativity is a measure of how capable an atom is of attracting a pair of bonding electrons. It refers to the fact that one atom exerts slightly more force in a bond than another, creating a dipole. If the electronegative difference between two atoms is small, the atoms will form a polar covalent bond. If the difference is large, the atoms will form an ionic bond. When there is no electronegativity, a pure nonpolar covalent bond is formed. Electronegativity can be discussed as a trend in the periodic table. Fluorine (F) has the greatest electronegativity, and elements to the left and below fluorine have lower levels of electronegativity. This property of elements is often measured using the Pauling scale, which ranges from 4.0 (fluorine) to 0.7 (francium). Elements with high electronegativity are highly reactive because they can capture electrons. The symbols δ^+ (delta plus) and δ^- (delta minus) stand for fractional charges.

Ionization energy is the energy required for an electron to free itself from the grip of its neutral atom. Ionization energy increases across a row. Groups on the left of the table have fewer valence electrons and noble gases have the maximum number of valence electrons (a filled outer shell). Ionization energy can be measured in kilojoules (kJ) per mole or electron volts (eV) per atom (1 kJ/mol = 0.010364 eV/atom). Elements with low ionization energies are highly reactive because they can easily give up electrons.

Electrons

Electrons are subatomic particles that orbit the nucleus at various levels commonly referred to as layers, shells, or clouds. The orbiting electron or electrons account for only a fraction of the atom's mass. They are much smaller than the nucleus, are negatively charged, and exhibit wave-like characteristics. Electrons are part of the lepton family of elementary particles. Electrons can occupy orbits that are varying distances away from the nucleus, and tend to occupy the lowest energy level they can. If an atom has all its electrons in the lowest available positions, it has a stable electron arrangement. The outermost electron shell of an atom in its uncombined state is known as the valence shell. The electrons there are called valence electrons, and it is their number that determines bonding behavior. Atoms tend to react in a manner that will allow them to fill or empty their valence shells.

Chemical bonds involve a negative-positive attraction between an electron or electrons and the nucleus of an atom or nuclei of more than one atom. The attraction keeps the atom cohesive, but also enables the formation of bonds among other atoms and molecules. Each of the four energy levels (or shells) of an atom has a maximum number of electrons they can contain. Each level must be completely filled before electrons can be added to the valence level. The farther away from the nucleus an electron is, the more energy it has. The first shell, or K-shell, can hold a maximum of 2 electrons; the second, the L-shell, can hold 8; the third, the M-shell, can hold 18; the fourth, the N-shell, can hold 32. The shells can also have subshells. Chemical bonds form and break between atoms when atoms gain, lose, or share an electron in the outer valence shell. Polar bond refers to a covalent type of bond with a separation of charge. One end is negative and the other is positive. The hydrogen-oxygen bond in water is one example of a polar bond.

There are seven electron shells. One is closest to the nucleus and seven is the farthest away. Electron shells can also be identified with the letters K, L, M, N, O, P, and Q. Traditionally, there were four subshells identified by the first letter of their descriptive name: s (sharp), p (principal), d (diffuse), and f (fundamental). The maximum number of electrons for each subshell is as follows: s is 2, p is 6, d is 10, and f is 14. Every shell has an s subshell, the second shell and those above also have a p subshell, the third shell and those above also have a d subshell, and so on. Each subshell contains atomic orbitals, which describes the wave-like characteristics of an electron or a pair of electrons expressed as two angles and the distance from the nucleus. Atomic orbital is a concept used to express the likelihood of an electron's position in accordance with the idea of wave-particle duality.

Electron configuration: This is a trend whereby electrons fill shells and subshells in an element in a particular order and with a particular number of electrons. The chemical properties of the elements reflect their electron configurations. Energy levels (shells) do not have to be completely filled before the next one begins to be filled. An example of electron configuration notation is $1s^22s^22p^5$, where the first number is the row (period), or shell. The letter refers to the subshell of the shell, and the number in superscript is the number of electrons in the subshell. A common shorthand method for electron configuration notation is to use a noble gas (in a bracket) to abbreviate the shells that elements have in common. For example, the electron configuration for neon is $1s^22s^22p^6$. The configuration for phosphorus is $1s^22s^22p^63s^23p^3$, which can be written as $[Ne]3s^23p^3$. Subshells are filled in the following manner: 1s, 2s, 2p, 3s, 3p, 4s, 3d, 4p, 5s, 4d, 5p, 6s, 4f, 5d, 6p, 7s, 5f, 6d, and 7p.

Most atoms are neutral since the positive charge of the protons in the nucleus is balanced by the negative charge of the surrounding electrons. Electrons are transferred between atoms when they come into contact with each other. This creates a molecule or atom in which the number of electrons does not equal the number of protons, which gives it a positive or negative charge. A negative ion is created when an atom gains electrons, while a positive ion is created when an atom loses electrons. An ionic bond is formed between ions with opposite charges. The resulting compound is neutral. Ionization refers to the process by which neutral particles are ionized into charged particles. Gases and plasmas can be partially or fully ionized through ionization.

Atoms interact by transferring or sharing the electrons furthest from the nucleus. Known as the outer or valence electrons, they are responsible for the chemical properties of an element. Bonds between atoms are created when electrons are paired up by being transferred or shared. If electrons are transferred from one atom to another, the bond is ionic. If electrons are shared, the bond is covalent. Atoms of the same element may bond together to form molecules or crystalline solids. When two or more different types of atoms bind together chemically, a compound is made. The physical properties of compounds reflect the nature of the interactions among their molecules. These interactions are determined by the structure of the molecule, including the atoms they consist of and the distances and angles between them.

Isotopes and Molecules

An isotope is a variation in the number of neutrons in an atom. Carbon, for example, always has the same number of protons (6), but does not always have the same number of neutrons. Its two most common isotopes are carbon-12 and carbon-13. The number after the element names refers to the total number of nucleons in the atom. Carbon's atomic number (Z) is always 6, but carbon-12 has 6 neutrons while carbon-13 has 7. An isotope can also be written by placing the number of nucleons in superscript before the element's symbol (^{13}C).

The important properties of water (H_2O) are high polarity, hydrogen bonding, cohesiveness, adhesiveness, high specific heat, high latent heat, and high heat of vaporization. It is essential to life as we know it, as water is one of the main if not the main constituent of many living things. Water is a liquid at room temperature. The high specific heat of water means it resists the breaking of its hydrogen bonds and resists heat and motion, which is why it has a relatively high boiling point and high vaporization point. It also resists temperature change. Water is peculiar in that its solid state floats in its liquid state. Most substances are denser in their solid forms. Water is cohesive, which means it is attracted to itself. It is also adhesive, which means it readily attracts other molecules. If water tends to adhere to another substance, the substance is said to be hydrophilic. Water makes a good solvent. Substances, particularly those with polar ions and molecules, readily dissolve in water.

Electrons in an atom can orbit different levels around the nucleus. They can absorb or release energy, which can change the location of their orbit or even allow them to break free from the atom. The outermost layer is the valence layer, which contains the valence electrons. The valence layer tends to have or share eight electrons. Molecules are formed by a chemical bond between atoms, a bond which occurs at the valence level. Two basic types of bonds are covalent and ionic. A covalent bond is formed when atoms share electrons. An ionic bond is formed when an atom transfers an electron to another atom. A hydrogen bond is a weak bond between a hydrogen atom of one molecule and an electronegative atom (such as nitrogen, oxygen, or fluorine) of another molecule. The Van der Waals force is a weak force between molecules. This type of force is much weaker than actual chemical bonds between atoms.

Reactions

Chemical reactions measured in human time can take place quickly or slowly. They can take fractions of a second or billions of years. The rates of chemical reactions are determined by how frequently reacting atoms and molecules interact. Rates are also influenced by the temperature and various properties (such as shape) of the reacting materials. Catalysts accelerate chemical reactions, while inhibitors decrease reaction rates. Some types of reactions release energy in the form of heat and light. Some types of reactions involve the transfer of either electrons or hydrogen ions between reacting ions, molecules, or atoms. In other reactions, chemical bonds are broken down by heat or light to form reactive radicals with electrons that will readily form new bonds. Processes such as the formation of ozone and greenhouse gases in the atmosphere and the burning and processing of fossil fuels are controlled by radical reactions.

Chemical equations describe chemical reactions. The reactants are on the left side before the arrow and the products are on the right side after the arrow. The arrow indicates the reaction or change. The coefficient, or stoichiometric coefficient, is the number before the element, and indicates the ratio of reactants to products in terms of moles. The equation for the formation of water from hydrogen and oxygen, for example, is $2H_2(g) + O_2(g) \rightarrow 2H_2O(l)$. The 2 preceding hydrogen and water is the coefficient, which means there are 2 moles of hydrogen and 2 of water. There is 1 mole of oxygen, which does not have to be indicated with the number 1. In parentheses, g stands for gas, l stands for liquid, s stands for solid, and aq stands for aqueous solution (a substance dissolved in water). Charges are shown in superscript for individual ions, but not for ionic compounds. Polyatomic ions are separated by parentheses so the ion will not be confused with the number of ions.

An unbalanced equation is one that does not follow the law of conservation of mass, which states that matter can only be changed, not created. If an equation is unbalanced, the numbers of atoms indicated by the stoichiometric coefficients on each side of the arrow will not be equal. Start by writing the formulas for each species in the reaction. Count the atoms on each side and determine if the number is equal. Coefficients must be whole numbers. Fractional amounts, such as half a molecule, are not possible. Equations can be balanced by multiplying the coefficients by a constant that will produce the smallest possible whole number coefficient. $H_2 + O_2 \rightarrow H_2O$ is an example of an unbalanced equation. The balanced equation is $2H_2 + O_2 \rightarrow 2H_2O$, which indicates that it takes two moles of hydrogen and one of oxygen to produce two moles of water.

One way to organize chemical reactions is to sort them into two categories: oxidation/reduction reactions (also called redox reactions) and metathesis reactions (which include acid/base reactions). Oxidation/reduction reactions can involve the transfer of one or more electrons, or they can occur as a result of the transfer of oxygen, hydrogen, or halogen atoms. The species that loses electrons is oxidized and is referred to as the reducing agent. The species that gains electrons is reduced and is referred to as the oxidizing agent. The element undergoing oxidation experiences an increase in its oxidation number, while the element undergoing reduction experiences a decrease in its oxidation number. Single replacement reactions are types of oxidation/reduction reactions. In a single replacement reaction, electrons are transferred from one chemical species to another. The transfer of electrons results in changes in the nature and charge of the species.

Single substitution, displacement, or replacement reactions are when one reactant is displaced by another to form the final product ($A + BC \rightarrow AB + C$). Single substitution reactions can be cationic or anionic. When a piece of copper (Cu) is placed into a solution of silver nitrate ($AgNO_3$), the solution turns blue. The copper appears to be replaced with a silvery-white material. The equation is $2AgNO_3 + Cu \rightarrow Cu(NO_3)2 + 2Ag$. When this reaction takes place, the copper dissolves and the silver in the silver nitrate solution precipitates (becomes a solid), thus resulting in copper nitrate and silver. Copper and silver have switched places in the nitrate.

Combination, or synthesis, reactions: In a combination reaction, two or more reactants combine to form a single product ($A + B \rightarrow C$). These reactions are also called synthesis or addition reactions. An example is burning hydrogen in air to produce water. The equation is $2H_2 (g) + O_2 (g) \rightarrow 2H_2O (l)$. Another example is when water and sulfur trioxide react to form sulfuric acid. The equation is $H_2O + SO_3 \rightarrow H_2SO_4$.

Double displacement, double replacement, substitution, metathesis, or ion exchange reactions are when ions or bonds are exchanged by two compounds to form different compounds ($AC + BD \rightarrow AD + BC$). An example of this is that silver nitrate and sodium chloride form two different products (silver chloride and sodium nitrate) when they react. The formula for this reaction is $AgNO_3 + NaCl \rightarrow AgCl + NaNO_3$.

Double replacement reactions are metathesis reactions. In a double replacement reaction, the chemical reactants exchange ions but the oxidation state stays the same. One of the indicators of this is the formation of a solid precipitate. In acid/base reactions, an acid is a compound that can donate a proton, while a base is a compound that can accept a proton. In these types of reactions, the acid and base react to form a salt and water. When the proton is donated, the base becomes water and the remaining ions form a salt. One method of determining whether a reaction is an oxidation/reduction or a metathesis reaction is that the oxidation number of atoms does not change during a metathesis reaction.

A neutralization, acid-base, or proton transfer reaction is when one compound acquires H^+ from another. These types of reactions are also usually double displacement reactions. The acid has an H^+ that is transferred to the base and neutralized to form a salt.

Decomposition (or desynthesis, decombination, or deconstruction) reactions; in a decomposition reaction, a reactant is broken down into two or more products ($A \rightarrow B + C$). These reactions are also called analysis reactions. Thermal decomposition is caused by heat. Electrolytic decomposition is due to electricity. An example of this type of reaction is the decomposition of water into hydrogen and oxygen gas. The equation is $2H_2O \rightarrow 2H_2 + O_2$. Decomposition is considered a chemical reaction whereby a single compound breaks down into component parts or simpler compounds. When a compound or substance separates into these simpler substances, the byproducts are often substances that are different from the original. Decomposition can be viewed as the opposite of combination reactions. Most decomposition reactions are endothermic. Heat needs to be added for the chemical reaction to occur. Separation processes can be mechanical or chemical, and usually involve re-organizing a mixture of substances without changing their chemical nature. The separated products may differ from the original mixture in terms of chemical or physical properties. Types of separation processes include filtration, crystallization, distillation, and chromatography. Basically, decomposition breaks down one compound into two or more compounds or substances that are different from the original; separation sorts the substances from the original mixture into like substances.

Catalysts, substances that help change the rate of reaction without changing their form, can increase reaction rate by decreasing the number of steps it takes to form products. The mass of the catalyst should be the same at the beginning of the reaction as it is at the end. The activation energy is the minimum amount required to get a reaction started. Activation energy causes particles to collide with sufficient energy to start the reaction. A catalyst enables more particles to react, which lowers the activation energy. Examples of catalysts in reactions are manganese oxide (MnO_2) in the decomposition of hydrogen peroxide, iron in the manufacture of ammonia using the Haber process, and concentrate of sulfuric acid in the nitration of benzene.

Endothermic reactions are chemical reactions that absorb heat and exothermic reactions are chemical reactions that release heat. Reactants are the substances that are consumed during a reaction, while products are the substances that are produced or formed. A balanced equation is one that uses reactants, products, and coefficients in such a way that the number of each type of atom (law of conservation of mass) and the total charge remains the same. The reactants are on the left side of the arrow and the products are on the right. The heat difference between endothermic and exothermic reactions is caused by bonds forming and breaking. If more energy is needed to break the reactant bonds than is released when they form, the reaction is endothermic. Heat is absorbed and the environmental temperature decreases. If more energy is released when product bonds form than is needed to break the reactant bonds, the reaction is exothermic. Heat is released and the environmental temperature increases.

The collision theory states that for a chemical reaction to occur, atoms or molecules have to collide with each other with a certain amount of energy. A certain amount of energy is required to breach the activation barrier. Heating a mixture will raise the energy levels of the molecules and the rate of reaction (the time it takes for a reaction to complete). Generally, the rate of reaction is doubled for every 10 degrees Celsius temperature increase. However, the increase needed to double a reaction rate increases as the temperature climbs. This is due to the increase in collision frequency that occurs as the temperature increases. Other factors that can affect the rate of reaction are surface area, concentration, pressure, and the presence of a catalyst.

The particles of an atom's nucleus (the protons and neutrons) are bound together by nuclear force, also known as residual strong force. Unlike chemical reactions, which involve electrons, nuclear reactions occur when two nuclei or nuclear particles collide. This results in the release or absorption of energy and products that are different from the initial particles. The energy released in a nuclear reaction can take various forms, including the release of kinetic energy of the product particles and the emission of very high energy photons known as gamma rays. Some energy may also remain in the nucleus. Radioactivity refers to the particles emitted from nuclei as a result of nuclear instability. There are many nuclear isotopes that are unstable and can spontaneously emit some kind of radiation. The most common types of radiation are alpha, beta, and gamma radiation, but there are several other varieties of radioactive decay.

Inorganic and Organic

The terms inorganic and organic have become less useful over time as their definitions have changed. Historically, inorganic molecules were defined as those of a mineral nature that were not created by biological processes. Organic molecules were defined as those that were produced biologically by a "life process" or "vital force." It was then discovered that organic compounds could be synthesized without a life process. Currently, molecules containing carbon are considered organic. Carbon is largely responsible for creating biological diversity, and is more capable than all other elements of forming large, complex, and diverse molecules of an organic nature. Carbon often completes its valence shell by sharing electrons with other atoms in four covalent bonds, which is also known as tetravalence.

The main trait of inorganic compounds is that they lack carbon. Inorganic compounds include mineral salts, metals and alloys, non-metallic compounds such as phosphorus, and metal complexes. A metal complex has a central atom (or ion) bonded to surrounding ligands (molecules or anions). The ligands sacrifice the donor atoms (in the form of at least one pair of electrons) to the central atom. Many inorganic compounds are ionic, meaning they form ionic bonds rather than share electrons. They may have high melting points because of this. They may also be colorful, but this is not an absolute identifier of an inorganic compound. Salts, which are inorganic compounds, are an example of inorganic bonding of cations and anions. Some examples of salts are magnesium chloride ($MgCl_2$) and sodium oxide (Na_2O). Oxides, carbonates, sulfates, and halides are classes of inorganic compounds. They are typically poor conductors, are very water soluble, and crystallize easily. Minerals and silicates are also inorganic compounds.

Two of the main characteristics of organic compounds are that they include carbon and are formed by covalent bonds. Carbon can form long chains, double and triple bonds, and rings. While inorganic compounds tend to have high melting points, organic compounds tend to melt at temperatures below 300° C. They also tend to boil, sublimate, and decompose below this temperature. Unlike inorganic compounds, they are not very water soluble. Organic molecules are organized into functional groups based on their specific atoms, which helps determine how they will react chemically. A few groups are alkanes, nitro, alkenes, sulfides, amines, and carbolic acids. The hydroxyl group (-OH) consists of alcohols. These molecules are polar, which increases their solubility. By some estimates, there are more than 16 million organic compounds.

Nomenclature refers to the manner in which a compound is named. First, it must be determined whether the compound is ionic (formed through electron transfer between cations and anions) or molecular (formed through electron sharing between molecules). When dealing with an ionic compound, the name is determined using the standard naming conventions for ionic compounds. This involves indicating the positive element first (the charge must be defined when there is more than one option for the valency) followed by the negative element plus the appropriate suffix. The rules for naming a molecular compound are as follows: write elements in order of increasing group number and determine the prefix by determining the number of atoms. Exclude mono for the first atom. The name for CO_2, for example, is carbon dioxide. The end of oxygen is dropped and "ide" is added to make oxide, and the prefix "di" is used to indicate there are two atoms of oxygen.

Acids and Bases

The potential of hydrogen (pH) is a measurement of the concentration of hydrogen ions in a substance in terms of the number of moles of H^+ per liter of solution. A lower pH indicates a higher H^+ concentration, while a higher pH indicates a lower H^+ concentration. Pure water has a neutral pH, which is 7. Anything with a pH lower than water (less than 7) is considered acidic. Anything with a pH higher than water (greater than 7) is a base. Drain cleaner, soap, baking soda, ammonia, egg whites, and sea water are common bases. Urine, stomach acid, citric acid, vinegar, hydrochloric acid, and battery acid are acids. A pH indicator is a substance that acts as a detector of hydrogen or hydronium ions. It is halochromic, meaning it changes color to indicate that hydrogen or hydronium ions have been detected.

When they are dissolved in aqueous solutions, some properties of acids are that they conduct electricity, change blue litmus paper to red, have a sour taste, react with bases to neutralize them, and react with active metals to free hydrogen. A weak acid is one that does not donate all of its protons or disassociate completely. Strong acids include hydrochloric, hydriodic, hydrobromic, perchloric, nitric, and sulfuric. They ionize completely. Superacids are those that are stronger than 100 percent sulfuric acid. They include fluoroantimonic, magic, and perchloric acids. Acids can be used in pickling, a process used to remove rust and corrosion from metals. They are also used as catalysts in the processing of minerals and the production of salts and fertilizers. Phosphoric acid (H_3PO_4) is added to sodas and other acids are added to foods as preservatives or to add taste.

When they are dissolved in aqueous solutions, some properties of bases are that they conduct electricity, change red litmus paper to blue, feel slippery, and react with acids to neutralize their properties. A weak base is one that does not completely ionize in an aqueous solution, and usually has a low pH. Strong bases can free protons in very weak acids. Examples of strong bases are hydroxide compounds such as potassium, barium, and lithium hydroxides. Most are in the first and second groups of the periodic table. A superbase is extremely strong compared to sodium hydroxide and cannot be kept in an aqueous solution. Superbases are organized into organic, organometallic, and inorganic classes. Bases are used as insoluble catalysts in heterogeneous reactions and as catalysts in hydrogenation.

Some properties of salts are that they are formed from acid base reactions, are ionic compounds consisting of metallic and nonmetallic ions, dissociate in water, and are comprised of tightly bonded ions. Some common salts are sodium chloride (NaCl), sodium bisulfate, potassium dichromate ($K_2Cr_2O_7$), and calcium chloride ($CaCl_2$). Calcium chloride is used as a drying agent, and may be used to absorb moisture when freezing mixtures. Potassium nitrate (KNO_3) is used to make fertilizer and in the manufacture of explosives. Sodium nitrate ($NaNO_3$) is also used in the making of fertilizer. Baking soda (sodium bicarbonate) is a salt, as are Epsom salts [magnesium sulfate ($MgSO_4$)]. Salt and water can react to form a base and an acid. This is called a hydrolysis reaction.

A buffer is a solution whose pH remains relatively constant when a small amount of an acid or a base is added. It is usually made of a weak acid and its conjugate base (proton receiver) or one of its soluble salts. It can also be made of a weak base and its conjugate acid (proton donator) or one of its salts. A constant pH is necessary in living cells because some living things can only live within a certain pH range. If that pH changes, the cells could die. Blood is an example of a buffer. A pKa is a measure of acid dissociation or the acid dissociation constant. Buffer solutions can help keep enzymes at the correct pH. They are also used in the fermentation process, in dyeing fabrics, and in the calibration of pH meters. An example of a buffer is HC_2H_3O (a weak acid) and $NaC_2H_3O_2$ (a salt containing the $C_2H_3O_2^-$ ion).

General Concepts

Aside from dark energy and dark matter, which are thought to account for all but four percent of the universe, the two most abundant elements in the universe are hydrogen (H) and helium (He). After hydrogen and helium, the most abundant elements are oxygen, neon, nitrogen, carbon, silicon, and magnesium. The most abundant isotopes in the solar system are hydrogen-1 and helium-4. Measurements of the masses of elements in the Earth's crust indicate that oxygen (O), silicon (Si), and aluminum (Al) are the most abundant on Earth. Hydrogen in its plasma state is the most abundant chemical element in stars in their main sequences, but is relatively rare on planet Earth.

Lewis formulas: These show the bonding or nonbonding tendency of specific pairs of valence electrons. Lewis dot diagrams use dots to represent valence electrons. Dots are paired around an atom. When an atom forms a covalent bond with another atom, the elements share the dots as they would electrons. Double and triple bonds are indicated with additional adjacent dots. Methane (CH_4), for instance, would be shown as a C with 2 dots above, below, and to the right and left and an H next to each set of dots. In structural formulas, the dots are single lines.

Kekulé diagrams: Like Lewis dot diagrams, these are two-dimensional representations of chemical compounds. Covalent bonds are shown as lines between elements. Double and triple bonds are shown as two or three lines and unbonded valence electrons are shown as dots.

Oxidation state and oxidation number are usually the same number. Even though they have different meanings, they are frequently used interchangeably. Oxidation numbers are Roman numerals in parentheses that are used as part of the naming scheme for inorganic compounds. Oxidation state refers to the hypothetical charge on an atom if all of its bonds are 100 percent ionic. They are integers that can occasionally be fractional numbers. Oxidation state is increased through oxidation (loss of electrons) and decreased through reduction (gain of electrons). The number for an oxidation state refers to a single atom or ion, and is a way to keep track of electrons. When using Lewis diagrams, shared electrons are generally assigned to the more electronegative element. In bonds involving two atoms of the same element, electrons are split between them. Lone pairs of electrons are assigned to the atom they are with.

Molar mass: This refers to the mass of one mole of a substance (element or compound), usually measured in grams per mole (g/mol). This differs from molecular mass in that molecular mass is the mass of one molecule of a substance relative to the atomic mass unit (amu).

Atomic mass unit (amu) is the smallest unit of mass, and is equal to 1/12 of the mass of the carbon isotope carbon-12. A mole (mol) is a measurement of molecular weight that is equal to the molecule's amu in grams. For example, carbon has an amu of 12, so a mole of carbon weighs 12 grams. One mole is equal to about 6.0221415×10^{23} elementary entities, which are usually atoms or molecules. This amount is also known as the Avogadro constant or Avogadro's number (N_A). Another way to say this is that one mole of a substance is the same as one Avogadro's number of that substance. One mole of chlorine, for example, is 6.0221415×10^{23} chlorine atoms. The charge on one mole of electrons is referred to as a Faraday.

The kinetic theory of gases assumes that gas molecules are small compared to the distances between them and that they are in constant random motion. The attractive and repulsive forces between gas molecules are negligible. Their kinetic energy does not change with time as long as the temperature remains the same. The higher the temperature is, the greater the motion will be. As the temperature of a gas increases, so does the kinetic energy of the molecules. In other words, gas will occupy a greater volume as the temperature is increased and a lesser volume as the temperature is decreased. In addition, the same amount of gas will occupy a greater volume as the temperature increases, but pressure remains constant. At any given temperature, gas molecules have the same average kinetic energy. The ideal gas law is derived from the kinetic theory of gases.

Charles's law: This states that gases expand when they are heated. It is also known as the law of volumes.

Boyle's law: This states that gases contract when pressure is applied to them. It also states that if temperature remains constant, the relationship between absolute pressure and volume is inversely proportional. When one increases, the other decreases. Considered a specialized case of the ideal gas law, Boyle's law is sometimes known as the Boyle-Mariotte law.

The ideal gas law is used to explain the properties of a gas under ideal pressure, volume, and temperature conditions. It is best suited for describing monatomic gases (gases in which atoms are not bound together) and gases at high temperatures and low pressures. It is not well-suited for instances in which a gas or its components are close to their condensation point. All collisions are perfectly elastic and there are no intermolecular attractive forces at work. The ideal gas law is a way to explain and measure the macroscopic properties of matter. It can be derived from the kinetic theory of gases, which deals with the microscopic properties of matter. The equation for the ideal gas law is $PV = nRT$, where "P" is absolute pressure, "V" is absolute volume, and "T" is absolute temperature. "R" refers to the universal gas constant, which is 8.3145 J/mol Kelvin, and "n" is the number of moles.

The crystalline structure of crystals is also known as a lattice. Crystal particles have symmetrical arrangements. Solidification may result in the formation of a single crystal or a group of crystals, which is known as a polycrystalline structure. The symmetry of a crystal is used to determine its classification. Although they are organized, structured, and symmetrical, crystals are imperfect and can have defects. Some may also have specific electrical properties. Crystal systems are grouped in accordance with their axial systems (there are three axes). The unique systems of crystals are cubic, hexagonal, rhombohedral, orthorhombic, monoclinic, and triclinic. Crystals in the cubic system are the most symmetric. The unit cell is the spatial arrangement of atoms. The spacing between unit cells is known as the lattice parameters. Salts form in cubic crystals. Common table salt (NaCl), for instance, forms a cubic lattice through ionic bonding. Rapid evaporation of a salt water solution results in small crystals, while slower evaporation leads to larger crystals.

Isomerization, or rearrangement, is the process of forming a compound's isomer. Within a compound, bonds are reformed. The reactant and product have the same molecular formula, but different structural formulas and different properties (A → B or A → A'). For example, butane (C_4H_{10}) is a hydrocarbon consisting of four carbon atoms in a straight chain. Heating it to 100° C or higher in the presence of a catalyst forms isobutane (methylpropane), which has a branched-chain structure. Boiling and freezing points are greatly different for butane and isobutane. A rearrangement reaction occurs within the molecule.

Common Measurements

A calorie is the amount of energy it takes to raise the temperature of a gram of water by one degree Celsius. A kilocalorie refers to the amount of energy it takes to raise the temperature of a kilogram of water by one degree Celsius. A calorie is equal to 4.184 joules. BTU stands for British thermal unit. It is a measurement of the amount of energy it takes to raise the temperature of a pound of water by one degree Fahrenheit. A BTU is equal to 252 calories or 1.054 kilojoules (kJ).

A calorimeter is a measurement device with a thermometer in which chemical or physical processes take place. The resulting change in temperature and the heat capacity can then be determined. Specific heat capacities have already been identified for many materials, and can be viewed in table form.

Enthalpy is a measure of heat content in a system. It is usually assumed that the system is closed and the pressure is constant. Enthalpy is represented by the symbol H. The heat of a reaction is the difference between the heat stored in the reactants and in the products. It is represented by ΔH.

Thermodynamics

Thermodynamics is a branch of physics that studies the conversion of energy into work and heat. It is especially concerned with variables such as temperature, volume, and pressure. Thermodynamic equilibrium refers to objects that have the same temperature because heat is transferred between them to reach equilibrium. Thermodynamics takes places within three different types of systems; open, isolated, and closed systems. Open systems are capable of interacting with a surrounding environment and can exchange heat, work (energy), and matter outside their system boundaries. A closed system can exchange heat and work, but not matter. An isolated system cannot exchange heat, work, or matter with its surroundings. Its total energy and mass stay the same. In physics, surrounding environment refers to everything outside a thermodynamic system (system). The terms "surroundings" and "environment" are also used. The term "boundary" refers to the division between the system and its surroundings.

The laws of thermodynamics are generalized principles dealing with energy and heat.
- The zeroth law of thermodynamics states that two objects in thermodynamic equilibrium with a third object are also in equilibrium with each other. Being in thermodynamic equilibrium basically means that different objects are at the same temperature.
- The first law deals with conservation of energy. It states that neither mass nor energy can be destroyed; only converted from one form to another.
- The second law states that the entropy (the amount of energy in a system that is no longer available for work or the amount of disorder in a system) of an isolated system can only increase. The second law also states that heat is not transferred from a lower-temperature system to a higher-temperature one unless additional work is done.
- The third law of thermodynamics states that as temperature approaches absolute zero, entropy approaches a constant minimum. It also states that a system cannot be cooled to absolute zero.

Thermal contact refers to energy transferred to a body by a means other than work. A system in thermal contact with another can exchange energy with it through the process of heat transfer. Thermal contact does not necessarily involve direct physical contact. Heat is energy that can be transferred from one body or system to another without work being done. Everything tends to become less organized and less useful over time (entropy). In all energy transfers, therefore, the overall result is that the heat is spread out so that objects are in thermodynamic equilibrium and the heat can no longer be transferred without additional work.

The laws of thermodynamics state that energy can be exchanged between physical systems as heat or work, and that systems are affected by their surroundings. It can be said that the total amount of energy in the universe is constant. The first law is mainly concerned with the conservation of energy and related concepts, which include the statement that energy can only be transferred or converted, not created or destroyed. The formula used to represent the first law is $\Delta U = Q - W$, where ΔU is the change in total internal energy of a system, Q is the heat added to the system, and W is the work done by the system. Energy can be transferred by conduction, convection, radiation, mass transfer, and other processes such as collisions in chemical and nuclear reactions. As transfers occur, the matter involved becomes less ordered and less useful. This tendency towards disorder is also referred to as entropy.

The second law of thermodynamics explains how energy can be used. In particular, it states that heat will not transfer spontaneously from a cold object to a hot object. Another way to say this is that heat transfers occur from higher temperatures to lower temperatures. Also covered under this law is the concept that systems not under the influence of external forces tend to become more disordered over time. This type of disorder can be expressed in terms of entropy. Another principle covered under this law is that it is impossible to make a heat engine that can extract heat and convert it all to useful work. A thermal bottleneck occurs in machines that convert energy to heat and then use it to do work. These types of machines are less efficient than ones that are solely mechanical.

Conduction is a form of heat transfer that occurs at the molecular level. It is the result of molecular agitation that occurs within an object, body, or material while the material stays motionless. An example of this is when a frying pan is placed on a hot burner. At first, the handle is not hot. As the pan becomes hotter due to conduction, the handle eventually gets hot too. In this example, energy is being transferred down the handle toward the colder end because the higher speed particles collide with and transfer energy to the slower ones. When this happens, the original material becomes cooler and the second material becomes hotter until equilibrium is reached. Thermal conduction can also occur between two substances such as a cup of hot coffee and the colder surface it is placed on. Heat is transferred, but matter is not.

Convection refers to heat transfer that occurs through the movement or circulation of fluids (liquids or gases). Some of the fluid becomes or is hotter than the surrounding fluid, and is less dense. Heat is transferred away from the source of the heat to a cooler, denser area. Examples of convection are boiling water and the movement of warm and cold air currents in the atmosphere and the ocean. Forced convection occurs in convection ovens, where a fan helps circulate hot air.

Radiation is heat transfer that occurs through the emission of electromagnetic waves, which carry energy away from the emitting object. All objects with temperatures above absolute zero radiate heat.

Heat is energy transfer (other than direct work) from one body or system to another due to thermal contact. Everything tends to become less organized and less orderly over time (entropy). In all energy transfers, therefore, the overall result is that the energy is spread out uniformly. This transfer of heat energy from hotter to cooler objects is accomplished by conduction, radiation, or convection. Temperature is a measurement of an object's stored heat energy. More specifically, temperature is the average kinetic energy of an object's particles. When the temperature of an object increases and its atoms move faster, kinetic energy also increases. Temperature is not energy since it changes and is not conserved. Thermometers are used to measure temperature.

There are three main scales for measuring temperature. Celsius uses the base reference points of water freezing at 0 degrees and boiling at 100 degrees. Fahrenheit uses the base reference points of water freezing at 32 degrees and boiling at 212 degrees. Celsius and Fahrenheit are both relative temperature scales since they use water as their reference point. The Kelvin temperature scale is an absolute temperature scale. Its zero mark corresponds to absolute zero. Water's freezing and boiling points are 273.15 Kelvin and 373.15 Kelvin, respectively. Where Celsius and Fahrenheit are measured is degrees, Kelvin does not use degree terminology.

- Converting Celsius to Fahrenheit: $°F = \frac{9}{5} °C + 32$
- Converting Fahrenheit to Celsius: $°C = \frac{5}{9} (°F - 32)$
- Converting Celsius to Kelvin: $K = °C + 273.15$
- Converting Kelvin to Celsius: $°C = K - 273.15$

Heat capacity, also known as thermal mass, refers to the amount of heat energy required to raise the temperature of an object, and is measured in Joules per Kelvin or Joules per degree Celsius. The equation for relating heat energy to heat capacity is $Q = C\Delta T$, where Q is the heat energy transferred, C is the heat capacity of the body, and ΔT is the change in the object's temperature. Specific heat capacity, also known as specific heat, is the heat capacity per unit mass. Every element and compound has its own specific heat. For example, it takes different amounts of heat energy to raise the temperature of the same amounts of magnesium and lead by one degree. The equation for relating heat energy to specific heat capacity is $Q = mc\Delta T$, where m represents the mass of the object, and c represents its specific heat capacity.

Some discussions of energy consider only two types of energy: kinetic energy (the energy of motion) and potential energy (which depends on relative position or orientation). There are, however, other types of energy. Electromagnetic waves, for example, are a type of energy contained by a field. Another type of potential energy is electrical energy, which is the energy it takes to pull apart positive and negative electrical charges. Chemical energy refers to the manner in which atoms form into molecules, and this energy can be released or absorbed when molecules regroup. Solar energy comes in the form of visible light and non-visible light, such as infrared and ultraviolet rays. Sound energy refers to the energy in sound waves.

Energy is constantly changing forms and being transferred back and forth. An example of a heat to mechanical energy transformation is a steam engine, such as the type used on a steam locomotive. A heat source such as coal is used to boil water. The steam produced turns a shaft, which eventually turns the wheels. A pendulum swinging is an example of both a kinetic to potential and a potential to kinetic energy transformation. When a pendulum is moved from its center point (the point at which it is closest to the ground) to the highest point before it returns, it is an example of a kinetic to potential transformation. When it swings from its highest point toward the center, it is considered a potential to kinetic transformation. The sum of the potential and kinetic energy is known as the total mechanical energy. Stretching a rubber band gives it potential energy. That potential energy becomes kinetic energy when the rubber band is released.

Motion and Force

Mechanics is the study of matter and motion, and the topics related to matter and motion, such as force, energy, and work. Discussions of mechanics will often include the concepts of vectors and scalars. Vectors are quantities with both magnitude and direction, while scalars have only magnitude. Scalar quantities include length, area, volume, mass, density, energy, work, and power. Vector quantities include displacement, velocity, acceleration, momentum, and force.

Motion is a change in the location of an object, and is the result of an unbalanced net force acting on the object. Understanding motion requires the understanding of three basic quantities: displacement, velocity, and acceleration.

Displacement
When something moves from one place to another, it has undergone *displacement*. Displacement along a straight line is a very simple example of a vector quantity. If an object

travels from position x = -5 cm to x = 5 cm, it has undergone a displacement of 10 cm. If it traverses the same path in the opposite direction, its displacement is -10 cm. A vector that spans the object's displacement in the direction of travel is known as a displacement vector.

Velocity
There are two types of velocity to consider: *average velocity* and *instantaneous velocity*. Unless an object has a constant velocity or we are explicitly given an equation for the velocity, finding the instantaneous velocity of an object requires the use of calculus. If we want to calculate the *average velocity* of an object, we need to know two things: the displacement, or the distance it has covered, and the time it took to cover this distance. The formula for average velocity is simply the distance traveled divided by the time required. In other words, the average velocity is equal to the change in position divided by the change in time. Average velocity is a vector and will always point in the same direction as the displacement vector (since time is a scalar and always positive).

Acceleration
Acceleration is the change in the velocity of an object. Typically, the acceleration will be a constant value. Like position and velocity, acceleration is a vector quantity and will therefore have both magnitude and direction.

Most motion can be explained by Newton's three laws of motion:

Newton's first law
An object at rest or in motion will remain at rest or in motion unless acted upon by an external force. This phenomenon is commonly referred to as inertia, the tendency of a body to remain in its present state of motion. In order for the body's state of motion to change, it must be acted on by an unbalanced force.

Newton's second law
An object's acceleration is directly proportional to the net force acting on the object, and inversely proportional to the object's mass. It is generally written in equation form $F = ma$, where F is the net force acting on a body, m is the mass of the body, and a is its acceleration. Note that since the mass is always a positive quantity, the acceleration is always in the same direction as the force.

Newton's third law
For every force, there is an equal and opposite force. When a hammer strikes a nail, the nail hits the hammer just as hard. If we consider two objects, A and B, then we may express any contact between these two bodies with the equation $F_{AB} = -F_{BA}$, where the order of the subscripts denotes which body is exerting the force. At first glance, this law might seem to forbid any movement at all since every force is being countered with an equal opposite force, but these equal opposite forces are acting on different bodies with different masses, so they will not cancel each other out.

Energy
The two types of energy most important in mechanics are potential and kinetic energy. Potential energy is the amount of energy an object has stored within itself because of its position or orientation. There are many types of potential energy, but the most common is gravitational potential energy. It is the energy that an object has because of its height (h)

above the ground. It can be calculated as $PE = mgh$, where m is the object's mass and g is the acceleration of gravity. Kinetic energy is the energy of an object in motion, and is calculated as $KE = mv^2/2$, where v is the magnitude of its velocity. When an object is dropped, its potential energy is converted into kinetic energy as it falls. These two equations can be used to calculate the velocity of an object at any point in its fall.

Work

Work can be thought of as the amount of energy expended in accomplishing some goal. The simplest equation for mechanical work (W) is $W = Fd$, where F is the force exerted and d is the displacement of the object on which the force is exerted. This equation requires that the force be applied in the same direction as the displacement. If this is not the case, then the work may be calculated as $W = Fd \cos(\theta)$, where θ is the angle between the force and displacement vectors. If force and displacement have the same direction, then work is positive; if they are in opposite directions, then work is negative; and if they are perpendicular, the work done by the force is zero.

As an example, if a man pushes a block horizontally across a surface with a constant force of 10 N for a distance of 20 m, the work done by the man is 200 N-m or 200 J. If instead the block is sliding and the man tries to slow its progress by pushing against it, his work done is -200 J, since he is pushing in the direction opposite the motion. If the man pushes vertically downward on the block while it slides, his work done is zero, since his force vector is perpendicular to the displacement vector of the block.

Friction

Friction is a force that arises as a resistance to motion where two surfaces are in contact. The maximum magnitude of the frictional force (f) can be calculated as $f = F_c\mu$, where F_c is the contact force between the two objects and μ is a coefficient of friction based on the surfaces' material composition. Two types of friction are static and kinetic. To illustrate these concepts, imagine a book resting on a table. The force of its weight (W) is equal and opposite to the force of the table on the book, or the normal force (N). If we exert a small force (F) on the book, attempting to push it to one side, a frictional force (f) would arise, equal and opposite to our force. At this point, it is a *static frictional force* because the book is not moving. If we increase our force on the book, we will eventually cause it to move. At this point, the frictional force opposing us will be a *kinetic frictional force*. Generally, the kinetic frictional force is lower than static frictional force (because the frictional coefficient for static friction is larger), which means that the amount of force needed to maintain the movement of the book will be less than what was needed to start it moving.

Gravitational force

Gravitational force is a universal force that causes every object to exert a force on every other object. The gravitational force between two objects can be described by the formula, $F = Gm_1m_2/r^2$, where m_1 and m_2 are the masses of two objects, r is the distance between them, and G is the gravitational constant, $G = 6.672 \times 10^{-11}$ N-m^2/kg^2. In order for this force to have a noticeable effect, one or both of the objects must be extremely large, so the equation is generally only used in problems involving planetary bodies. For problems involving objects on the earth being affected by earth's gravitational pull, the force of gravity is simply calculated as $F = mg$, where g is 9.81 m/s^2 toward the ground.

Electrical force

Electrical force is a universal force that exists between any two electrically charged objects. Opposite charges attract one another and like charges repel one another. The magnitude of the force is directly proportional to the magnitude of the charges (q) and inversely proportional to the square of the distance (r) between the two objects: $F = kq_1q_2/r^2$, where k = 9×10^9 N-m^2/C^2. Magnetic forces operate on a similar principle.

Buoyancy

The key determiner as to whether an object will float or sink in water is its density. The general rule is that if an object is less dense than water, it floats; if it is denser than water, it sinks. The density of an object is equal to its mass divided by its volume (d = m/v). It is important to note the difference between an object's density and a material's density. Water has a density of one gram per cubic centimeter, while steel has a density approximately eight times that. Despite having a much higher material density, an object made of steel may still float. A hollow steel sphere, for instance, will float easily because the density of the object includes the air contained within the sphere. An object may also float only in certain orientations. An ocean liner that is placed in the water upside down, for instance, may not remain afloat. An object will float only if it can displace a mass of water equal to its own mass.

Archimedes's principle states that a buoyant (upward) force on a submerged object is equal to the weight of the liquid displaced by the object. This principle of buoyancy can also be used to calculate the volume of an irregularly shaped object. The mass of the object (m) minus its apparent mass in the water (m_a) divided by the density of water (ρ_w), gives the object's volume: $V = (m-m_a)/\rho_w$.

Machines

Simple machines include the inclined plane, lever, wheel and axle, and pulley. These simple machines have no internal source of energy. More complex or compound machines can be formed from them. Simple machines provide a force known as a mechanical advantage and make it easier to accomplish a task. The inclined plane enables a force less than the object's weight to be used to push an object to a greater height. A lever enables a multiplication of force. The wheel and axle allows for movement with less resistance. Single or double pulleys allows for easier direction of force. The wedge and screw are forms of the inclined plane. A wedge turns a smaller force working over a greater distance into a larger force. The screw is similar to an incline that is wrapped around a shaft.

A certain amount of work is required to move an object. The amount cannot be reduced, but by changing the way the work is performed a mechanical advantage can be gained. A certain amount of work is required to raise an object to a given vertical height. By getting to a given height at an angle, the effort required is reduced, but the distance that must be traveled to reach a given height is increased. An example of this is walking up a hill. One may take a direct, shorter, but steeper route, or one may take a more meandering, longer route that requires less effort. Examples of wedges include doorstops, axes, plows, zippers, and can openers.

A lever consists of a bar or plank and a pivot point or fulcrum. Work is performed by the bar, which swings at the pivot point to redirect the force. There are three types of levers: first, second, and third class. Examples of a first-class lever include balances, see-saws, nail extractors, and scissors (which also use wedges). In a second-class lever the fulcrum is placed at one end of the bar and the work is performed at the other end. The weight or load to be moved is in between. The closer to the fulcrum the weight is, the easier it is to move. Force is increased, but the distance it is moved is decreased. Examples include pry bars, bottle openers, nutcrackers, and wheelbarrows. In a third-class lever the fulcrum is at one end and the positions of the weight and the location where the work is performed are reversed. Examples include fishing rods, hammers, and tweezers.

The center of a wheel and axle can be likened to a fulcrum on a rotating lever. As it turns, the wheel moves a greater distance than the axle, but with less force. Obvious examples of the wheel and axle are the wheels of a car, but this type of simple machine can also be used to exert a greater force. For instance, a person can turn the handles of a winch to exert a greater force at the turning axle to move an object. Other examples include steering wheels, wrenches, faucets, waterwheels, windmills, gears, and belts. Gears work together to change a force. The four basic types of gears are spur, rack and pinion, bevel, and worm gears. The larger gear turns slower than the smaller, but exerts a greater force. Gears at angles can be used to change the direction of forces.

A single pulley consists of a rope or line that is run around a wheel. This allows force to be directed in a downward motion to lift an object. This does not decrease the force required, just changes its direction. The load is moved the same distance as the rope pulling it. When a combination pulley is used, such as a double pulley, the weight is moved half the distance of the rope pulling it. In this way, the work effort is doubled. Pulleys are never 100% efficient because of friction. Examples of pulleys include cranes, chain hoists, block and tackles, and elevators.

An electric motor converts electric energy into mechanical energy. Energy can be provided by an AC or DC source. The power provided has many practical applications. The basic premise of a motor is that the electric current passing through a wire or coil creates a magnetic field that opposes the poles of a permanent magnet. The repelling forces between one pole of the electromagnet and the opposing pole of the fixed magnet cause the coil to move about ½ a turn. As it approaches the pole of like attraction, the coil would normally stop moving. In a motor, however, the current is reversed at this time, which reverses the poles and again forces rotation. In a DC motor, a switch or commuter can be used to reverse the charge. In an AC motor, the charge alternates on its own. The coil is attached to a shaft that is rotated, which provides the mechanical energy necessary to do work.

An electrical generator is the opposite of a motor in that it transforms magnetic force into electrical energy. Like a motor, however, it uses an electromagnetic field and a permanent magnet to achieve electromagnetic induction. Generators do not create electricity, but rather convert mechanical energy into electric energy. Smaller gas generators are used as backup or primary power sources of electricity for equipment, homes, and other small-scale applications. Larger generators may use mechanical energy from many different sources, including water, steam, wind, compressed air, or even a hand crank.

Electrical Charges

Measured in watts, electric power refers to the rate at which electrical energy is transferred by an electric circuit. It can be calculated using Joule's law: $P = V*I$, where "P" is power, "V" is the potential difference (in volts) and "I" is current (in amps). Power can be generated, transmitted, and converted into various forms of light.

A watt is the unit used to measure power. One watt is equal to one joule of energy per second. A transformer is a device that uses induction to transfer current from one circuit to another. Two wound coils act as a pair of inductors. Voltage can be modified to be transferred to another circuit (as in transmission lines) or to a load, such as an electrical device plugged into a socket.

Models that can be used to explain the flow of electric current, potential, and circuits include water, gravity, and roller coasters. For example, just as gravity is a force and a mass can have a potential for energy based on its location, so can a charge within an electrical field. Just as a force is required to move an object uphill, a force is also required to move a charge from a low to high potential. Another example is water. Water does not flow when it is level. If it is lifted to a point and then placed on a downward path, it will flow. A roller coaster car requires work to be performed to transport it to a point where it has potential energy (the top of a hill). Once there, gravity provides the force for it to flow (move) downward. If either path is broken, the flow or movement stops or is not completed.

A glass rod and a plastic rod can illustrate the concept of static electricity due to friction. Both start with no charge. A glass rod rubbed with silk produces a positive charge, while a plastic rod rubbed with fur produces a negative charge. The electron affinity of a material is a property that helps determine how easily it can be charged by friction. Materials can be sorted by their affinity for electrons into a triboelectric series. Materials with greater affinities include celluloid, sulfur, and rubber. Materials with lower affinities include glass, rabbit fur, and asbestos. In the example of a glass rod and a plastic one, the glass rod rubbed with silk acquires a positive charge because glass has a lower affinity for electrons than silk. The electrons flow to the silk, leaving the rod with fewer electrons and a positive charge. When a plastic rod is rubbed with fur, electrons flow to the rod and result in a negative charge.

The attractive force between the electrons and the nucleus is called the electric force. A positive (+) charge or a negative (-) charge creates a field of sorts in the empty space around it, which is known as an electric field. The direction of a positive charge is away from it and the direction of a negative charge is towards it. An electron within the force of the field is pulled towards a positive charge because an electron has a negative charge. A particle with a positive charge is pushed away, or repelled, by another positive charge. Like charges repel each other and opposite charges attract. Lines of force show the paths of charges. Electric force between two objects is directly proportional to the product of the charge magnitudes and inversely proportional to the square of the distance between the two objects. Electric charge is measured with the unit Coulomb (C). It is the amount of charge moved in one second by a steady current of one ampere ($1C = 1A \times 1s$).

Insulators are materials that prevent the movement of electrical charges, while conductors are materials that allow the movement of electrical charges. This is because conductive materials have free electrons that can move through the entire volume of the conductor. This allows an external charge to change the charge distribution in the material. In induction, a neutral conductive material, such as a sphere, can become charged by a positively or negatively charged object, such as a rod. The charged object is placed close to the material without touching it. This produces a force on the free electrons, which will either be attracted to or repelled by the rod, polarizing (or separating) the charge. The sphere's electrons will flow into or out of it when touched by a ground. The sphere is now charged. The charge will be opposite that of the charging rod.

Charging by conduction is similar to charging by induction, except that the material transferring the charge actually touches the material receiving the charge. A negatively or positively charged object is touched to an object with a neutral charge. Electrons will either flow into or out of the neutral object and it will become charged. Insulators cannot be used to conduct charges. Charging by conduction can also be called charging by contact. The law of conservation of charge states that the total number of units before and after a charging process remains the same. No electrons have been created. They have just been moved around. The removal of a charge on an object by conduction is called grounding.

Circuits

Electric potential, or electrostatic potential or voltage, is an expression of potential energy per unit of charge. It is measured in volts (V) as a scalar quantity. The formula used is $V = E/Q$, where V is voltage, E is electrical potential energy, and Q is the charge. Voltage is typically discussed in the context of electric potential difference between two points in a circuit. Voltage can also be thought of as a measure of the rate at which energy is drawn from a source in order to produce a flow of electric charge.

A circuit is a closed path along which electrons can travel with minimal resistance except at particular locations. Electric current is the sustained flow of electrons that are part of an electric charge moving along a path in a circuit. This differs from a static electric charge, which is a constant non-moving charge rather than a continuous flow. The rate of flow of electric charge is expressed using the ampere (amp or A) and can be measured using an ammeter. A current of 1 ampere means that 1 coulomb of charge passes through a given area every second. Electric charges typically only move from areas of high electric potential to areas of low electric potential. To get charges to flow into a high potential area, you must to connect it to an area of higher potential, by introducing a battery or other voltage source.

Electric currents experience resistance as they travel through a circuit. Different objects have different levels of resistance. The ohm (Ω) is the measurement unit of electric resistance. The symbol is the Greek letter omega. Ohm's Law, which is expressed as $I = V/R$, states that current flow (I, measured in amps) through an object is equal to the potential difference from one side to the other (V, measured in volts) divided by resistance (R, measured in ohms). An object with a higher resistance will have a lower current flow through it given the same potential difference.

Movement of electric charge along a path between areas of high electric potential and low electric potential, with a resistor or load device between them, is the definition of a simple circuit. It is a closed conducting path between the high and low potential points, such as the positive and negative terminals on a battery. One example of a circuit is the flow from one terminal of a car battery to the other. The electrolyte solution of water and sulfuric acid provides work in chemical form to start the flow. A frequently used classroom example of circuits involves using a D cell (1.5 V) battery, a small light bulb, and a piece of copper wire to create a circuit to light the bulb.

Series circuits are circuits in which there is only one path through which electrons can flow. If a load in this type of circuit is removed, disabled, or switched off, the circuit is open and electricity does not flow. A parallel circuit is one in which there is more than one path through which electrons can travel. In a series circuit, the same current flows through all components. In a parallel circuit, on the other hand, the same voltage exists across all parallel paths, though the current may be vastly different among them. An example of a series circuit is a string of old-fashioned Christmas tree lights. If one bulb breaks or comes loose, the entire string will not work.

Electricity concepts and devices

Direct current (DC) is the flow of an electric charge in one direction. Batteries and solar cells typically use direct current.

Alternating current (AC) is current that periodically reverses direction. AC is typically used in houses and other buildings.

A diode is an electronic device used to conduct electric current in one direction. The process of conduction in one direction is known as rectification. A rectifier is used to convert alternating current to direct current. Diodes are also used to remove modulation from radio signals.

An inverter is the opposite of a rectifier in that it converts direct current to alternating current.
Electromotive force (emf) is what causes electrons to move when there is potential difference between two points (voltage). Devices that can provide emf include batteries, voltaic cells, thermoelectric devices, solar cells, electrical generators, transformers, and Van de Graaff generators.

Transistor is a device made of a semiconductive material that can amplify or switch an electric charge.

Semiconductor is a material with conductivity between an insulator and a conductor. These materials replaced earlier electric devices such as vacuum tubes.

Used in modern circuits, solid state devices are solid materials in which the charge carriers, or electrons, are contained entirely within the material. Examples include transistors, microprocessors, integrated circuits, light-emitting diodes (LEDs), and liquid-crystal displays (LCDs).

Magnets

A magnet is a piece of metal, such as iron, steel, or magnetite (lodestone) that can affect another substance within its field of force that has like characteristics. Magnets can either

- 89 -

attract or repel other substances. Magnets have two poles: north and south. Like poles repel and opposite poles (pairs of north and south) attract. The magnetic field is a set of invisible lines representing the paths of attraction and repulsion. Magnetism can occur naturally, or ferromagnetic materials can be magnetized. Certain matter that is magnetized can retain its magnetic properties indefinitely and become a permanent magnet. Other matter can lose its magnetic properties. For example, an iron nail can be temporarily magnetized by stroking it repeatedly in the same direction using one pole of another magnet. Once magnetized, it can attract or repel other magnetically inclined materials, such as paper clips. Dropping the nail repeatedly will cause it to lose its charge.

The motions of subatomic structures (nuclei and electrons) produce a magnetic field. It is the direction of the spin and orbit that indicate the direction of the field. The strength of a magnetic field is known as the magnetic moment. As electrons spin and orbit a nucleus, they produce a magnetic field. Pairs of electrons that spin and orbit in opposite directions cancel each other out, creating a net magnetic field of zero. Materials that have an unpaired electron are magnetic. Those with a weak attractive force are referred to as paramagnetic materials, while ferromagnetic materials have a strong attractive force. A diamagnetic material has electrons that are paired, and therefore does not typically have a magnetic moment. There are, however, some diamagnetic materials that have a weak magnetic field.

A magnetic field can be formed not only by a magnetic material, but also by electric current flowing through a wire. When a coiled wire is attached to the two ends of a battery, for example, an electromagnet can be formed by inserting a ferromagnetic material such as an iron bar within the coil. When electric current flows through the wire, the bar becomes a magnet. If there is no current, the magnetism is lost. A magnetic domain occurs when the magnetic fields of atoms are grouped and aligned. These groups form what can be thought of as miniature magnets within a material. This is what happens when an object like an iron nail is temporarily magnetized. Prior to magnetization, the organization of atoms and their various polarities are somewhat random with respect to where the north and south poles are pointing. After magnetization, a significant percentage of the poles are lined up in one direction, which is what causes the magnetic force exerted by the material.

Waves

Waves are divided into types based on the direction of particle motion in a medium and the direction of wave propagation. Longitudinal waves are waves that travel in the same direction as the particle movement. They are sometimes called pressure, compressional, or density waves. Longitudinal sound waves are the easiest to produce and have the highest speed. A longitudinal wave consists of compressions and rarefactions, such as those seen by extending and collapsing a Slinky toy.

Shear or transverse waves waves move perpendicular to the direction of the particle movement. For example, if the particles in a medium move up and down, a transverse wave will move forward. Transverse waves are possible only in solids and are slower than longitudinal waves. Surface (circular) waves travel at the surface of a material and move in elliptical orbits. They are a little slower than shear waves. Plate waves move in elliptical orbits and only occur in very thin pieces of material.

Waves can be in phase or out of phase, which is similar to the concept of being in sync or out of sync. For example, if two separate waves originate from the same point and the peaks (crests) and valleys (troughs) are exactly aligned, they are said to be in phase. If the peak of a wave aligns with the valley of another wave, they are out of phase. When waves are in phase their displacement is doubled. If they are out of phase they cancel each other out. If they are somewhere in between being completely in phase and completely out of phase, the wave interaction is a wave that is the sum of the amplitudes of all points along the wave. If waves originate from different points, the amplitude of particle displacement is the combined sum of the particle displacement amplitude of each individual wave.

When waves traveling in the same medium interact, it is known as wave interference. While a single wave generally remains the same in terms of waveform, frequency, amplitude, and wavelength, several waves traveling through particles in a medium take on a more complicated appearance after they interact. The final properties of a wave are dependent on many factors, such as the points of origin of waves and whether they are in phase, out of phase, or somewhere in between. Constructive interference refers to what happens when two crests or two troughs of a wave meet. The resulting amplitude of the crest or trough is doubled. Destructive interference is what happens when the crest of one wave and the trough of another that are the same shape meet. When this occurs, the two waves cancel each other out. An example of destructive interference is when two unlike sound waves reduce the volume of the sound.

Waves have energy and can transfer energy when they interact with matter. Although waves transfer energy, they do not transport matter. They are a disturbance of matter that transfers energy from one particle to an adjacent particle. There are many types of waves, including sound, seismic, water, light, micro, and radio waves. The two basic categories of waves are mechanical and electromagnetic. Mechanical waves are those that transmit energy through matter. Electromagnetic waves can transmit energy through a vacuum. A transverse wave provides a good illustration of the features of a wave, which include crests, troughs, amplitude, and wavelength.

There are a number of important attributes of waves. Frequency is a measure of how often particles in a medium vibrate when a wave passes through the medium with respect to a certain point or node. Usually measured in Hertz (Hz), frequency might refer to cycles per second, vibrations per second, or waves per second. One Hz is equal to one cycle per second.

Period is a measure of how long it takes to complete a cycle. It is the inverse of frequency; where frequency is measure in cycles per second, period can be thought of as seconds per cycle, though it is measured in units of time only.

Speed refers to how fast or slow a wave travels. It is measured in terms of distance divided by time. While frequency is measured in terms of cycles per second, speed might be measured in terms of meters per second.

Amplitude is the maximum amount of displacement of a particle in a medium from its rest position, and corresponds to the amount of energy carried by the wave. High-energy waves have greater amplitudes; low energy waves have lesser amplitudes. Amplitude is a measure of a wave's strength.

Rest position, also called equilibrium, is the point at which there is neither positive nor negative displacement. Crest, also called the peak, is the point at which a wave's positive or upward displacement from the rest position is at its maximum. Trough, also called a valley, is the point at which a wave's negative or downward displacement from the rest position is at its maximum. A wavelength is one complete wave cycle. It could be measured from crest to crest, trough to trough, rest position to rest position, or any point of a wave to the corresponding point on the next wave.

Sound is a pressure disturbance that moves through a medium in the form of mechanical waves, which transfer energy from one particle to the next. Sound requires a medium to travel through, such as air, water, or other matter since it is the vibrations that transfer energy to adjacent particles, not the actual movement of particles over a great distance. Sound is transferred through the movement of atomic particles, which can be atoms or molecules. Waves of sound energy move outward in all directions from the source. Sound waves consist of compressions (particles are forced together) and rarefactions (particles move farther apart and their density decreases). A wavelength consists of one compression and one rarefaction. Different sounds have different wavelengths. Sound is a form of kinetic energy.

Pitch is the quality of sound determined by frequency. For example, a musical note can be tuned to a specific frequency. A, for instance, has a frequency of 440 Hz, which is a higher frequency than middle C. Humans can detect frequencies between about 20 Hz to 20,000 Hz.

Loudness is a human's perception of sound intensity. Sound intensity is measured as the sound power per unit area, and can be expressed in decibels.

Timbre is a human's perception of the type or quality of sound. Oscillation is a measurement, usually of time, against a basic value, equilibrium, or rest point.

The Doppler effect refers to the effect the relative motion of the source of the wave and the location of the observer has on waves. The Doppler effect is easily observable in sound waves. What a person hears when a train approaches or a car honking its horn passes by are examples of the Doppler effect. The pitch of the sound is different not because the emitted frequency has changed, but because the received frequency has changed. The frequency is higher (as is the pitch) as the train approaches, the same as emitted just as it passes, and lower as the train moves away. This is because the wavelength changes. The Doppler effect can occur when an observer is stationary, and can also occur when two trains approach and pass each other. Electromagnetic waves are also affected in this manner. The motion of the medium can also affect the wave. For waves that do not travel in a medium, such as light waves, it is the difference in velocity that determines the outcome.

The electromagnetic spectrum is defined by frequency (f) and wavelength (λ). Frequency is typically measured in hertz and wavelength is usually measured in meters. Because light travels at a fairly constant speed, frequency is inversely proportional to wavelength, a relationship expressed by the formula $f = c/\lambda$, where c is the speed of light (about 300 million meters per second). Frequency multiplied by wavelength equals the speed of the wave; for electromagnetic waves, this is the speed of light, with some variance for the medium in which it is traveling. Electromagnetic waves include (from largest to smallest wavelength) radio waves, microwaves, infrared radiation (radiant heat), visible light, ultraviolet radiation, x-rays, and gamma rays. The energy of electromagnetic waves is carried in packets that have a magnitude inversely proportional to the wavelength. Radio waves have a range of wavelengths, from about 10^{-3} to 10^5 meters, while their frequencies range from 10^3 to about 10^{11} Hz.

Atoms and molecules can gain or lose energy only in particular, discrete amounts. Therefore, they can absorb and emit light only at wavelengths that correspond to these amounts. Using a process known as spectroscopy, these characteristic wavelengths can be used to identify substances.

Light is the portion of the electromagnetic spectrum that is visible because of its ability to stimulate the retina. It is absorbed and emitted by electrons, atoms, and molecules that move from one energy level to another. Visible light interacts with matter through molecular electron excitation (which occurs in the human retina) and through plasma oscillations (which occur in metals). Visible light is between ultraviolet and infrared light on the spectrum. The wavelengths of visible light cover a range from 380 nm (violet) to 760 nm (red). Different wavelengths correspond to different colors.

The human brain interprets or perceives visible light, which is emitted from the sun and other stars, as color. For example, when the entire wavelength reaches the retina, the brain perceives the color white. When no part of the wavelength reaches the retina, the brain perceives the color black. The particular color of an object depends upon what is absorbed and what is transmitted or reflected. For example, a leaf consists of chlorophyll molecules, the atoms of which absorb all wavelengths of the visible light spectrum except for green, which is why a leaf appears green. Certain wavelengths of visible light can be absorbed when they interact with matter. Wavelengths that are not absorbed can be transmitted by transparent materials or reflected by opaque materials.

When light waves encounter an object, they are either reflected, transmitted, or absorbed. If the light is reflected from the surface of the object, the angle at which it contacts the surface will be the same as the angle at which it leaves, on the other side of the perpendicular. If the ray of light is perpendicular to the surface, it will be reflected back in the direction from which it came. When light is transmitted through the object, its direction may be altered upon entering the object. This is known as refraction. When light waves are refracted, or bent, an image can appear distorted. The degree to which the light is refracted depends on the speed at which light travels in the object. Light that is neither reflected nor transmitted will be absorbed by the surface and stored as heat energy. Nearly all instances of light hitting an object will involve a combination of two or even all three of these.

Diffraction refers to the bending of waves around small objects and the spreading out of waves past small openings. The narrower the opening, the greater the level of diffraction will be. Larger wavelengths also increase diffraction. A diffraction grating can be created by placing a number of slits close together, and is used more frequently than a prism to separate light. Different wavelengths are diffracted at different angles.

The various properties of light have numerous real life applications. For example, polarized sunglasses have lenses that help reduce glare, while non-polarized sunglasses reduce the total amount of light that reaches the eyes. Polarized lenses consist of a chemical film of molecules aligned in parallel. This allows the lenses to block wavelengths of light that are intense, horizontal, and reflected from smooth, flat surfaces. The "fiber" in fiber optics refers to a tube or pipe that channels light. Because of the composition of the fiber, light can be transmitted greater distances before losing the signal. The fiber consists of a core, cladding, and a coating. Fibers are bundled, allowing for the transmission of large amounts of data.

Geometric optics uses the concept of rays to determine how light will propagate. Ray diagrams can illustrate the path of light through a lens. Different types of lenses refract light, either convergently or divergently, to form images. After passing through a lens, rays converge at a focal point. Collimated rays are nearly parallel, and can be thought of as having no focal point. There are many types and combinations of lenses. Convergent lenses, also called positive lenses, are thicker in the middle and thinner at the edges. Rays are focused to a point. Divergent lenses, also called negative lenses, are thicker at the ends and thinner in the middle. Rays are spread apart, or diverged. A convex lens is bowed outward, either at one vertical surface or both. A convex lens with two convex surfaces may also be termed biconvex or double convex. A concave lens is bowed inward, while a planar lens is flat.

Rocks and minerals

The physical properties (as opposed to chemical structures) used to identify minerals are hardness, luster, color, cleavage, streak, form (the external shape), and other special properties. Senses other than sight, such as touch, taste, and smell, may be used to observe physical properties. Hardness is the resistance a mineral has to scratches. The Mohs Hardness Scale is used to rate hardness from 1 to 10. Color can often not be determined definitively as some minerals can be more than one color. Luster is determined by reflected light. Luster can be described as metallic (shiny), sub-metallic (dull), non-metallic (vitreous, like glass), or earthy (like dirt or powder). Streak is the true color of the mineral in powdered form. It can be determined by rubbing the specimen across an unglazed porcelain tile. Fracture or cleavage is how a mineral reacts to stress, such as being struck with a hammer. Other properties that can be used to identify rocks and minerals include magnetism, a salty taste, or a pungent odor in a streak test.

Minerals are naturally occurring, inorganic solids with a definite chemical composition and an orderly internal crystal structure. A polymorph is two minerals with the same chemical composition, but a different crystal structure. Rocks are aggregates of one or more minerals, and may also contain mineraloids (minerals lacking a crystalline structure) and organic remains. The three types of rocks are sedimentary, igneous, and metamorphic. Rocks are classified based on their formation and the minerals they contain. Minerals are classified by their chemical composition. Geology is the study of the planet Earth as it pertains to the composition, structure, and origin of its rocks. Petrology is the study of rocks, including their composition, texture, structure, occurrence, mode of formation, and history. Mineralogy is the study of minerals.

Sedimentary rock

Sedimentary rocks are formed by the process of lithification, which involves compaction, the expulsion of liquids from pores, and the cementation of the pre-existing rock. It is pressure and temperature that are responsible for this process. Sedimentary rocks are often formed in layers in the presence of water, and may contain organic remains, such as fossils. Sedimentary rocks are organized into three groups: detrital, biogenic, and chemical. Texture refers to the size, shape, and grains of sedimentary rock. Texture can be used to determine how a particular sedimentary rock was created. Composition refers to the types of minerals present in the rock. The origin of sedimentary rock refers to the type of water that was involved in its creation. Marine deposits, for example, likely involved ocean environments, while continental deposits likely involved dry land and lakes.

Mineral classification

Minerals are classified by chemical composition and internal crystalline structure. They are organized into classes. Native elements such as gold and silver are not classified in this manner. The eight classes are sulfides, oxides\hydroxides, halides, carbonates, sulfates, phosphates, and silicates. These classes are based on the dominant anion (negatively charged ion) or anionic group. Minerals are classified in this way for three main reasons. First, minerals with the same anion have unmistakable resemblances. Second, minerals with the same anion are often found in the same geologic environment. For example, calcite and dolomite, which belong to the same group, are often found together. Last, this method is similar to the naming convention used to identify inorganic compounds in chemistry. Minerals can be further separated into groups on the basis of internal structure.

Metamorphic rock

Metamorphic rock is that which has been changed by great heat and pressure. This results in a variety of outcomes, including deformation, compaction, destruction of the characteristics of the original rock, bending, folding, and formation of new minerals because of chemical reactions, and changes in the size and shape of the mineral grain. For example, the igneous rock ferromagnesian can be changed into schist and gneiss. The sedimentary rock carbonaceous can be changed into marble. The texture of metamorphic rocks can be classified as foliated and unfoliated. Foliation, or layering, occurs when rock is compressed along one axis during recrystallization. This can be seen in schist and shale. Unfoliated rock does not include this banding. Rocks that are compressed equally from all sides or lack specific minerals will be unfoliated. An example is marble.

Igneous rock

Igneous rock is formed from magma, which is molten material originating from beneath the Earth's surface. Depending upon where magma cools, the resulting igneous rock can be classified as intrusive, plutonic, hypabyssal, extrusive, or volcanic. Magma that solidifies at a depth is intrusive, cools slowly, and has a coarse grain as a result. An example is granite. Magma that solidifies at or near the surface is extrusive, cools quickly, and usually has a fine grain. An example is basalt. Magma that actually flows out of the Earth's surface is called lava. Some extrusive rock cools so quickly that crystals do not have time to form. These rocks have a glassy appearance. An example is obsidian. Hypabyssal rock is igneous rock that is formed at medium depths.

Earth's structure

The Earth is ellipsoid, not perfectly spherical. This means the diameter is different through the poles and at the equator. Through the poles, the Earth is about 12,715 km in diameter. The approximate center of the Earth is at a depth of 6,378 km. The Earth is divided into a crust, mantle, and core. The core consists of a solid inner portion. Moving outward, the molten outer core occupies the space from about a depth of 5,150 km to a depth of 2,890 km. The mantle consists of a lower and upper layer. The lower layer includes the D' (D prime) and D" (D double-prime) layers. The solid portion of the upper mantle and crust together form the lithosphere, or rocky sphere. Below this, but still within the mantle, is the asthenosphere, or weak sphere. These layers are distinguishable because the lithosphere is relatively rigid, while the asthenosphere resembles a thick liquid.

Maps

Traditional maps represent land in two dimensions, while topographic maps represent elevation through the use of contour lines. Contour lines help show changes to elevations above the surface of the Earth and on the ocean floor. They also help show the shape of Earth's surface features. The United States Geological Survey (USGS) produces frequently used quadrangle maps in various scales. A quadrangle topographic map is bounded by two lines of latitude and two lines of longitude. A 7.5-minute map shows an area that spans 7.5 minutes of latitude and 7.5 minutes of longitude. The name of the quadrangle map appears at the top, and usually indicates the name of a prominent feature. Topographic maps that show much less detail are also available. They might show a much larger area, such as a country or state. USGS quad maps also refer to adjacent quad maps. Other information contained on quad maps includes the projection and grid used, scale, contour intervals, and magnetic declination, which is the difference between true north and magnetic north.

Earth's chemical composition

The Earth's core consists of hot iron and forms of nickel. The mantle consists of different materials, including iron, magnesium, and calcium. The crust covers the mantle, consists of a thin layer of much lighter rocks, and is further subdivided into continental and oceanic portions. The continental portion consists mainly of silicates, such as granite. The oceanic portion consists of heavier, volcanic rocks, such as basalt. The upper 10 miles of the lithosphere layer (the crust and part of the mantle) is made up of 95% igneous rock (or its metamorphic equivalent), 4% shale, 0.75% sandstone, and 0.25% limestone. There are over 4,000 known minerals, but only about 20 make up some 95% of all rocks. There are, however, more than 3,000 individual kinds of minerals in the Earth's crust. Silicates are the largest group of minerals.

Mountains

Orogeny refers to the formation of mountains, particularly the processes of folding and faulting caused by plate tectonics. Folding is when layers of sedimentary rock are pressed together by continental plate movements. Sections of rock that are folded upward are called anticlines. Sections of rock that are folded downward are called synclines. Examples of folded mountains are the Alps and the Himalayans. Fault-block mountains are created when tectonic plate movement produces tension that results in displacement. Mountains in the

- 96 -

Southwest United States are examples of fault-blocking mountains. Mountains can also be caused by volcanic activity and erosion.

Tectonic Convection

Heat is transferred through the process of convection, which is a cycle. Hot material rises and spreads, cooling as it spreads. The cool material then sinks, where it is heated again. The process of convection can be seen in a pot of boiling water. It is believed this same process is happening deep within the Earth. Greater depths are associated with more pressure and heat. The weight of all the rocks causes the increase in pressure, while the decay of heavy radioactive elements such as uranium produces heat. This creates hot areas of molten material that find their way upward and to the surface in an effort to equalize, which means pressure and temperature are reduced. This causes the processes involved in plate tectonics.

Plate tectonic theory

The theory of plate tectonics states that the lithosphere, the solid portion of the mantle and Earth's crust, consists of major and minor plates. These plates are on top of and move with the viscous upper mantle, which is heated because of the convection cycle that occurs in the interior of the Earth. There are different estimates as to the exact number of major and minor plates. The number of major plates is believed to be between 9 and 15, and it is thought that there may be as many as 40 minor plates. The United States is atop the North American plate. The Pacific Ocean is atop the Pacific plate. The point at which these two plates slide horizontally along the San Andreas fault is an example of a transform plate boundary. The other two types of boundaries are divergent (plates that are spreading apart and forming new crust) and convergent (the process of subduction causes one plate to go under another). The movement of plates is what causes other features of the Earth's crust, such as mountains, volcanoes, and earthquakes.

Volcanic activities and plate tectonics

Volcanoes can occur along any type of tectonic plate boundary. At a divergent boundary, as plates move apart, magma rises to the surface, cools, and forms a ridge. An example of this is the mid-Atlantic ridge. Convergent boundaries, where one plate slides under another, are often areas with a lot of volcanic activity. The subduction process creates magma. When it rises to the surface, volcanoes can be created. Volcanoes can also be created in the middle of a plate over hot spots. Hot spots are locations where narrow plumes of magma rise through the mantle in a fixed place over a long period of time. The Hawaiian Islands and Midway are examples. The plate shifts and the island moves. Magma continues to rise through the mantle, however, which produces another island. Volcanoes can be active, dormant, or extinct. Active volcanoes are those that are erupting or about to erupt. Dormant volcanoes are those that might erupt in the future and still have internal volcanic activity. Extinct volcanoes are those that will not erupt.

Types of volcanoes

The three types of volcanoes are shield, cinder cone, and composite. A shield volcano is created by a long-term, relatively gentle eruption. This type of volcanic mountain is created by each progressive lava flow that occurs over time. A cinder cone volcano is created by explosive eruptions. Lava is spewed out of a vent into the air. As it falls to the ground, the lava cools into cinders and ash, which build up around the volcano in a cone shape. A composite volcano is a combination of the other two types of volcanoes. In this type, there are layers of lava flows and layers of ash and cinder.

Seismic deformation and seismic waves

There are two types of deformations created by an earthquake fault rupture: static and dynamic. Static deformation permanently displaces the ground. Examples are when a road or railroad track becomes distorted by an earthquake. Plate tectonics stresses the fault by creating tension with slow plate movements. An earthquake releases the tension. Plate tectonics also cause a second type of deformation. This type results in dynamic motions that take the form of seismic waves. These sound waves can be compressional waves, also known as primary or P waves, or shear waves, also known as secondary or S waves. P waves travel fastest, with speeds ranging between 1.5 and 8 kilometers per second. Shear waves are slower. P waves shake the ground in the direction they are propagating. S waves shake perpendicularly or transverse to the direction of propagation. Seismographs use a simple pendulum to record earthquake movement in a record called a seismogram. A seismogram can help seismologists estimate the distance, direction, Richter magnitude, and type of faulting of an earthquake.

Earthquakes plate tectonics

Most earthquakes are caused by tectonic plate movement. They occur along fractures called faults or fault zones. Friction in the faults prevents smooth movement. Tension builds up over time, and the release of that tension results in earthquakes. Faults are grouped based on the type of slippage that occurs. The types of faults are dip-slip, strike-slip, and oblique-slip. A dip-slip fault involves vertical movement along the fault plane. In a normal dip-slip fault, the wall that is above the fault plane moves down. In a reverse dip-slip fault, the wall above the fault plane moves up. A strike-slip fault involves horizontal movement along the fault plane. Oblique-slip faults involve both vertical and horizontal movement. The Richter magnitude scale measures how much seismic energy was released by an earthquake.

Erosion

Erosion is the wearing away of rock materials from the Earth's surface. Erosion can be classified as natural geologic erosion and erosion due to human activity. Natural geologic erosion occurs due to weathering and gravity. Factors involved in natural geologic erosion are typically long term forces. Human activity such as development, farming, and deforestation occurs over shorter periods of time. Soil, which supports plant growth, is the topmost layer of organic material. One type of erosion is sheet erosion, which is the gradual and somewhat uniform removal of surface soil. Rills are small rivulets that cut into soil. Gullies are rills that have become enlarged due to extended water run-off. Sandblows are caused by wind blowing away particles. Negative effects of erosion include sedimentation in rivers, which can pollute water and damage ecosystems. Erosion can also result in the removal of topsoil, which destroys crops and prevents plants from growing. This reduces food production and alters ecosystems.

Hydrologic cycle

The hydrologic, or water, cycle refers to water movement on, above, and in the Earth. Water can be in any one of its three states during different phases of the cycle. The three states of water are liquid water, frozen ice, and water vapor. Processes involved in the hydrologic cycle include precipitation, canopy interception, snow melt, runoff, infiltration, subsurface flow, evaporation, sublimation, advection, condensation, and transpiration. Precipitation is when condensed water vapor falls to Earth. Examples include rain, fog drip, and various forms of snow, hail, and sleet. Canopy interception is when precipitation lands on plant foliage instead of falling to the ground and evaporating. Snow melt is runoff produced by melting snow. Infiltration occurs when water flows from the surface into the ground. Subsurface flow refers to water that flows underground. Evaporation is when water in a liquid state changes to a gas. Sublimation is when water in a solid state (such as snow or ice) changes to water vapor without going through a liquid phase. Advection is the movement of water through the atmosphere. Condensation is when water vapor changes to liquid water. Transpiration is when water vapor is released from plants into the air.

Deposition

Deposition, or sedimentation, is the geological process in which previously eroded material is transported or added to a land form or land mass. Erosion and sedimentation are complementary geological processes. Running water causes a substantial amount of deposition of transported materials in both fresh water and coastal areas. Examples include gravity transporting material down the slope of a mountain and depositing it at the base of the slope. Another example is when sandstorms deposit particles in other locations. When glaciers melt and retreat, it can result in the deposition of sediments. Evaporation is also considered to cause deposition since dissolved materials are left behind when water evaporates. Deposition can include the build up of organic materials. For example, chalk is partially made up of the small calcium carbonate skeletons of marine plankton, which helps create more calcium carbonate from chemical processes.

Weathering

There are two basic types of weathering: mechanical and chemical. Weathering is a very prominent process on the Earth's surface. Materials weather at different rates, which are known as differential weathering. Mechanical and chemical weathering is interdependent. For example, chemical weathering can loosen the bonds between molecules and allow mechanical weathering to take place. Mechanical weathering can expose the surfaces of land masses and allow chemical weathering to take place. Impact, abrasion, frost wedging, root wedging, salt wedging, and uploading are types of mechanical weathering. Types of chemical weathering are dissolution, hydration, hydrolysis, oxidation, biological, and carbonation. The primary type of chemical weathering is caused by water dissolving a mineral. The more acidic water is, the more effective it is at weathering. Carbonic and sulfuric acids can enter rain when they are present in the atmosphere. This lowers the pH value of rain, making it more acidic. Normal rain water has a pH value of 5.5. Acid rain has a pH value of 4 or less.

Radioactive dating

Radioactive dating, also known as radiometric dating, is a technique that can be used to determine the age of rocks and even the Earth itself. The process compares the amount of radioactive material in a rock to the amount of material that has "decayed." Decay refers to the fact that the nuclide of an element loses subatomic particles over time. The process includes a parent element that undergoes changes to create a daughter element, also known as the decay product. The daughter element can also be unstable and lose particles, creating another daughter element. This is known as a decay chain. Decay occurs until all the elements are stable. Three types of dating techniques are radiocarbon dating, potassium-argon dating, and uranium-lead dating. These techniques can be used to date a variety of natural and manmade materials, including archaeological artifacts.

Mass extinction

Mass extinction, also known as an extinction event, is a decrease in the number of species over a short period of time. While there are many theories as to the causes of mass extinction, it occurs when a relatively large number of species die off or when fewer species evolve than expected. Extinction events are classified as major and minor. It is generally accepted that there have been five major extinction events in Earth's history. The five most significant mass extinction events are Ordovician-Silurian, Permian-Triassic, Late Devonian, Triassic-Jurassic, and Cretaceous-Tertiary.

Uniformitarianism, catastrophism, and superposition

Uniformitarianism: Also known as gradualism, uniformitarianism is the belief among modern geologists that the forces, processes, and laws that we see today have existed throughout geologic time. It involves the belief that the present is the key to the past, and that relatively slow processes have shaped the geological features of Earth.

Catastrophism: This is the belief that the Earth was shaped by sudden, short-term catastrophic events.

Superposition: In geology, and in the field of stratigraphy in particular, the law of superposition is that underground layers closer to the surface were deposited more recently.

Geologic time scale

One year is 365.25 days long. The International System of Units (SI) suggests the symbol "a" for a standard year or annum. The prefixes "M" for mega and "G" for giga are used to refer to one million and one billion years, respectively. Ma stands for a megannum (10^6 years) and Ga stands for a gigannum (10^9 years). For example, it can be said that the Earth was formed 4.5 billion years ago, or 4.5 Ga. The term "ago" is understood. Use of the abbreviation "mya" for millions of years (ago) is discouraged, but it is still occasionally used. The abbreviation "BP" stands for "before present." The "present" is defined as January 1, 1950, since present changes from year to year. Another abbreviation used is BCE, which stands for "Before the Common Era." Christian and current can also be used in place of common.

Geologists use the geologic time scale when discussing Earth's chronology and the formation of rocks and minerals. Age is calculated in millions of years before the present time. Units of time are often delineated by geologic or paleontologic events. Smaller units of time such as eras are distinguished by the abundance and/or extinction of certain plant and animal life. For example, the extinction of the dinosaurs marks the end of the Mesozoic era and the beginning of the Cenozoic, the present, era. We are in the Holocene epoch. The supereon encompasses the greatest amount of time. It is composed of eons. Eons are divided into eras, eras into periods, and periods into epochs. Layers of rock also correspond to periods of time in geochronology. Current theory holds that the Earth was formed 4.5 billion years ago.

Development of geologic time scale

The first known observations of stratigraphy were made by Aristotle, who lived before the time of Christ. He observed seashells in ancient rock formations and on the beach, and concluded that the fossilized seashells were similar to current seashells. Avicenna, a Persian scholar from the 11th century, also made early advances in the development of stratigraphy with the concept of superposition. Nicolas Steno, a Danish scientist from the 17th century, expounded upon this with the belief that layers of rock are piled on top of each other. In the 18th century, Abraham Werner categorized rocks from four different periods: the Primary, Secondary, Tertiary, and Quaternary periods. This fell out of use when the belief emerged that rock layers containing the same fossils had been deposited at the same time, and were therefore from the same age. British geologists created the names for many of the time divisions in use today. For example, the Devonian period was named after the county of Devon, and the Permian period was named after Perm, Russia.

Relative and absolute time

A numerical, or "absolute," age is a specific number of years, such as 150 million years ago. A "relative" age refers to a time range, such as the Mesozoic era. It is used to determine whether one rock formation is older or younger than another formation. Radioactive dating is a form of absolute dating and stratigraphy is a form of relative dating. Radioactive dating techniques have provided the most information about the absolute age of rocks and other geological features. Together, geochronologists have created a geologic time scale. Biostratigraphy uses plant and animal fossils within rock to determine its relative age.

Stratigraphy

Stratigraphy is a branch of geology that involves the study of rock layers and layering. Sedimentary rocks are the primary focus of stratigraphy. Subfields include lithostratigraphy, which is the study of the vertical layering of rock types, and biostratigraphy, which is the study of fossil evidence in rock layers. Magnetostratigraphy is the study of changes in detrital remnant magnetism (DRM), which is used to measure the polarity of Earth's magnetic field at the time a stratum was deposited. Chronostratigraphy focuses on the relative dating of rock strata based on the time of rock formation. Unconformity refers to missing layers of rock.

Fossils

Fossils provide a wealth of information about the past, particularly about the flora and fauna that once occupied the Earth, but also about the geologic history of the Earth itself and how Earth and its inhabitants came to be. Some fossilized remains in the geohistorical record exemplify ongoing processes in the Earth's environment, such as weathering, glaciation, and volcanism. These have all led to evolutionary changes in plants and animals. Other fossils support the theory that catastrophic events caused drastic changes in the Earth and its living creatures. One example of this type of theory is that a meteor struck the Earth and caused dinosaurs to become extinct. Both types of fossils provide scientists with a way to hypothesize whether these types of events will happen again.

Fossils are preservations of plants, animals, their remains, or their traces that date back to about 10,000 years ago. Fossils and where they are found in rock strata makes up the fossil record. Fossils are formed under a very specific set of conditions. The fossil must not be damaged by predators and scavengers after death, and the fossil must not decompose. Usually, this happens when the organism is quickly covered with sediment. This sediment builds up and molecules in the organism's body are replaced by minerals. Fossils come in an array of sizes, from single-celled organisms to large dinosaurs.

Atmospheric layers

Earth's atmosphere has five main layers. From lowest to highest, these are the troposphere, the stratosphere, the mesosphere, the thermosphere, and the exosphere. Between each pair of layers is a transition layer called a pause. The troposphere includes the tropopause, which is the transitional layer of the stratosphere. Energy from Earth's surface is transferred to the troposphere. Temperature decreases with altitude in this layer. In the stratosphere, the temperature is inverted, meaning that it increases with altitude. The stratosphere includes the ozone layer, which helps block ultraviolet light from the Sun. The stratopause is the transitional layer to the mesosphere. The temperature of the mesosphere decreases with height. It is considered the coldest place on Earth, and has an average temperature of -85 degrees Celsius. Temperature increases with altitude in the thermosphere, which includes the thermopause. Just past the thermosphere is the exobase, the base layer of the exosphere. Beyond the five main layers are the ionosphere, homosphere, heterosphere, and magnetosphere.

Earth's atmosphere

The atmosphere consists of 78% nitrogen, 21% oxygen, and 1% argon. It also includes traces of water vapor, carbon dioxide and other gases, dust particles, and chemicals from Earth. The atmosphere becomes thinner the farther it is from the Earth's surface. It becomes difficult to breathe at about 3 km above sea level. The atmosphere gradually fades into space. The lowest layer of the atmosphere is called the troposphere. Its thickness varies at the poles and the equator, varying from about 7 to 17 km. This is where most weather occurs. The stratosphere is next, and continues to an elevation of about 51 km. The mesosphere extends from the stratosphere to an elevation of about 81 km. It is the coldest layer and is where meteors tend to ablate. The next layer is the thermosphere. It is where the International Space Station orbits. The exosphere is the outermost layer, extends to 10,000 km, and mainly consists of hydrogen and helium.

Tropospheric circulation

Most weather takes place in the troposphere. Air circulates in the atmosphere by convection and in various types of "cells." Air near the equator is warmed by the Sun and rises. Cool air rushes under it, and the higher, warmer air flows toward Earth's poles. At the poles, it cools and descends to the surface. It is now under the hot air, and flows back to the equator. Air currents coupled with ocean currents move heat around the planet, creating winds, weather, and climate. Winds can change direction with the seasons. For example, in Southeast Asia and India, summer monsoons are caused by air being heated by the Sun. This air rises, draws moisture from the ocean, and causes daily rains. In winter, the air cools, sinks, pushes the moist air away, and creates dry weather.

Layers above Earth's surface

The ozone layer, although contained within the stratosphere, is determined by ozone (O_3) concentrations. It absorbs the majority of ultraviolet light from the Sun. The ionosphere is part of both the exosphere and the thermosphere. It is characterized by the fact that it is a plasma, a partially ionized gas in which free electrons and positive ions are attracted to each other, but are too energetic to remain fixed as a molecule. It starts at about 50 km above Earth's surface and goes to 1,000 km. It affects radio wave transmission and auroras. The ionosphere pushes against the inner edge of the Earth's magnetosphere, which is the highly magnetized, non-spherical region around the Earth. The homosphere encompasses the troposphere, stratosphere, and mesosphere. Gases in the homosphere are considered well mixed. In the heterosphere, the distance that particles can move without colliding is large. As a result, gases are stratified according to their molecular weights. Heavier gases such as oxygen and nitrogen occur near the bottom of the heterosphere, while hydrogen, the lightest element, is found at the top.

Hydrosphere

Much of Earth is covered by a layer of water or ice called the hydrosphere. Most of the hydrosphere consists of ocean water. The water cycle and the many processes involved in it take place in the hydrosphere. There are several theories regarding how the Earth's hydrosphere was formed. Earth contains more surface water than other planets in the inner solar system. Outgassing, the slow release of trapped water vapor from the Earth's interior, is one theory used to explain the existence of water on Earth. This does not really account for the quantity of water on Earth, however. Another hypothesis is that the early Earth was subjected to a period of bombardment by comets and water-rich asteroids, which resulted in the release of water into the Earth's environment. If this is true, much of the water on the surface of the Earth today originated from the outer parts of the solar system beyond Neptune.

Formation of Earth's atmosphere

It is generally believed that the Earth's atmosphere evolved into its present state. Some believe Earth's early atmosphere contained hydrogen, helium, methane, ammonia, and some water vapor. These elements also played a role in planet formation. Earth's early atmosphere was developed before the emergence of living organisms as we know them today. Eventually, the hot hydrogen and helium escaped Earth's gravity and drifted off.

Others believe the early atmosphere contained a large amount of carbon dioxide. Either way, there was probably little oxygen at the time. One theory is that a second stage of the atmosphere evolved over several hundred million years through a process during which methane, ammonia, and water vapor broke down and reformed into nitrogen, hydrogen, and carbon dioxide. About two billion years ago, higher levels of oxygen were found in the atmosphere, which is indicated by large deposits of iron ore. At the same time, iron ores created in oxygen-poor environments stopped forming. The oxygen in the atmosphere today comes mainly from plants and microorganisms such as algae.

Paleozoic era

The Paleozoic era began about 542 Ma and lasted until 251 Ma. It is further divided into six periods. The Paleozoic era began after the supercontinent Pannotia started to break up and at the end of a global ice age. By the end of the era, the supercontinent Pangaea had formed. The beginning of the Paleozoic era is marked by Cambrian Explosion, a time when there were abundant life forms according to the fossil record. The end of the era is marked by one of the major extinction events, the Permian extinction, during which almost 90 percent of the species living at the time became extinct. Many plant and animal forms appeared on the land and in the sea during this era. It is also when large land plants first appeared in the fossil record. There are many invertebrates found in the fossil record of the Paleozoic era, and fish, amphibians, and reptiles also first appeared in the fossil record during this era. There were also large swamps and forests, some of which were formed into coal deposits that exist today.

Earth's formation

Earth's early development began after a supernova exploded. This led to the formation of the Sun out of hydrogen gas and interstellar dust. These same elements swirled around the newly-formed Sun and formed the planets, including Earth. Scientists theorize that about 4.5 billion years ago, Earth was a chunk of rock surrounded by a cloud of gas. It is believed it lacked water and the type of atmosphere that exists today. Heat from radioactive materials in the rock and pressure in the Earth's interior melted the interior. This caused the heavier materials, such as iron, to sink. Lighter silicate-type rocks rose to the Earth's surface. These rocks formed the Earth's earliest crust. Other chemicals also rose to the Earth's surface, helping to form the water and atmosphere. There is one material that has been dated by scientists and found to be 4.4 billion years old. The material is zircon, which consists of zirconium, silicon, and oxygen. Zircon is a mineral that has a high resistance to weathering.

Cenozoic era

The Cenozoic era began about 65.5 Ma and continues to the present. It is marked by the Cretaceous-Tertiary extinction event (extinction of the dinosaurs as well as many invertebrates and plants). The Cenozoic era is further divided into the Paleogene, Neogene, and Quaternary periods. During the Cenozoic era, Pangaea continued to drift, and the plates eventually moved into their present positions. The Pleistocene Ice Age, also known as Quaternary glaciation or the current ice age began about 2.58 Ma and includes the glaciation occurring today. Mammals continued to evolve and other plants and animals came into existence during this era. The fossil record includes the ancestors of the horse, rhinoceros, and camel. It also includes the first dogs and cats and the first humanlike creatures. The first humans appeared less than 200,000 years ago.

Mesozoic era

The Mesozoic era is known as the Age of the Dinosaurs. It is also the era during which the dinosaurs became extinct. The fossil record also shows the appearance of mammals and birds. Trees that existed included gymnosperms, which have uncovered seeds and are mostly cone bearing, and angiosperms, which have covered seeds and are flowering plants. The angiosperm group is currently the dominant plant group. It was also during this era that the supercontinent Pangaea divided into the continental pieces that exist today. During the Cretaceous period, sea levels rose until one-third of the Earth's present land mass was underwater, and then receded. This period created huge marine deposits and chalk. The extinction of the dinosaurs happened about 65 Ma, and was believed to have been triggered by the impact of an asteroid.

Ocean

The ocean is the salty body of water that encompasses the Earth. It has a mass of 1.4×10^{24} grams. Geographically, the ocean is divided into three large oceans: the Pacific Ocean, the Atlantic Ocean, and the Indian Ocean. There are also other divisions, such as gulfs, bays, and various types of seas, including Mediterranean and marginal seas. Ocean distances can be measured by latitude, longitude, degrees, meters, miles, and nautical miles. The ocean accounts for 70.8% of the surface of the Earth, amounting to 361,254,000 km^2. The ocean's depth is greatest at Challenger Deep in the Mariana Trench. The ocean floor here is 10,924 meters below sea level. The depths of the ocean are mapped by echo sounders and satellite altimeter systems. Echo sounders emit a sound pulse from the surface and record the time it takes to return. Satellite altimeters provide better maps of the ocean floor.

Ocean's importance

The ocean covers 71 percent of the Earth's surface and contains 97 percent of the planet's water. The ocean is an important part of the biosphere, the hydrologic cycle, and tropospheric circulation. It also plays a key role in Earth's weather and climate, which influence the daily lives of humans. The main uses of the ocean and coastal areas for humans are food, transport, oil, gas, and recreation. It is estimated that the ocean provides a means of support for almost 50 percent of all species on Earth. Roughly 20 percent of the animal protein in human diets comes from the ocean.

Seawater

Salinity is a measure of the amount of dissolved salts in ocean water. It is defined in terms of conductivity. Salinity is influenced by the geologic formations in the area, with igneous formations leading to lower salinity and sedimentary formations leading to higher salinity. Dryer areas with greater rates of evaporation also have higher salt concentrations. Areas where fresh water mixes with ocean water have lower salt concentrations. Hydrogen and oxygen make up about 96.5% of sea water. The major constituents of the dissolved solids of sea water at an atomic level are chlorine (55.3%), sodium (30.8%), magnesium (3.7%), sulfur (2.6%), calcium (1.2%), and potassium (1.1%). The salinity of ocean water is fairly constant, ranging from 34.60 to 34.80 parts per thousand, which is 200 parts per million. Measuring variation on this small of a scale requires instruments that are accurate to about one part per million.

Ocean floor

The ocean floor includes features similar to those found on land, such as mountains, ridges, plains, and canyons. The oceanic crust is a thin, dense layer that is about 10 km thick. The greatest volume of water is contained in the basins with lesser volumes that occupy the low-lying areas of the continents, which are known as the continental shelves. The continental slope connects the shelf to the ocean floor of the basin. The continental rise is a slightly sloping area between the slope and the basin. A seamount is an undersea volcanic peak that rises to a height of at least 1,000 meters. A guyot is a seamount with a flat top. A mid-ocean ridge is a continuous undersea mountain chain. Sills are low parts of ridges separating ocean basins or other seas. Trenches are long, narrow troughs. Many isolated peaks and seamounts are scattered throughout the ocean basins, and interrupt ocean currents.

Gyres and the Coriolis effect

Gyres are surface ocean currents that form large circular patterns. In the Northern Hemisphere, they flow clockwise. In the Southern Hemisphere, they flow counterclockwise. These directions are caused by the Coriolis effect. The Coriolis effect occurs due to the fact that the Earth is a rotating object. In the Northern Hemisphere, currents appear to be curving to the right. In the Southern Hemisphere, currents appear to be curving to the left. This is because the Earth is rotating. Gyres tend to flow in the opposite direction near the Earth's poles. In the portion of the Pacific Ocean north of the equator, the major currents are North Pacific, California, North Equatorial, and Kuroshio. In the South Pacific, they are South Equatorial, East Australia, South Pacific, and Peru. In the North Atlantic, they are the North Atlantic Drift, Canary, North Equatorial, and Gulf Stream. In the South Atlantic, they are South Equatorial, Brazil, South Atlantic, and Benguela.

Ocean currents

Surface currents are caused by winds. Subsurface currents, which occur deep beneath the ocean's surface, are caused by land masses and the Earth's rotation. The density of ocean water can also affect currents. Sea water with a higher salinity is denser than sea water with a lower salinity. Water from denser areas flows to areas with water that is less dense. Currents are classified by temperature. Colder polar sea water flows south towards warmer water, forming cold currents. Warm water currents swirl around the basins and equator. In turn, heat lost and gained by the ocean creates winds. Ocean currents play a significant role in transferring this heat toward the poles, which aids in the development of many types of weather phenomena.

Upwelling and Ekman transport

Upwelling occurs where wind blows parallel to a coast. This causes the ocean surface to move away from the coast. Deep-sea water, which is usually cold and rich in nutrients, rises to takes its place. Ekman transport refers to the impact of the Coriolis effect when wind moves water. Wind blowing in one direction tries to move the surface layer of water in a straight line, but the rotation of the Earth causes water to move in a curved direction. The wind continues to blow the surface of the water and the surface water turns slightly. Below the surface, the water turns even more, eventually creating a spiral. This creates water movement at a right angle to the wind direction. The importance of upwelling is that it brings the nutrient-rich dead and rotting sea creatures closer to the ocean's surface. Here, they are consumed by phytoplankton, which is in turn eaten by zooplankton. Fish eat the zooplankton, and larger creatures and humans eat the fish. Downwelling is the opposite of upwelling.

Deep sea currents

Deep sea currents are often likened to a conveyor belt because they circumnavigate the entire ocean, albeit weakly, and slowly mix deeper and shallower water. In the winter, deep circulation carries cold water from high latitudes to lower latitudes throughout the world. This takes place in areas where most water is at a depth of between 4 and 5 km. This water mass can be as cold as or colder than 4°C. Surface ocean temperatures average about 17°C, but can vary from -2°C to 36°C. The vast cold mass of sea water is also dense and has a high saline content, which forces it to sink at high latitudes. It spreads out, stratifies, and fills the ocean basins. Deep mixing occurs and then the water upwells. The manner in which deep sea currents move can be described as abyssal circulation.

Ocean waves

Most waves in the ocean are formed by winds. The stronger the winds are, the larger the waves will be. The highest point of a wave is the crest. The lowest point of a wave is the trough. The wavelength is measured from crest to crest. The wave height is measured from the trailing trough to the peak of the crest. The wave frequency refers to the number of wave crests passing a designated point each second. A wave period is the time it takes for a wave crest to reach the point of the wave crest of the previous wave. The energy in the wave runs into the shallow sea floor. This causes the wave to become steeper and then fall over, or break.

Other types of waves

Waves that reach the shore are not all the same size. They can be larger or smaller than average. About once an hour, there is usually a wave that is twice the size of others. There are even larger, but rare, rogue waves, which often travel alone and in a direction different than other waves. Swells are waves that have traveled a great distance. These types of waves are usually large waves with flatter crests. They are very regular in shape and size. The sea level slowly rises and falls over the period of a day. These types of waves on the sea surface are known as tides. Tides have wavelengths of thousands of kilometers. They differ from other wave types in that they are created by slow and very small changes in gravity due to the motion of the Sun and the Moon relative to Earth.

Tsunamis

Seismic sea waves or tsunamis (sometimes mistakenly called tidal waves) are formed by seismic activity. A tsunami is a series of waves with long wavelengths and long periods. Far out at sea, the heights of these waves are typically less than one meter. The wavelength may be 100 km and the wave period may range from five minutes to one hour. However, as seismic sea waves approach the shoreline, the bottom of the wave is slowed down by the shallower sea floor. The top is not slowed as much, and wave height increases to as much as 20 meters. These waves can hit the shore at speeds of up to 30 miles per hour. Tsunamis are caused by earthquakes, submarine landslides, and volcanic eruptions.

Beaufort wind scale

The Beaufort wind scale assigns a numerical value to wind conditions and the appearance of the sea. Zero represents a calm, mirror-like sea with no measurable wind. Twelve is the maximum on the Beaufort scale, and represents hurricane force winds with speeds of 35.2 meters per second (m/s). Visibility is greatly reduced, the sea air is filled with foam, and the sea is completely white with driving spray. The scale is as follows: 1 is light wind with a speed of 1.2 m/s; 2 is a light breeze of 2.8 m/s; 3 is a gentle breeze of 4.9 m/s; 4 is a moderate breeze of 7.7 m/s; and 5 is a fresh breeze of 10.5 m/s. At 5, there are moderate waves, many white caps, and some spray. Six is a strong breeze of 13.1 m/s; 7 is a near gale with wind speeds of 15.8 m/s; 8 is gale force winds of 18.8 m/s; 9 is strong gales of 22.1 m/s; 10 is considered a storm with wind speeds of 25.9 m/s; and 11 is a violent storm.

Shoreline

The area where land meets the sea is called the shoreline. This marks the average position of the ocean. Longshore currents create longshore drift or transport (also called beach drift). This is when ocean waves move toward a beach at an angle, which moves water along the coast. Sediment is eroded from some areas and deposited in others. In this way, it is moved along the beach. Rip currents are strong, fast currents that occur when part of longshore current moves away from the beach. Hard, man-made structures built perpendicular to the beach tend to trap sand on the up-current side. Erosion occurs on the down-current side. Features formed by the sediment deposited by waves include spits, bay-mouth bars, tombolos, barrier islands, and buildups. Sand is composed of weather-resistant, granular materials like quartz and orthoclase. In some locations, it is composed of rock and basalt.

Tides

The gravitational pull of the Sun and Moon causes the oceans to rise and fall each day, creating high and low tides. Most areas have two high tides and two low tides per day. Because the Moon is closer to the Earth than the Sun, its gravitational pull is much greater. The water on the side of the Earth that is closest to the Moon and the water on the opposite side experience high tide. The two low tides occur on the other sides. This changes as the Moon revolves around the Earth. Tidal range is the measurement of the height difference between low and high tide. Tidal range also changes with the location of the Sun and Moon throughout the year, creating spring and neap tides. When all these bodies are aligned, the combined gravitational pull is greater and the tidal range is also greater. This is what creates the spring tide. The neap tide is when the tidal range is at its lowest, which occurs when the Sun and Moon are not at right angles.

Black smokers

Black smokers are a relatively recently discovered feature of the ocean floor. They were first identified in 1977. A black smoker is a type of hydrothermal vent formed when superheated water from below Earth's crust emerges from the ocean floor. This hot water is also rich in sulfides and other minerals from the Earth's crust. When the hot water comes in contact with the cold ocean water, it creates a black chimney-like structure around the vent. Water temperatures around black smokers have been recorded at 400°C. However, water pressure is too great on the sea floor to allow for boiling. The water is also very acidic (twice that of vinegar). It is estimated that the yearly volume of water passing through black smokers is 1.4×10^{14} kg.

Carbon cycle

The carbon and nutrient cycles of the ocean are processes that are due in part to the deep currents, mixing, and upwelling that occur in the ocean. Carbon dioxide (CO_2) from the atmosphere is dissolved into the ocean at higher latitudes and distributed to the denser deep water. Where upwelling occurs, CO_2 is brought back to the surface and emitted into the tropical air. Phytoplankton are typically single-celled organisms that are nourished by the Sun. They are photosynthetic autotrophs, meaning they convert water, carbon dioxide, and solar energy into food. They drift with the currents, produce oxygen as a byproduct, and serve as a food source. Zooplankton feed on phytoplankton. Zooplankton are heterotrophic organisms, meaning they do not synthesize their own food. Zooplankton can be single-celled creatures or much larger organisms, such as jellyfish, mollusks, and crustaceans.

El Niño-Southern Oscillation (ENSO)

The El Niño-Southern Oscillation (ENSO) is a climate pattern of the Pacific Ocean area that lasts 6 to 18 months and causes weather that is different from the expected seasonal patterns and variations. There are two sets of events associated with ENSO: El Niño and La Niña. The usual weather patterns for the Pacific Ocean involve the movement of sea water by winds from the eastern part of the tropical Pacific to the western part of the Pacific Ocean. This pattern causes cold deep water upwells in the eastern Pacific. This creates wet weather and is considered a low-pressure system. Conversely, the eastern Pacific is a dry, high-pressure system. El Niño weakens upwelling because equalization in air pressure leads to less wind, which leads to more water staying in the eastern Pacific. La Niña increases upwelling because winds grow stronger because of higher air pressures across the Pacific. Both El Niño and La Niña cause extreme weather events such as droughts, heavy rain, and flooding.

Rift valley

Rift valleys occur both on land and in the ocean. They are a result of plate tectonics, and occur when plates are spreading apart. In the ocean, this is part of the crust development cycle in which new crust is created at mid-ocean ridges and old crust is lost at the trenches. The Mid-Atlantic Ridge is an example of this. It occurs at divergent Eurasian and North American plates and in the South Atlantic, African, and South American plates. The East Pacific Rise is also a mid-oceanic ridge. The most extensive rift valley is located along the crest of the mid-ocean ridge system. It is a result of sea floor spreading.

Beaches

Weathering erodes the parent material of beaches, rock and soil, into sand, which is typically quartz. Other parts of the soil such as clay and silt are deposited in areas of the continental shelf. The larger sand particles get deposited in the form of a beach. This includes a near shore, which is underwater, a fore shore, the area typically considered the beach, and a back shore. The offshore starts about 5 meters from the shoreline and extends to about 20 meters. The beach also includes wet and dry parts and a fore dune and rear dune. Waves typically move sand from the sea to the beach, and gravity and wave action move it back again. Wind gradually pushes sand particles uphill in a jumping motion called saltation. Sand stays deposited in the form of dunes and the dunes appear as if they roll backward. Storms can both erode a beach and provide additional deposition.

North Atlantic Oscillation (NAO)

The North Atlantic Oscillation is a climatic occurrence that affects winter weather in the Northern Hemisphere, particularly in the east coast regions of the United States, Europe, and North Africa. Atmospheric pressure over the North Atlantic caused by the Icelandic Low and the high pressure Azores leads to the North Atlantic Oscillation. There is both a "positive" and "negative" phase of the NAO. The positive phase is when strong winds caused by a large difference in air pressure send wet winter storms from eastern North America to northern Europe. Weaker winds associated with a smaller difference in air pressure cause eastern North America and northern Europe to have fewer winter storms. Instead, the weather is rainy in southern Europe and North Africa.

Weather, climate, and meteorology

Meteorology is the study of the atmosphere, particularly as it pertains to forecasting the weather and understanding its processes. Weather is the condition of the atmosphere at any given moment. Most weather occurs in the troposphere. Weather includes changing events such as clouds, storms, and temperature, as well as more extreme events such as tornadoes, hurricanes, and blizzards. Climate refers to the average weather for a particular area over time, typically at least 30 years. Latitude is an indicator of climate. Changes in climate occur over long time periods.

Weather phenomena

Common atmospheric conditions that are frequently measured are temperature, precipitation, wind, and humidity. These weather conditions are often measured at permanently fixed weather stations so weather data can be collected and compared over time and by region. Measurements may also be taken by ships, buoys, and underwater instruments. Measurements may also be taken under special circumstances. The measurements taken include temperature, barometric pressure, humidity, wind speed, wind direction, and precipitation. Usually, the following instruments are used: A thermometer is used for measuring temperature; a barometer is used for measuring barometric/air pressure; a hygrometer is used for measuring humidity; an anemometer is used for measuring wind speed; a weather vane is used for measuring wind direction; and a rain gauge is used for measuring precipitation.

Latitudinal variation of solar radiation

Latitude is a measurement of the distance from the equator. The distance from the equator indicates how much solar radiation a particular area receives. The equator receives more sunlight, while polar areas receive less. The Earth tilts slightly on its rotational axis. This tilt determines the seasons and affects weather. There are eight biomes or ecosystems with particular climates that are associated with latitude. Those in the high latitudes, which get the least sunlight, are tundra and taiga. Those in the mid latitudes are grassland, temperate forest, and chaparral. Those in latitudes closest to the equator are the warmest. The biomes are desert and tropical rain forest. The eighth biome is the ocean, which is unique because it consists of water and spans the entire globe. Insolation refers to incoming solar radiation. Diurnal variations refer to the daily changes in insolation. The greatest insolation occurs at noon.

Tilt of the Earth

The tilt of the Earth on its axis is 23.5°. This tilt causes the seasons and affects the temperature because it affects the amount of Sun the area receives. When the Northern or Southern Hemispheres are tilted toward the Sun, the hemisphere tilted toward the sun experiences summer and the other hemisphere experiences winter. This reverses as the Earth revolves around the Sun. Fall and spring occur between the two extremes. The equator gets the same amount of sunlight every day of the year, about 12 hours, and doesn't experience seasons. Both poles have days during the winter when they are tilted away from the Sun and receive no daylight. The opposite effect occurs during the summer. There are 24 hours of daylight and no night. The summer solstice, the day with the most amount of sunlight, occurs on June 21st in the Northern Hemisphere and on December 21st in the Southern Hemisphere. The winter solstice, the day with the least amount of sunlight, occurs on December 21st in the Northern Hemisphere and on June 21st in the Southern Hemisphere.

Breezes

Sea breezes and land breezes help influence an area's prevailing winds, particularly in areas where the wind flow is light. Sea breezes, also called onshore breezes, are the result of the different capacities for absorbing heat of the ocean and the land. The sea can be warmed to a greater depth than the land. It warms up more slowly than the land's surface. Land heats air above it as its temperature increases. This heated; warmer is less dense and rises as a result. The cooler air above the sea and higher sea level pressure create a wind flow in the direction of the land. Coastal areas often receive these cooler breezes. Land cools slower at night than the ocean, and coastal breezes weaken at this time. When the land becomes so cool that it is cooler than the sea surface, the pressure over the ocean is lower than the land. This creates a land breeze. This can cause rain and thunderstorms over the ocean.

Wind

Winds are the result of air moving by convection. Masses of warm air rise, and cold air sweeps into their place. The warm air also moves, cools, and sinks. The term "prevailing wind" refers to the wind that usually blows in an area in a single direction. Dominant winds are the winds with the highest speeds. Belts or bands that run latitudinal and blow in a specific direction are associated with convection cells. Hadley cells are formed directly north and south of the equator. The Farrell cells occur at about 30° to 60°. The jet stream runs between the Farrell cells and the polar cells. At the higher and lower latitudes, the direction is easterly. At mid latitudes, the direction is westerly. From the North Pole to the south, the surface winds are Polar High Easterlies, Subpolar Low Westerlies, Subtropical High or Horse Latitudes, North-East Trade winds, Equatorial Low or Doldrums, South-East Trades, Subtropical High or Horse Latitudes, Subpolar Low Easterlies, and Polar High.

Thunderstorms

A thunderstorm is one of the many weather phenomena that can be created during the ongoing process of heat moving through Earth's atmosphere. Thunderstorms form when there is moisture to form rain clouds, unstable air, and lift. Unstable air is usually caused by warm air rising quickly through cold air. Lift can be caused by fronts, sea breezes, and elevated terrain, such as mountains. Single cell thunderstorms have one main draft. Multicell clusters have clusters of storms. Multicell lines have severe thunderstorms along a squall line. Supercell thunderstorms are large and severe, and have the capacity to produce destructive tornadoes. Thunder is a sonic shock wave caused by the rapid expansion of air around lightning. Lightning is the discharge of electricity during a thunderstorm. Lightning can also occur during volcanic eruptions or dust storms.

Atmospheric variations

Terrain affects several local atmospheric conditions, including temperature, wind speed, and wind direction. When there are land forms, heating of the ground can be greater than the heating of the surrounding air than it would be at the same altitude above sea level. This creates a thermal low in the region and amplifies any existing thermal lows. It also changes the wind circulation. Terrain such as hills and valleys increase friction between the air and the land, which disturbs the air flow. This physical block deflects the wind, and the resulting air flow is called a barrier jet. Just as the heating of the land and air affect sea and land breezes along the coast, rugged terrain affects the wind circulation between mountains and valleys.

Cyclones

Cyclones generally refer to large air masses rotating in the same direction as the Earth. They are formed in low pressure areas. Cyclones vary in size. Some are mesoscale systems, which vary in size from about 5 km to hundreds of kilometers. Some are synoptic scale systems, which are about 1,000 km in size. The size of subtropical cyclones is somewhere in between. Cold-core polar and extratropical cyclones are synoptic scale systems. Warm-core tropical, polar low and mesocyclones are mesoscale systems. Extratropical cyclones, sometimes called mid-latitude cyclones or wave cyclones, occur in the middle latitudes. They have neither tropical nor polar characteristics. Extratropical cyclones are everyday phenomena which, along with anticyclones, drive the weather over much of the Earth. They can produce cloudiness, mild showers, heavy gales, and thunderstorms. Anticyclones occur when there is a descending pocket of air of higher than average pressure. Anticyclones are usually associated with clearing skies and drier, cooler air.

Tornados

During a tornado, wind speeds can be upward of 300 miles per hour. Tornados are rotating funnel-like clouds. They have a very high energy density, which means they are very destructive to a small area. They are also short-lived. About 75% of the world's tornadoes occur in the United States, mostly in an area of the Great Plains known as Tornado Alley. If there are two or more columns of air, it is referred to as a multiple vortex tornado. A satellite tornado is a weak tornado that forms near a larger one within the same mesocyclone. A waterspout is a tornado over water. The severity of tornadoes is measured using the Enhanced Fujita Scale. An EF-0 rating is associated with a 3-second wind gust between 65 and 85 miles per hour, while an EF-5 is associated with wind speeds of greater than 200 mph.

Humidity

Humidity refers to water vapor contained in the air. The amount of moisture contained in air depends upon its temperature. The higher the air temperature, the more moisture it can hold. These higher levels of moisture are associated with higher humidity. Absolute humidity refers to the total amount of moisture air is capable of holding at a certain temperature. Relative humidity is the ratio of water vapor in the air compared to the amount the air is capable of holding at its current temperature. As temperature decreases, absolute humidity stays the same and relative humidity increases. A hygrometer is a device used to measure humidity. The dew point is the temperature at which water vapor condenses into water at a particular humidity.

Hurricanes

A hurricane is one of the three weather phenomena that can occur as a result of a tropical cyclone. A tropical cyclone is a warm-core, low-pressure condition that circles in the same direction as the Earth. A tropical depression has sustained winds of up to 30 miles per hour (mph), with rotational winds around a center. A tropical storm appears more circular and has more rotation than a tropical depression. Its winds range from 39 to 73 mph. A hurricane appears well-organized and sometimes has a recognizable eye with strong rotation. Its wind speed is more than 73 mph. Hurricanes are classified using the Saffir-Simpson Scale, which ranges from category 1 to category 5. A category 5 hurricane has wind speeds greater than 155 mph. Hurricanes are named alphabetically through the season starting with "A." The letters "Q," "U," and "Z" are not used. There are six lists of names that are used from year to year. The names of devastating hurricanes are retired from the list.

Precipitation

After clouds reach the dew point, precipitation occurs. Precipitation can take the form of a liquid or a solid. It is known by many names, including rain, snow, ice, dew, and frost. Liquid forms of precipitation include rain and drizzle. Rain or drizzle that freezes on contact is known as freezing rain or freezing drizzle. Solid or frozen forms of precipitation include snow, ice needles or diamond dust, sleet or ice pellets, hail, and graupel or snow pellets. Virga is a form of precipitation that evaporates before reaching the ground. It usually looks like sheets or shafts falling from a cloud. The amount of rainfall is measured with a rain gauge. Intensity can be measured according to how fast precipitation is falling or by how severely it limits visibility. Precipitation plays a major role in the water cycle since it is responsible for depositing much of the Earth's fresh water.

Heat waves

A heat wave is a stretch of hotter than normal weather. Some heat waves may involve high humidity and last longer than a week. Heat waves can form if a warm high-pressure weather system stalls in an area. The jet stream is a flow that moves air through the middle latitudes. When this shifts, it can bring a pattern of unusually warm weather into a region, creating a heat wave. Heat can be trapped by cities. If there is no rain or clouds to help cool the weather, the heat wave can linger. In humans, heat waves can lead to heat stroke, heat exhaustion, cramps, dehydration, and even death. Plants can dry up and crops can fail. There is also a greater threat of fires during a heat wave in dry areas.

Cloud types

Most clouds can be classified according to the altitude of their base above Earth's surface. High clouds occur at altitudes between 5,000 and 13,000 meters. Middle clouds occur at altitudes between 2,000 and 7,000 meters. Low clouds occur from the Earth's surface to altitudes of 2,000 meters. Types of high clouds include cirrus (Ci), thin wispy mare's tails that consist of ice; cirrocumulus (Cc), small, pillow-like puffs that often appear in rows; and cirrostratus (Cs), thin, sheetlike clouds that often cover the entire sky. Types of middle clouds include altocumulus (Ac), gray-white clouds that consist of liquid water; and altostratus (As), grayish or blue-gray clouds that span the sky. Types of low clouds include stratus (St), gray and fog-like clouds consisting of water droplets that take up the whole sky; stratocumulus (Sc), low-lying, lumpy gray clouds; and nimbostratus (Ns), dark gray clouds with uneven bases that indicate rain or snow. Two types of clouds, cumulus (Cu) and cumulonimbus (Cb), are capable of great vertical growth. They can start at a wide range of altitudes, from the Earth's surface to altitudes of 13,000 meters.

Cloud formation

Clouds form when air cools and warm air is forced to give up some of its water vapor because it can no longer hold it. This vapor condenses and forms tiny droplets of water or ice crystals called clouds. Particles, or aerosols, are needed for water vapor to form water droplets. These are called condensation nuclei. Clouds are created by surface heating, mountains and terrain, rising air masses, and weather fronts. Clouds precipitate, returning the water they contain to Earth. Clouds can also create atmospheric optics. They can scatter light, creating colorful phenomena such as rainbows, colorful sunsets, and the green flash phenomenon.

Air masses and weather fronts

Air masses are large volumes of air in the troposphere of the Earth. They are categorized by their temperature and by the amount of water vapor they contain. Arctic and Antarctic air masses are cold, polar air masses are cool, and tropical and equatorial air masses are hot. Other types of air masses include maritime and monsoon, both of which are moist and unstable. There are also continental and superior air masses, which are dry. A weather front separates two masses of air of different densities. It is the principal cause of meteorological phenomena. Air masses are quickly and easily affected by the land they are above. They can have certain characteristics, and then develop new ones when they get blown over a different area.

Nonstandard cloud types

Contrails, or condensation trails, are thin white streaks caused by jets. These are created from water vapor condensing and freezing the jet's exhaust particles. Contrails can be further classified as short-lived, persistent non-spreading, and persistent. Lenticular or lee wave, clouds are created by an air current over an obstacle, such as a mountain. They appear to be stationary, but are actually forming, dissipating, and reforming in the same place. Kelvin-Helmholtz clouds are formed by winds with different speeds or directions. They look like ocean waves. Mammatus clouds hang down from the base of a cloud, usually a cumulonimbus cloud. They often occur during the warmer months.

Pressure systems

The concept of atmospheric pressure involves the idea that air exerts a force. An imaginary column of air 1 square inch in size rising through the atmosphere would exert a force of 14.7 pounds per square inch (psi). Both temperature and altitude affect atmospheric pressure. Low and high pressure systems tend to want to equalize. Air tends to move from areas of high pressure to areas of low pressure. When air moves into a low pressure system, the air that was there gets pushed up, creating lower temperatures and pressures. Water vapor condenses and forms clouds and possibly rain and snow. A barometer is used to measure air pressure.

Bergeron system

The Bergeron classification system uses three sets of letters to identify the following characteristics of air masses: moisture content, thermal characteristics from where they originated, and the stability of the atmosphere. The first, moisture content, uses the following letters: "c" represents the dry continental air masses and "m" stands for the moist maritime air masses. The second set of abbreviations are as follows: "T" indicates the air mass is tropical in origin; "P" indicates the air mass is polar in origin; "A" indicates the air mass is Antarctic in origin; "M" stands for monsoon; "E" indicates the air mass is equatorial in origin; and "S" is used to represent superior air, which is dry air formed by a downward motion. The last set of symbols provides an indicator of the stability of the mass. "K" indicates the mass is colder than the ground below it, while "w" indicates the mass is warmer than the ground. For example, cP is a continental polar air mass, while cPk is a polar air mass blowing over the Gulf Stream, which is warmer than the mass.

Frontal systems

A cold front is a mass of cold air, usually fast moving and dense, that moves into a warm air front, producing clouds. This often produces a temperature drop and rain, hail (frozen rain), thunder, and lightning. A warm front is pushed up by a fast moving cold front. It is often associated with high wispy clouds, such as cirrus and cirrostratus clouds. A stationary front forms when a warm and cold front meet, but neither is strong enough to move the other. Winds blowing parallel to the fronts keep the front stationary. The front may remain in the same place for days until the wind direction changes and both fronts become a single warm or cold front. In other cases, the entire front dissipates. An occluded front is when a cold front pushes into a warm front. The warm air rises and the two masses of cool air join. These types of fronts often occur in areas of low atmospheric pressure.

Weather fronts and maps

A weather front is the area between two differing masses of air that affects weather. Frontal movements are influenced by the jet stream and other high winds. Movements are determined by the type of front. Cold fronts move up to twice as fast as warm ones. It is in the turbulent frontal area that commonplace and dramatic weather events take place. This area also creates temperature changes. Weather phenomena include rain, thunderstorms, high winds, tornadoes, cloudiness, clear skies, and hurricanes. Different fronts can be plotted on weather maps using a set of designated symbols. Surface weather maps can also include symbols representing clouds, rain, temperature, air pressure, and fair weather.

Cold fronts are represented on weather maps as a blue line. Solid blue triangles are used to indicate the direction of movement. Warm fronts are represented with a red line. Solid red semi-circles are used to indicate the direction of the front. The cold and warm front symbols are merged and alternated to point in opposite directions to indicate a stationary front. An occluded front is represented by a purple line with alternating solid purple triangles and semi-circles. A surface trough is represented by an orange dashed line. A squall or shear line is represented by a red line. Two dots and a dash are alternated to form the line. A dry line is represented by an orange line with semi-circles in outline form. A tropical wave is represented by a straight orange line. An "L" is used to indicate an area of low atmospheric pressure and an "H" is used to indicate an area of high atmospheric pressure.

Weather phenomena

Shearline: This evolves from a stationary front that has gotten smaller. Wind direction shifts over a short distance.

Dry line or dew point line: This separates two warm air masses of differing moisture content. At lower altitudes, the moist air mass wedges under the drier air. At higher altitudes, the dry air wedges under the moist air. This is a frequent occurrence in the Midwest and Canada, where the dry air of the Southwest and the moister air of the Gulf of Mexico meet. This can lead to extreme weather events, including tornadoes and thunderstorms.

Squall line: Severe thunderstorms can form at the front of or ahead of a cold front. In some cases, severe thunderstorms can also outrun cold fronts. A squall line can produce extreme weather in the form of heavy rain, hail, lightning, strong winds, tornadoes, and waterspouts.

Tropical waves or easterly waves: These are atmospheric troughs or areas of low air pressure that travel westward in the tropics, causing clouds and thunderstorms.

Astronomy

Astronomy is the scientific study of celestial objects and their positions, movements, and structures. Celestial does not refer to the Earth in particular, but does include its motions as it moves through space. Other objects include the Sun, the Moon, planets, satellites, asteroids, meteors, comets, stars, galaxies, the universe, and other space phenomena. The term astronomy has its roots in the Greek words "astro" and "nomos," which means "laws of the stars."

Weather forecasting

Short and long-term weather forecasting is important because the day-to-day weather greatly affects humans and human activity. Severe weather and natural events can cause devastating harm to humans, property, and sources of livelihood, such as crops. The persistence method of forecasting can be used to create both short and long-term forecasts in areas that change very little or change slowly. It assumes that the weather tomorrow will be similar to the weather today. Barometric pressure is measured because a change in air pressure can indicate the arrival of a cold front that could lead to precipitation. Long-term forecasts based on climate data are useful to help people prepare for seasonal changes and severe events such as hurricanes.

Universe structure

What can be seen of the universe is believed to be at least 93 billion light years across. To put this into perspective, the Milky Way galaxy is about 100,000 light years across. Our view of matter in the universe is that it forms into clumps. Matter is organized into stars, galaxies, clusters of galaxies, superclusters, and the Great Wall of galaxies. Galaxies consist of stars, some with planetary systems. Some estimates state that the universe is about 13 billion years old. It is not considered dense, and is believed to consist of 73 percent dark energy, 23 percent cold dark matter, and 4 percent regular matter. Cosmology is the study of the universe. Interstellar medium (ISM) is the gas and dust in the interstellar space between a galaxy's stars.

Universe origin

The universe can be said to consist of everything and nothing. The universe is the source of everything we know about space, matter, energy, and time. There are likely still phenomena that have yet to be discovered. The universe can also be thought of as nothing, since a vast portion of the known universe is empty space. It is believed that the universe is expanding. The Big Bang theory, which is widely accepted among astronomers, was developed to explain the origin of the universe. There are other theories regarding the origin of the universe, such as the Steady-State theory and the Creationist theory. The Big Bang theory states that all the matter in the universe was once in one place. This matter underwent a huge explosion that spread the matter into space. Galaxies formed from this material and the universe is still expanding.

Stars

Black hole: A black hole is a space where the gravitational field is so powerful that everything, including light, is pulled into it. Once objects enter the surface, the event horizon, they cannot escape.

Quasar: Quasar stands for quasi-stellar radio source, which is an energetic galaxy with an active galactic nucleus. Quasars were first identified by their emissions of large amounts of electromagnetic energy, such as radio waves and visible light. These emissions differed from those associated with other galaxies.

Blazar: A blazar is a very violent phenomenon in galaxies with supermassive black holes. Dark matter: Although its existence has not yet been proven, dark matter may account for a large proportion of the universe's mass. It is undetectable because it does not emit any radiation, but is believed to exist because of gravitational forces exerted on visible objects.

Galaxies

Galaxies consist of stars, stellar remnants, and dark matter. Dwarf galaxies contain as few as 10 million stars, while giant galaxies contain as many as 1 trillion stars. Galaxies are gravitationally bound, meaning the stars, star systems, other gases, and dust orbits the galaxy's center. The Earth exists in the Milky Way galaxy and the nearest galaxy to ours is the Andromeda galaxy. Galaxies can be classified by their visual shape into elliptical, spiral, irregular, and starburst galaxies. It is estimated that there are more than 100 billion galaxies in the universe ranging from 1,000 to 100,000 parsecs in diameter. Galaxies can be megaparsecs apart. Intergalactic space consists of a gas with an average density of less than one atom per cubic meter. Galaxies are organized into clusters which form superclusters. Dark matter may account for up to 90% of the mass of galaxies. Dark matter is still not well understood.

Time measurements

A sidereal day is four minutes shorter than a solar day. A solar day is the time it takes the Earth to complete one revolution and face the Sun again. From noon to noon is 24 hours. A sidereal day is measured against a distant "fixed" star. As the Earth completes one rotation, it has also completed part of its revolution around the Sun, so it completes a sidereal rotation in reference to the fixed star before it completes a solar rotation. The Sun travels along the ecliptic in 365.25 days. This can be tracked day after day before dawn. After one year, the stars appear back in their original positions. As a result, different constellations are viewable at different times of the year. Sidereal years are slightly longer than tropical years. The difference is caused by the precession of the equinoxes. A calendar based on the sidereal year will be out of sync with the seasons at a rate of about one day every 71 years.

Large units of distance

An astronomical unit, also known as AU, is a widely used measurement in astronomy. One AU is equal to the distance from the Earth to the Sun, which is 150 million km, or 93 million miles. These distances can also be expressed as 149.60×10^9 m or 92.956×10^6 mi. A light year (ly) is the distance that light travels in a vacuum in one year. A light year is equal to about 10 trillion km, or 64,341 AU, and is used to measure large astronomical units. Also used for measuring large distances is the parsec (pc), which is the preferred unit since it is better suited for recording observational data. A parsec is the parallax of one arcsecond, and is about 31 trillion km (about 19 trillion miles), or about 3.26 light years. It is used to calculate distances by triangulation. The AU distance from the Earth to the Sun is used to form the side of a right triangle.

Star life cycle

There are different life cycle possibilities for stars after they initially form and enter into the main sequence stage. Small, relatively cold red dwarfs with relatively low masses burn hydrogen slowly, and will remain in the main sequence for hundreds of billions of years. Massive, hot supergiants will leave the main sequence after just a few million years. The Sun is a mid-sized star that may be in the main sequence for 10 billion years. After the main sequence, the star expands to become a red giant. Depending upon the initial mass of the star, it can become a black dwarf (from a medium-sized star), and then a small, cooling white dwarf. Massive stars become red supergiants (and sometimes blue supergiants), explode in a supernova, and then become neutron stars. The largest stars can become black holes.

Star birth

A nebula is a cloud of dust and gas that is composed primarily of hydrogen (97%) and helium (3%). Gravity causes parts of the nebula to clump together. This accretion continues adding atoms to the center of an unstable protostar. Equilibrium between gravity pulling atoms and gas pressure pushing heat and light away from the center is achieved. A star dies when it is no longer able to maintain equilibrium. A protostar may never become a star if it does not reach a critical core temperature. It may become a brown dwarf or a gas giant instead. If nuclear fusion of hydrogen into helium begins, a star is born. The "main sequence" of a star's life involves nuclear fusion reactions. During this time, the star contracts over billions of years to compensate for the heat and light energy lost. In the star's core, temperature, density, and pressure increase as the star contracts and the cycle continues.

Hertzsprung-Russell diagram

A Hertzsprung-Russell diagram (H-R diagram or HRD) is a plot or scattergraph depicting stars' temperatures and comparing them with stars' luminosities or magnitudes. This can help determine the age and evolutionary state of a star. A Hertzsprung-Russell diagram is also known as a color-magnitude diagram (CMD). It helps represent the life cycles of stars. In these plots, temperatures are plotted from highest to lowest, which aids in the comparison of H-R diagrams and observations. Hertzsprung-Russell diagrams can have many variations. Most of the stars in these diagrams lie along the line called main sequence, which contains stars that are fusing hydrogen. Other groupings include white dwarfs, subgiants, giants, and supergiants.

Spectral classification

Stars use the Morgan-Keenan classification system, which is based on spectral traits that indicate the ionization of the chromosphere. The following letter designations are used to indicate temperature, from hottest to coolest: O, B, A, F, G, K, and M. The phrase "Oh, be a fine girl/guy, kiss me" can be used as a memory aid. Different types of stars also have different corresponding colors. O stars are blue; A stars are white; G stars are yellow; and M stars are red. The numbers 0 to 9 are used to indicate tenths between two star classes. Zero indicates 0/10 and 9 indicates 9/10. Luminosity output is an indicator of size, and is expressed with the Roman numerals I, II, III, IV, and V. Supergiants are included in class I, giants are included in class III, and main sequence stars are included in class V. Using the Sun as an example, the spectral type G2V could be expressed as "a yellow two-tenths towards an orange main sequence star."

Sun

The Sun is at the center of the solar system. It is composed of 70% hydrogen (H) and 28% helium (He). The remaining 2% is made up of metals. The Sun is one of 100 billion stars in the Milky Way galaxy. Its diameter is 1,390,000 km, its mass is 1.989×10^{30} kg, its surface temperature is 5,800 K, and its core temperature is 15,600,000 K. The Sun represents more than 99.8% of the total mass of the solar system. At the core, the temperature is 15.6 million K, the pressure is 250 billion atmospheres, and the density is more than 150 times that of water. The surface is called the photosphere. The chromosphere lies above this, and the corona, which extends millions of kilometers into space, is next. Sunspots are relatively cool regions on the surface with a temperature of 3,800 K. Temperatures in the corona are over 1,000,000 K. Its magnetosphere, or heliosphere, extends far beyond Pluto.

Solar system formation

A planetary system consists of the various non-stellar objects orbiting a star, such as planets, dwarf planets, moons, asteroids, meteoroids, comets, and cosmic dust. The Sun, together with its planetary system, which includes Earth, is known as the solar system. The theory of how the solar system was created is that it started with the collapse of a cloud of interstellar gas and dust, which formed the solar nebula. This collapse is believed to have occurred because the cloud was disturbed. As it collapsed, it heated up and compressed at the center, forming a flatter protoplanetary disk with a protostar at the center. Planets formed as a result of accretion from the disk. Gas cooled and condensed into tiny particles of rock, metal, and ice. These particles collided and formed into larger particles, and then into object the size of small asteroids. Eventually, some became large enough to have significant gravity.

Solar system components

The solar system is a planetary system of objects that exist in an ecliptic plane. Objects orbit around and are bound by gravity to a star called the Sun. Objects that orbit around the Sun include: planets, dwarf planets, moons, asteroids, meteoroids, cosmic dust, and comets. The definition of planets has changed. At one time, there were nine planets in the solar system. There are now eight. Planetary objects in the solar system include four inner, terrestrial planets: Mercury, Venus, Earth, and Mars. They are relatively small, dense, rocky, lack rings, and have few or no moons. The four outer, or Jovian, planets are Jupiter, Saturn, Uranus, and Neptune, which are large and have low densities, rings, and moons. They are also known as gas giants. Between the inner and outer planets is the asteroid belt. Beyond Neptune is the Kuiper belt. Within these belts are five dwarf planets: Ceres, Pluto, Haumea, Makemake, and Eris.

Sun's energy

The Sun's energy is produced by nuclear fusion reactions. Each second, about 700,000,000 tons of hydrogen are converted (or fused) to about 695,000,000 tons of helium and 5,000,000 tons of energy in the form of gamma rays. In nuclear fusion, four hydrogen nuclei are fused into one helium nucleus, resulting in the release of energy. In the Sun, the energy proceeds towards the surface and is absorbed and re-emitted at lower and lower temperatures. Energy is mostly in the form of visible light when it reaches the surface. It is estimated that the Sun has used up about half of the hydrogen at its core since its birth. It is expected to radiate in this fashion for another 5 billion years. Eventually, it will deplete its hydrogen fuel, grow brighter, expand to about 260 times its diameter, and become a red giant. The outer layers will ablate and become a dense white dwarf the size of the Earth.

Inner terrestrial planets

Mercury: Mercury is the closest to the Sun and is also the smallest planet. It orbits the Sun every 88 days, has no satellites or atmosphere, has a Moon-like surface with craters, appears bright, and is dense and rocky with a large iron core.

Venus: Venus is the second planet from the Sun. It orbits the Sun every 225 days, is very bright, and is similar to Earth in size, gravity, and bulk composition. It has a dense atmosphere composed of carbon dioxide and some sulfur. It is covered with reflective clouds made of sulfuric acid and exhibits signs of volcanism. Lightning and thunder have been recorded on Venus's surface.

Earth: Earth is the third planet from the Sun. It orbits the Sun every 365 days. Approximately 71% of its surface is salt-water oceans. The Earth is rocky, has an atmosphere composed mainly of oxygen and nitrogen, has one moon, and supports millions of species. It contains the only known life in the solar system.

Mars: Mars it the fourth planet from the Sun. It appears reddish due to iron oxide on the surface, has a thin atmosphere, has a rotational period similar to Earth's, and has seasonal cycles. Surface features of Mars include volcanoes, valleys, deserts, and polar ice caps. Mars has impact craters and the tallest mountain, largest canyon, and perhaps the largest impact crater yet discovered.

Solar system size

The Earth is about 12,765 km (7,934 miles) in diameter. The Moon is about 3,476 km (2,160 mi) in diameter. The distance between the Earth and the Moon is about 384,401 km (238,910 mi). The diameter of the Sun is approximately 1,390,000 km (866,000 mi). The distance from the Earth to the Sun is 149,598,000 km, also known as 1 Astronomical Unit (AU). The star that is nearest to the solar system is Proxima Centauri. It is about 270,000 AU away. Some distant galaxies are so far away that their light takes several billion years to reach the Earth. In other words, people on Earth see them as they looked billions of years ago.

Oort Cloud, asteroid belt, and Kuiper Belt

The asteroid belt is between Mars and Jupiter. The many objects contained within are composed of rock and metal similar to those found on the terrestrial planets. The Kuiper Belt is beyond Neptune's orbit, but the influence of the gas giants may cause objects from the Kuiper Belt to cross Neptune's orbit. Objects in the Kuiper Belt are still being discovered. They are thought to be composed of the frozen forms of water, ammonia, and methane, and may be the source of short-period comets. It is estimated that there are 35,000 Kuiper Belt objects greater than 100 km in diameter and perhaps 100 million objects about 20 km in diameter. There is also a hypothetical Oort Cloud that may exist far beyond the Kuiper Belt and act as a source for long-period comets.

Outer planets

Jupiter: Jupiter is the fifth planet from the Sun and the largest planet in the solar system. It consists mainly of hydrogen, and 25% of its mass is made up of helium. It has a fast rotation and has clouds in the tropopause composed of ammonia crystals that are arranged into bands sub-divided into lighter-hued zones and darker belts causing storms and turbulence. Jupiter has wind speeds of 100 m/s, a planetary ring, 63 moons, and a Great Red Spot, which is an anticyclonic storm.

Saturn: Saturn is the sixth planet from the Sun and the second largest planet in the solar system. It is composed of hydrogen, some helium, and trace elements. Saturn has a small core of rock and ice, a thick layer of metallic hydrogen, a gaseous outer layer, wind speeds of up to 1,800 km/h, a system of rings, and 61 moons.

Uranus: Uranus is the seventh planet from the Sun. Its atmosphere is composed mainly of hydrogen and helium, and also contains water, ammonia, methane, and traces of hydrocarbons. With a minimum temperature of 49 K, Uranus has the coldest atmosphere. Uranus has a ring system, a magnetosphere, and 13 moons.

Neptune: Neptune is the eighth planet from the Sun and is the planet with the third largest mass. It has 12 moons, an atmosphere similar to Uranus, a Great Dark Spot, and the strongest sustained winds of any planet (wind speeds can be as high as 2,100 km/h). Neptune is cold (about 55 K) and has a fragmented ring system.

Meteors, meteoroids, and meteorites

A meteoroid is the name for a rock from space before it enters the Earth's atmosphere. Most meteoroids burn up in the atmosphere before reaching altitudes of 80 km. A meteor is the streak of light from a meteoroid in the Earth's atmosphere, and is also known as a shooting star. Meteor showers are associated with comets, happen when the Earth passes through the debris of a comet, and are associated with a higher than normal number of meteors. Meteorites are rocks that reach the Earth's surface from space. Fireballs are very bright meteors with trails that can last as long as 30 minutes. A bolide is a fireball that burns up

Copyright © Mometrix Media. You have been licensed one copy of this document for personal use only. Any other reproduction or redistribution is strictly prohibited. All rights reserved.

when it enters Earth's atmosphere. There are many types of meteorites, and they are known to be composed of various materials. Iron meteorites consist of iron and nickel with a criss-cross, or Widmanstatten, internal metallic crystalline structure. Stony iron meteorites are composed of iron, nickel, and silicate materials. Stony meteorites consist mainly of silicate and also contain iron and nickel.

Comets

A comet consists of frozen gases and rocky and metallic materials. Comets are usually small and typically have long tails. A comet's tail is made of ionized gases. It points away from the Sun and follows the comet as it approaches the Sun. The tail precedes the head as the comet moves away from the Sun. It is believed that as many as 100 billion comets exist. About 12 new ones are discovered each year. Their orbits are elliptical, not round. Some scientists theorize that short-period comets originate from the Kuiper Belt and long-period comets originate from the Oort Cloud, which is thought to be 100,000 AU away. Comets orbit the Sun in time periods varying from a few years to hundreds of thousands of years. A well-known comet, Halley's Comet, has an orbit of 76 years. It is 80 percent water, and consists of frozen water, carbon dioxide (dry ice), ammonia, and methane.

Earth-Moon-Sun system

The Earth-Moon-Sun system is responsible for eclipses. From Earth, the Sun and the Moon appear to be about the same size. An eclipse of the Sun occurs during a new Moon, when the side of the Moon facing the Earth is not illuminated. The Moon passes in front of the Sun and blocks its view from Earth. Eclipses do not occur every month because the orbit of the Moon is at about a 5° angle to the plane of Earth's orbit. An eclipse of the Moon happens during the full Moon phase. The Moon passes through the shadow of the Earth and blocks sunlight from reaching it, which temporarily causes darkness. During a lunar eclipse, there are two parts to the shadow. The umbra is the dark, inner region. The sun is completely blocked in this area. The penumbra is a partially lighted area around the umbra. Earth's shadow is four times longer than the Moon's shadow.

Natural satellites

There are about 335 moons, or satellites, that orbit the planets and objects in the solar system. Many of these satellites have been recently discovered, a few are theoretical, some are asteroid moons (moons orbiting asteroids), some are moonlets (small moons), and some are moons of dwarf planets and objects that have not been definitively categorized, such as trans-Neptunian objects. Mercury and Venus do not have any moons. There are several moons larger than the dwarf planet Pluto and two larger than Mercury. Some consider the Earth and Moon a pair of double planets rather than a planet and a satellite. Some satellites may have started out as asteroids. They were eventually captured by a planet's gravity and became moons.

Remote sensing

Remote sensing refers to the gathering of data about an object or phenomenon without physical or intimate contact with the object being studied. The data can be viewed or recorded and stored in many forms (visually with a camera, audibly, or in the form of data).

Gathering weather data from a ship, satellite, or buoy might be thought of as remote sensing. The monitoring of a fetus through the use of ultrasound technology provides a remote image. Listening to the heartbeat of a fetus is another example of remote sensing. Methods for remote sensing can be grouped as radiometric, geodetic, or acoustic. Examples of radiometric remote sensing include radar, laser altimeters, light detection and ranging (LIDAR) used to determine the concentration of chemicals in the air, and radiometers used to detect various frequencies of radiation. Geodetic remote sensing involves measuring the small fluctuations in Earth's gravitational field. Examples of acoustic remote sensing include underwater sonar and seismographs.

Phases of the Moon

It takes about one month for the Moon to go through all its phases. Waxing refers to the two weeks during which the Moon goes from a new moon to a full moon. About two weeks is spent waning, going from a full moon to a new moon. The lit part of the Moon always faces the Sun. The phases of waxing are: new moon, during which the Moon is not illuminated and rises and sets with the Sun; crescent moon, during which a tiny sliver is lit; first quarter, during which half the Moon is lit and the phase of the Moon is due south on the meridian; gibbous, during which more than half of the Moon is lit and has a shape similar to a football; right side, during which the Moon is lit; and full moon, during which the Moon is fully illuminated, rises at sunset, and sets at sunrise. After a full moon, the Moon is waning. The phases of waning are: gibbous, during which the left side is lit and the Moon rises after sunset and sets after sunrise; third quarter, during which the Moon is half lit and rises at midnight and sets at noon; crescent, during which a tiny sliver is lit; and new moon, during which the Moon is not illuminated and rises and sets with the Sun.

Tropic of Cancer, Tropic of Capricorn; Antarctic and Arctic Circles

Tropic of Cancer: This is located at 23.5 degrees north. The Sun is directly overhead at noon on June 21st in the Tropic of Cancer, which marks the beginning of summer in the Northern Hemisphere.

Tropic of Capricorn: This is located at 23.5 degrees south. The Sun is directly overhead at noon on December 21st in the Tropic of Capricorn, which marks the beginning of winter in the Northern Hemisphere.

Arctic Circle: This is located at 66.5 degrees north, and marks the start of when the Sun is not visible above the horizon. This occurs on December 21st, the same day the Sun is directly over the Tropic of Capricorn.

Antarctic Circle: This is located at 66.5 degrees south, and marks the start of when the Sun is not visible above the horizon. This occurs on June 21st, which marks the beginning of winter in the Southern Hemisphere and is when the Sun is directly over the Tropic of Cancer.

Latitude, longitude, and equator

For the purposes of tracking time and location, the Earth is divided into sections with imaginary lines. Lines that run vertically around the globe through the poles are lines of longitude, sometimes called meridians. The Prime Meridian is the longitudinal reference point of 0. Longitude is measured in 15-degree increments toward the east or west. Degrees are further divided into 60 minutes, and each minute is divided into 60 seconds. Lines of latitude run horizontally around the Earth parallel to the equator, which is the 0 reference point and the widest point of the Earth. Latitude is the distance north or south from the equator, and is also measured in degrees, minutes, and seconds.

Geosynchronous and geostationary orbits

A geosynchronous orbit around the Earth has an orbital period matching the Earth's sidereal rotation period. Sidereal rotation is based on the position of a fixed star, not the Sun, so a sidereal day is slightly shorter than a 24-hour solar day. A satellite in a geosynchronous orbit appears in the same place in the sky at the same time each day. Technically, any object with an orbit time period equal to the Earth's rotational period is geosynchronous. A geostationary orbit is a geosynchronous orbit that is circular and at zero inclination, which means the object is located directly above the equator. Geostationary orbits are useful for communications satellites because they are fixed in the same spot relative to the Earth. A semisynchronous orbit has an orbital period of half a sidereal day.

Equinox, solstice, perihelion, and aphelion

Equinox: This occurs twice each year when the Sun crosses the plane of the Earth's celestial equator. During an equinox, Earth is not tilted away from or towards the Sun. The length of day and night are roughly equal. The two equinoxes are the March equinox and the September equinox.

Solstice: The summer solstice, the day with the most amount of sunlight, occurs on June 21st in the Northern Hemisphere and on December 21st in the Southern Hemisphere. The winter solstice, the day with the least amount of sunlight, occurs on December 21st in the Northern Hemisphere and on June 21st in the Southern Hemisphere.

Perihelion: This is the point in an object's orbit when it is closest to the Sun.
Aphelion: This is the point in an object's orbit when it is farthest from the Sun.

Piloted space missions

The Soviet space program successfully completed the first space flight by orbiting Yuri Gagarin in 1961 on Vostok 1. His orbit lasted 1 hour, 48 minutes. Later in 1961, the U.S. completed its first piloted space flight by launching Alan Shepard into space in the Mercury-Redstone 3. This space mission was suborbital. The first woman in space was Valentina Tereshkova, who orbited the Earth 48 times aboard Vostok 6 in 1963. The first space flight with more than one person and also the first that didn't involve space suits took place on the Voskhod in 1964. The first person on the Moon was American Neil Armstrong. In 1969, he traveled to the Moon on Apollo 11, which was the 11th manned space flight completed in the Apollo program, which was conducted from 1968 to 1972. In 2003, Yang Liwei became the first person from China to go into space. He traveled onboard the Shenzhou 5. The Space Shuttle Orbiter has included piloted space shuttles from 1981 until the present. The program was suspended after two space shuttle disasters: Challenger in 1986 and Columbia in 2003.

Notable satellites

The first satellite to orbit the Earth was the Soviet Union's Sputnik 1 in 1957. Its two radio transmitters emitted beeps that were received by radios around the world. Analysis of the radio signals was used to gather information about the electron density of the ionosphere. Soviet success escalated the American space program. In 1958, the U.S. put Explorer 1 into orbit. The Osumi was the first Japanese satellite, which was put into orbit in 1970. The Vanguard 1 is the satellite that has orbited the Earth the longest. It was put into orbit in 1958 and was still in orbit in June, 2009. The Mir Space Station orbited Earth for 11 years, and was assembled in space starting in 1986. It was almost continuously occupied until 1999. The International Space Station began being assembled in orbit in 1998. At 43,000 cubic feet, it is the largest manned object sent into space. It circles the Earth every 90 minutes.

Limitations of space exploration

There are many limitations of space exploration. The main limitation is knowledge. Space exploration is currently time-consuming, dangerous, and costly. Manned and unmanned missions, even within the solar system, take years of planning and years to complete. The associated financial costs are great. Interstellar travel and intergalactic is not yet realistically feasible. Technological advances are needed before these types of missions can be carried out. By some estimates, it would take more than 70 years to travel to Proxima Centauri (the nearest star) using the fastest rocket technology available. It would take much longer using less advanced technologies. Space travel is dangerous for many reasons. Rocket fuel is highly explosive. Non-Earth environments are uninhabitable for humans. Finally, astronauts are exposed to larger than usual amounts of radiation.

Unpiloted space missions

The first artificial object to reach another space object was Luna 2. It crashed on the Moon in 1959. The first automatic landing was by Luna 9. It landed on the Moon in 1966. Mariner 2's flyby of Venus in 1962 was the first successful interplanetary flyby. Venera 7 landing on and transmitting data from Venus was the first interplanetary surface landing, which took place in 1970. The first soft landing on Mars was in 1971. Unpiloted spacecraft have also made successful soft landings on the asteroids Eros and Itokawa, as well as Titan, a moon of Saturn. The first flyby of Jupiter was in 1973 by Pioneer 10. Pioneer 10 was also the first craft of its kind to leave the solar system. The first flyby of Mercury was in 1974 by Mariner. The first flyby of Saturn was in 1979 by Pioneer 11. The first flyby of Uranus was in 1986 by Voyager 2, which also flew by Neptune in 1989.

Granite and basalt

Both granite and basalt are plentiful igneous rocks, but granite is intrusive and basalt is extrusive. Intrusive rocks come from magma within the Earth's crust and cool slowly. Extrusive rocks are formed from lava on the Earth's surface and cool more quickly than intrusive rocks. Granite is an igneous rock with a medium to coarse texture that is formed from magma. It can be a variety of colors. It is intrusive, massive, hard, and coarse grained. It forms a major part of continental crust. It can be composed of potassium feldspar, plagioclase feldspar, and quartz, as well as various amounts of muscovite, biotite, and hornblende-type amphiboles. Basalt is extrusive and usually colored gray to black. It has a fine grain due to quicker cooling. Basalt is porphyritic, meaning it contains larger crystals in a fine matrix. Basalt is usually composed of amphibole and pyroxene, and sometimes of plagioclase, feldspathoids, and olivine.

Moon facts

The Moon is the fifth largest satellite in the solar system. It orbits the Earth about every 27.3 days. The changes of the Earth, Sun, and Moon in relation to each other cause the phases of the Moon, which repeat every 29.5 days. The Moon's gravitational pull (along with the Sun's) is responsible for the tides on Earth. Its diameter is about 3,474 km and its gravity is about 17% of Earth's. The lunar maria (plural of mare) on the Moon's surface is dark thin layers composed of dark basalt. They were formed by ancient volcanoes. There are many impact craters on the Moon. There were numerous impact craters on Earth at one time, but they have been transformed by erosion over time. Very few are still visible

Greenhouse effect

The greenhouse effect refers to a naturally occurring and necessary process. Greenhouse gasses, which are ozone, carbon dioxide, water vapor, and methane, trap infrared radiation that is reflected toward the atmosphere. This is actually beneficial in that warm air is trapped. Without the greenhouse effect, it is estimated that the temperature on Earth would be 30 degrees less on average. The problem occurs because human activity generates more greenhouse gases than necessary. The practices that increase the amount of greenhouse gases are the burning of natural gas and oil, farming practices that result in the release of methane and nitrous oxide, factory operations that produce gases, and deforestation practices that decrease the amount of oxygen available to offset greenhouse gases. Population growth also increases the volume of gases released. Excess greenhouse gases cause more infrared radiation to become trapped, which increases the temperature at the Earth's surface.

Ecosystems

Human impacts on ecosystems take many forms and have many causes. They include widespread disruptions and specific niche disturbances. Humans practice many forms of environmental manipulation that affect plants and animals in many biomes and ecosystems. Many human practices involve the consumption of natural resources for food and energy production, the changing of the environment to produce food and energy, and the intrusion on ecosystems to provide shelter. These general behaviors include a multitude of specific behaviors, including the use and overuse of pesticides, the encroachment upon habitat, over hunting and over fishing, the introduction of plant and animal species into non-native ecosystems, not recycling, and the introduction of hazardous wastes and chemical byproducts into the environment. These behaviors have led to a number of consequences, such as acid rain, ozone depletion, deforestation, urbanization, accelerated species loss, genetic abnormalities, endocrine disruption in populations, and harm to individual animals.

Human affairs and the environment

Since the industrial revolution, science and technology has had a profound impact on human affairs. There has been a rapid increase in the number of discoveries in many fields. Many major and minor discoveries have led to a great improvement in the quality of life of many people. This includes longer life spans because of better nutrition, access to medical care, and a decrease in workplace health hazards. Not all of these problems have been solved, and many still exist in one form or another. For example, even though there are means to recycle, not every business does so because of economic factors. These advances, while improving the lives of many humans, have also taken their toll on the environment. A possible solution may arise when the carrying capacity for humans on Earth is reached. The population will decline, and solutions will have to be found. Otherwise, an immediate halt or decrease in the human behaviors that are causing environmental damage will need to happen.

Global warming

Rising temperatures may lead to an increase in sea levels as polar ice melts, lower amounts of available fresh water as coastal areas flood, species extinction because of changes in habitat, increases in certain diseases, and a decreased standard of living for humans. Less fresh water and losses of habitat for humans and other species can also lead to decreased agricultural production and food supply shortages. Increased desertification leads to habitat loss for humans and certain other species. Decreases in animal populations from losses of habitat and increased hunting by other species can lead to extinction. Increases in severe weather, such as huge sustained snowstorms, may also occur at unlikely latitudes. Even though global warming results in weather that is drier and warmer overall, it still gets cold enough to snow. There may be more moisture in the atmosphere due to evaporation. Global warming may cause the permanent loss of glaciers and permafrost. There might also be increases in air pollution and acid rain.

Waste disposal methods

Landfills: Methane (CH_4) is a greenhouse gas emitted from landfills. Some is used to generate electricity and some gets into the atmosphere. CO_2 is also emitted, and landfill gas can contain nitrogen, oxygen, water vapor, sulfur, mercury, and radioactive contaminants such as tritium. Landfill leachate contains acids from car batteries, solvents, heavy metals, pesticides, motor oil, paint, household cleaning supplies, plastics, and many other potentially harmful substances. Some of these are dangerous when they get into the ecosystem. Lead, mercury, and others are toxic.

Incinerators: These contribute to air pollution in that they can release nitric and sulfuric oxides, which cause acid rain.

Sewage: When dumped in raw form into oceans, sewage can introduce fecal contaminants and pathogenic organisms, which can harm ocean life and cause disease in humans.

Price of consumerism

The economics of capitalism and even of communism with an increased tendency to a market economy are such that economic growth and quality of living are associated with a wasteful cycle of production. Goods are produced as cheaply as possible with little or no regard for the ecological effects. The ultimate goal is profitability. The production process is wasteful, and often introduces hazardous byproducts into the environment. Furthermore, after the product (which is not necessary for survival) has been consumed, it may be dumped into a landfill instead of recycled. When consumer products get dumped in landfills, they can leach contamination into groundwater. Landfills can also leach gases. These are or have been dumping grounds for illegal substances, business and government waste, construction industry waste, and medical waste. These items also get dumped at illegal dump sites in urban and remote areas.

Ethical and moral issues

Ethical and moral concerns related to genetic engineering arise in the scientific community and in smaller communities within society. Religious and moral beliefs can conflict with the economic interests of businesses, and with research methods used by the scientific community. For example, the United States government allows genes to be patented. A company has patented the gene for breast and ovarian cancer and will only make it available to researchers for a fee. This leads to a decrease in research, a decrease in medical solutions, and possibly an increase in the occurrence of breast and ovarian cancers. The possibility of lateral or incidental discoveries as a result of research is also limited. For example, a researcher working on a genetic solution to treat breast cancer might accidentally discover a cure for prostate cancer. This, however, would not occur if the researcher could not use the patented gene in the first place.

Types of energy production

Coal-fired power plants: These generate electricity, and are the largest source of greenhouse gases, including sulfur oxides responsible for acid rain, carbon dioxide, mercury, and nitrogen oxides.

Nuclear power plants: Spent nuclear waste (fuel rods) is incredibly toxic to humans, causing burns, sickness, and hair loss at low levels. Higher levels result in death. Storage facilities tend to be placed on Native American lands and in communities of color. Dirty bombs can be made with uranium. The process of uranium mining (as well as the processes used to mine other precious metals) pollutes, introducing chemicals into the surrounding area and drastically changing its natural balance and beauty. Tailings can contaminate ground, surface, and well water. Some nuclear waste can remain harmful for billions of years. Strontium-90 is one radioactive pollutant. Other radioactive isotopes are also released. A huge amount of water is necessary for cooling.

Gasoline: The burning of gas and other fossil fuels releases carbon dioxide (a greenhouse gas) into the atmosphere.

Practice Test

Practice Questions

DIRECTIONS: Read each question or incomplete sentence and select the best response.

1. A student is working on a science project and is going through each step of the scientific method. After the student conducts his or her first experiment and records the results of the experimental test, what should the student do next?
a. Communicate the results
b. Draw a conclusion
c. Repeat the experiment
d. Create a hypothesis

Use the following information to answer questions 2 and 3.

A student is conducting an experiment using a ball that is attached to the end of a string on a pendulum. The student pulls the ball back so that it is at an angle to its resting position. As the student releases the ball, it swings forward and backward. The student measures the time it takes the ball to make one complete period. A period is defined as the time it takes the ball to swing forward and back again to its starting position. This is repeated using different string lengths.

2. The student formed the following hypothesis:

Lengthening the string of the pendulum increases the time it takes the ball to make one complete period.

What correction would you have the student make to the hypothesis?
a. Turn it into an "if/then" statement.
b. Add the word "will" in the middle after the word "pendulum."
c. Switch the order of the sentence so that the phrase about the period comes first, and the phrase about the string's length is last.
d. No corrections are needed.

3. What would be an appropriate control variable for this experiment?
a. The period
b. The length of the string
c. The mass of the ball
d. The color of the ball

4. Once a hypothesis has been verified and accepted, it becomes a _____.
a. fact
b. law
c. conclusion
d. theory

5. A student has collected data on the width of tree trunks and average precipitation rates for different locations. The student wants to show the relationship between these two variables. What type of graph should the student use?
    a. A multi-line graph with the width measurements on the x-axis and precipitation rates on the y-axis.
    b. A scatter plot with the width measurements on the y-axis and precipitation rates on the x-axis.
    c. A bar graph with the width measurements on the y-axis and precipitation rates on the x-axis.
    d. A pie chart with the width of tree shown as a percentage at different precipitation rates.

6. A student is measuring morning and afternoon temperatures for a school project using a thermal infrared gun instrument. The instrument is calibrated incorrectly and produces a cold bias of 7/10 of a degree in all the temperature measurements. How should the student deal with this error?
    a. The student should recalibrate the instrument and redo the project.
    b. Since it is not a major error, the student can ignore it.
    c. This is a systematic error and the student should take it into consideration when analyzing the results by increasing the temperatures 7/10 of a degree.
    d. This is a random error so the student should only mention it as a potential problem in interpreting the results.

7. Make the following metric conversion:
5 decimeters = _____ decameters
    a. 0.5
    b. 0.05
    c. 50
    d. 500

8. Which of the data sets could be plotted on a pie chart?
    a. The total population of the top five largest U.S. cities.
    b. The incubation period of a penguin colony as it relates to hours of daylight.
    c. The distribution of weight among players of a football team.
    d. The percent of vegetation cover and precipitation rates in different national parks.

9. Which of the following processes uses electrical charges to separate substances?
    a. Spectrophotometry
    b. Chromatography
    c. Centrifugation
    d. Electrophoresis

10. When using a light microscope, how is the total magnification determined?
    a. By multiplying the ocular lens power times the objective being used.
    b. By looking at the objective you are using only.
    c. By looking at the ocular lens power only.
    d. By multiplying the objective you are using times two.

11. When performing a dissection in class, which of the following procedures is incorrect?
   a. Rinse the specimen before handling.
   b. Dispose of harmful chemicals according to district regulations.
   c. Decaying specimens are never permitted but unknown specimens are sometimes permitted.
   d. Students with open sores on their hands that cannot be covered should be excused from the dissection.

12. After a science laboratory exercise, some solutions remain unused and are left over. What should be done with these solutions?
   a. Dispose of the solutions according to local disposal procedures.
   b. Empty the solutions into the sink and rinse with warm water and soap.
   c. Ensure the solutions are secured in closed containers and throw away.
   d. Store the solutions in a secured, dry place for later use.

13. The volume of water in a bucket is 2.5 liters. When an object with an irregular shape and a mass of 40 grams is submerged in the water, the volume of the water is 4.5 liters. What is the density of the object?
   a. 1/10 g/L
   b. 2 g/L
   c. 20 g/L
   d. 80 g/L

14. Which of the following represents a chemical change?
   a. Sublimation of water
   b. A spoiling apple
   c. Dissolution of salt in water
   d. Pulverized rock

15. The amount of potential energy an object has depends on all of the following except its
   a. mass.
   b. height above ground.
   c. gravitational attraction.
   d. temperature.

16. Elements on the periodic table are arranged into groups and periods and ordered according to
   a. atomic number.
   b. number of protons.
   c. reactivity.
   d. All of the above

- 132 -

17. The specific heat capacity of ice is half as much as that of liquid water. What is the result of this?

    a. It takes half the amount of energy to increase the temperature of a 1 kg sample of ice by 1°C than a 1 kg sample of water.

    b. It takes twice the amount of energy to increase the temperature of a 1 kg sample of ice by 1°C than a 1 kg sample of water.

    c. It takes a quarter the amount of energy to increase the temperature of a 1 kg sample of ice by 1°C than a 1 kg sample of water.

    d. It takes the same amount of energy to increase the temperature of a 1 kg sample of ice and a 1 kg sample of water by 1°C.

18. What happens to the temperature of a substance as it is changing phase from a liquid to a solid?

    a. Its temperature increases due to the absorption of latent heat.

    b. Its temperature decreases due to the heat of vaporization.

    c. Its temperature decreases due to the latent heat of fusion.

    d. Its temperature remains the same due to the latent heat of fusion.

19. A long nail is heated at one end. After a few seconds, the other end of the nail becomes equally hot. What type of heat transfer does this represent?

    a. Radiation

    b. Conduction

    c. Convection

    d. Entropy

20. Which of the following statements about heat transfer is not true?

    a. As the energy of a system changes, its thermal energy must change or work must be done.

    b. Heat transfer from a warmer object to a cooler object can occur spontaneously.

    c. Heat transfer can never occur from a cooler object to a warmer object.

    d. If two objects reach the same temperature, energy is no longer available for work.

21. The measure of energy within a system is called _____.

    a. temperature

    b. heat

    c. entropy

    d. thermodynamics

22. Which of the following is true of an isotope?

    a. It has a different number of protons than its element.

    b. It has a different number of electrons than its element.

    c. It has a different charge as compared to its element.

    d. It has a different number of neutrons than its element.

23. If an atom's outer shell is filled, what must be true?

    a. It reacts with other atoms through chemical reactions.

    b. It exchanges electrons to form bonds with other atoms.

    c. It has 32 electrons in its outer shell.

    d. It is a stable atom.

24. Which type of nuclear process features atomic nuclei splitting apart to form smaller nuclei?
    a. Fission
    b. Fusion
    c. Decay
    d. Ionization

25. Electrons with greater amounts of energy are found _____ the nucleus than electrons with less energy.
    a. closer to
    b. farther from
    c. more often inside
    d. more randomly around

26. The process whereby a radioactive element releases energy slowly over a long period of time to lower its energy and become more stable is best described as _____.
    a. combustion
    b. fission
    c. fusion
    d. decay

27. Which of the following is a type of simple machine?
    a. A bicycle
    b. A pair of scissors
    c. A screw
    d. A shovel

28. In which of the following scenarios is work not applied to the object?
    a. Mario moves a book from the floor to the top shelf.
    b. A book drops off the shelf and falls to the floor.
    c. Mario pushes a box of books across the room.
    d. Mario balances a book on his head and walks across the room.

29. A ball is resting on the front end of a boat. The boat is moving straight forwards toward a dock. According to Newton's first law of motion, when the front of the boat hits the dock, how will the ball's motion change?
    a. The ball will remain at rest.
    b. The ball will move backwards.
    c. The ball will move forwards.
    d. The ball will move sideways.

30. What two things are required for circular motion to occur?
    a. Acceleration and centripetal force
    b. Acceleration and gravitational force
    c. Constant speed and centripetal force
    d. Constant speed and gravitational force

31. According to Bernoulli's Principle, where will a gas flowing through a pipe exert the least amount of pressure?
    a. Where the pipe is widest
    b. Where the pipe is narrowest
    c. Where its velocity is lowest
    d. Where its kinetic energy is lowest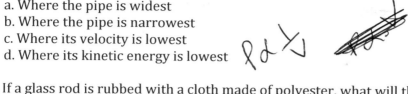

32. If a glass rod is rubbed with a cloth made of polyester, what will the resulting charge be on each material?
    a. The charge on the glass rod is positive and the charge on the cloth is negative.
    b. The charge on the glass rod is negative and the charge on the cloth is positive.
    c. The charge on the glass rod is neutral and the charge on the cloth is positive.
    d. The charge on the glass rod and the cloth both become neutral.

33. According to Ohm's Law, how are voltage and current related in an electrical circuit?
    a. Voltage and current are inversely proportional to one another.
    b. Voltage and current are directly proportional to one another.
    c. Voltage acts to oppose the current along an electrical circuit.
    d. Voltage acts to decrease the current along an electrical circuit.

34. A material becomes magnetic when the individual electrons of an atom _____, allowing their magnetic fields to add together.
    a. spin in pairs in opposite directions
    b. spin in pairs in the same direction
    c. spin unpaired
    d. stop spinning

35. In a parallel circuit, there are three paths: A, B and C. Path A has a resistance of 10 ohms, path B a resistance of 5 ohms and part C a resistance of 2 ohms. How do the voltage and current change for each path?
    a. Voltage and current are kept the same in each path.
    b. Voltage is greatest in path A and current is greatest in path C.
    c. Voltage is lowest in path C and current is greatest in path C.
    d. Voltage is the same for each path and current is greatest in path C.

36. A rock concert is taking place outdoors. In which of the following conditions will the sound travel the farthest?
    a. High temperature and low humidity
    b. High temperature and humidity
    c. Low temperature and humidity
    d. Low temperature and high humidity

37. Which of the following would cause a high angle of reflection of a light wave?
    a. A high angle of incidence of the wave
    b. A low angle of incidence of the wave
    c. A wave that travels through a medium of higher density
    d. A wave with a very short wavelength

38. What term is used to describe two waves that are out of phase as they come together to produce a new wave?
    a. Incomplete interference
    b. Distorted interference
    c. Constructive interference
    d. Destructive interference

39. What would happen to light waves if they hit a convex lens?
    a. They will be refracted and converge.
    b. They will be refracted and diverge.
    c. They will be reflected and converge.
    d. They will be reflected and diverge.

40. If an astronomer observing the stars detects a blue shift, what could he conclude?
    a. The star is moving farther away from him.
    b. The star is moving closer or toward him.
    c. The star is cooling down and becoming smaller.
    d. The star is heating up and becoming larger.

41. Salts are made from a combination of what two types of elements?
    a. A metal and a nonmetal
    b. A nonmetal and an alkaline earth metal
    c. A cation from a base and an anion from an acid
    d. A metal and a halogen

42. What group of the periodic table makes up the alkaline earth metals?
    a. Group 1
    b. Group 2
    c. Group 13
    d. Group 17

43. Which of the following elements is not a noble gas?
    a. Neon.
    b. Argon
    c. Astatine
    d. Krypton

44. If an atom has a neutral charge, what must be true of the atom?
    a. The nucleus contains only neutrons and no protons.
    b. The atomic mass is equal to the number of neutrons.
    c. The atomic number is equal to the number of neutrons.
    d. The atomic number is equal to the number of electrons.

45. Most organic molecules have all of the following properties except
    a. high solubility in water.
    b. a tendency to melt.
    c. covalently bonded.
    d. high flammability.

46. In a single replacement reaction, what products could result from these reactants in the following chemical equation?

2Al + Fe2 O3 ---->

    a. AlO3 + Fe2
    b. 2Fe2 + 2AlO3
    c. Al2O3 + 2Fe
    d. 2AlFeO3

47. What type of compound is formed by the combination of two or more non-metallic elements with one another?
    a. Organic
    b. Ionic
    c. Covalent
    d. Chemical

48. Which of the following descriptions of Lewis dot structures is not correct?
    a. They show the bonding between atoms of a molecule.
    b. They show all the electrons of each atom of a molecule.
    c. The total number of electrons is equal to the sum of the number of valence electrons on each atom.
    d. They show any lone pairs of electrons that may exist in a molecule that are not bonded to another atom.

49. Which of the following does not describe a carboxyl group correctly?
    a. A carbon atom attached to an oxygen atom by a double bond and to a hydroxyl group by a single bond.
    b. A carbonyl group bonded to a hydroxyl group.
    c. A set of four atoms bonded together and abbreviated as CO2H.
    d. A carbon atom attached to a hydrogen atom by a double bond and to an oxygen atom by a double bond.

50. A gas is held in a closed container and held at constant temperature. What is the effect of increasing the volume of the container by 3 times?
    a. The pressure is tripled.
    b. The pressure increases by one third.
    c. The pressure decreases by one third.
    d. The pressure remains constant.

Use the following information to answer questions 51 and 52.

> Four identical liquid samples inside of identical sealed containers initially at room temperature were placed in four isolated environments, each with its own maintained temperature. After each liquid sample is allowed sufficient time to assume the temperature of its environment, the samples changed as follows: In sample A, the liquid vaporized and is now a gas. In sample B, the liquid is boiling. In sample C, the liquid is now a solid. In sample D, the liquid remains a liquid.

51. Which sample's container has the greatest pressure?
    a. Sample A
    b. Sample B
    c. Sample C
    d. All containers have equal pressure

52. If the temperature in each environment were increased by 10 degrees Celsius and each sample were allowed time to assume the new temperature, which of the following events is MOST likely to occur?
    a. Sample A would become a liquid
    b. Sample B would become a gas
    c. Sample D would begin to boil
    d. None of these are likely to occur

53. Which statement best describes the molecular arrangement of a liquid crystal?
    a. The molecular arrangement is random in some directions and regular in others.
    b. The molecular arrangement is a regularly, repeating pattern in all directions.
    c. The molecular arrangement is random in all directions.
    d. The molecular arrangement is reduced to one layer with a random pattern.

54. Which of the following is not true of a chemical reaction?
    a. Matter is never gained or lost.
    b. Heat may be absorbed or released.
    c. The rate of the reaction increases with temperature.
    d. There may be a different number of atoms for the products and the reactants.

55. Which of the following would increase the reaction rate of a chemical reaction?
    a. Low kinetic energy
    b. Low temperature
    c. High concentration
    d. High activation energy

56. Copper is added to silver nitrate, which reacts to form copper nitrate and silver. What type of reaction has occurred?
    a. Compound
    b. Decomposition
    c. Single Replacement
    d. Double Replacement

57. Which statement accurately describes an electrolysis reaction?
    a. A reaction that changes the charge of the atoms.
    b. A reaction that uses electricity to drive it.
    c. A reaction that creates electricity as a by-product.
    d. A reaction that lowers the pH of the substances.

58. Examine the following reaction. What are the possible products?

ABC ----> ____ + ____

a. 2AB + C
b. AB + CD
c. A + BC
d. B + C

59. Which action will help dissolve a gas in a liquid if the gas and liquid are placed in a sealed container?

a. Heat the liquid.
b. Cool the liquid.
c. Shake the container.
d. Decrease the pressure on the lid.

60. What type of substance is least likely to be soluble in water?

a. Ionic
b. Polar
c. Hydrophilic
d. Non-polar

61. How does adding a solute to a liquid solvent affect the vapor pressure of the liquid?

a. The vapor pressure increases by an amount proportional to the amount of solute.
b. The vapor pressure increases by an amount proportional to the amount of solvent.
c. The vapor pressure decreases by an amount proportional to the amount of solute.
d. The amount of solute present in a liquid solvent does not have any effect on vapor pressure.

62. Which of the following liquids will have the highest electrical conductivity?

a. Pure water
b. Water plus salt
c. Water plus vinegar
d. Water plus carbonated soda

63. The main function of _____ is it to reduce the number of chromosomes to half the number of parent cells?

a. mitosis
b. telophase
c. meiosis I
d. meiosis II

64. This organelle contains digestive enzymes that break down food and unneeded substances. They are also thought to be linked to the aging process. What part of a cell does this describe?

a. Lysosomes
b. Chromatin
c. Plastids
d. Golgi Apparatus

65. Which of the following describes the difference between an anabolism reaction and a catabolism reaction?
    a. Anabolism undergoes ionic reactions, while catabolism undergoes covalent reactions.
    b. Anabolism undergoes condensation reactions, while catabolism undergoes hydrolysis.
    c. Anabolism reactions use water, while catabolism reactions do not.
    d. Anabolism reactions release glucose, while catabolism reactions release water.

66. Plant A undergoes C4 photosynthesis. What type of environment would the plant most likely live in?
    a. Plant A lives in a very moist environment.
    b. Plant A lives in a very arid environment.
    c. Plant A lives in a marine environment.
    d. Plant A lives in a dark environment that lacks solar energy.

67. Where is the type of RNA that carries and positions amino acids for further assembly located in the cell?
    (Sill 3.2)
    a. Cytoplasm
    b. Nucleus
    c. Ribosome
    d. Mitochondria

68. The following is the anticodon sequence formed during translation. What is the original codon sequence?
    A C G U A C G C U

    a. T G C A T G C G A
    b. U G C T U G C G T
    c. U G C A U G C G A
    d. U C G A U C G C A

69. A diybrid cross is made between the dominant genes for Brown eyes (B) and Blonde hair (S), and the recessive genes for blue eyes (b) and red hair (s). What fraction of offspring would have the genotype BbSs in the F2 generation?
    a. 1/16
    b. 3/16
    c. 4/16
    d. 9/16

70. What type of mutation is represented by the following sequence?
    1 5 4 3 2 6

    a. Breakage
    b. Deletion
    c. Insertion
    d. Inversion

71. Many people have their wisdom teeth removed because they no longer serve a function in humans and may cause problems if left in. What are wisdom teeth an example of?
    a. Analogous structure
    b. Homologous structure
    c. Vestigial structure
    d. Divergent structure

72. Which statement best explains the Biological Species Concept (BSC)?
    a. It states that the status of species is based on the ability to pass on the most successful traits to their offspring.
    b. It states that the status of species is based on the reproductive isolation of populations.
    c. It states that the status of species is based on the ability of populations to mix and produce fertile hybrids.
    d. It states that the status of a species is due to the theory of natural selection.

73. What is the result of allopatric speciation?
    a. New species due to geographic isolation.
    b. New species due to geographic overlap.
    c. Hybrid species due to geographic overlap.
    d. Loss of diversity of a species due to geographic divergence.

74. How did Jean Baptiste Lamarck's theory of evolution compare to Darwin's theory of natural selection?
    a. He expanded Darwin's theory of natural selection by stating that some genes allow for better survival than others.
    b. He proposed an alternate theory by stating that favorable traits developed due to environmental conditions and the desire and needs of the organisms.
    c. He provided evidence to Darwin's belief that the desires and needs of organisms affected evolution of populations.
    d. He opposed Darwin's view that evolution was predetermined and believed that the selection of traits was more random.

75. Which of the following would not be used as evidence for evolution?
    a. Fossil record
    b. DNA sequences
    c. Anatomical structures
    d. Reproductive habits

76. In which taxonomic group are organisms most alike?
    a. Phylum
    b. Family
    c. Class
    d. Order

TSMTAEM

77. Which division of plants produces seeds for reproduction?
    a. Anthophyta
    b. Lycophyta
    c. Sphenophyta
    d. Pterophyta

78. What do all animals belonging to the Echinodermata phylum have in common?
    a. They use multiple appendages for locomotion.
    b. They use tube feet for locomotion and feeding.
    c. They have an exoskeleton made of chitin.
    d. They must shed their outer layer of skin to grow.

79. Where are the reproductive organs of a plant?
    a. Style
    b. Stigma
    c. Flowers
    d. Sepals

80. Plants begin to break down the products of photosynthesis through respiration. What is the result of respiration?
    a. Water
    b. Oxygen and glucose
    c. Carbon dioxide and sugar
    d. Carbon dioxide and water

81. Which of the following is not an advantage angiosperms show over other types of plants?
    a. Larger leaves
    b. Double fertilization
    c. Dormant seeds
    d. Lower seed dispersal

82. How are animals of the Mollusca phylum able to respire?
    a. Through gills
    b. Through a trachea
    c. Through lungs
    d. Through muscle contraction

83. What part of a plant system responds to stimuli by releasing water via transpiration, except during adverse conditions like a drought when it closes up to prevent the plant from dehydration?
    a. Pith
    b. Stomata
    c. Guard cells
    d. Sepals

84. Which of the following animal structures is not paired to its correct function?
    a. Muscle System – controls movement through three types of muscle tissue
    b. Nervous System – controls sensory responses by carrying impulses away from and toward the cell body
    c. Digestive System – breaks down food for absorption into the blood stream where it is delivered to cells for respiration
    d. Circulatory System – exchanges gases with the environment by delivering oxygen to the bloodstream and releasing carbon dioxide

85. If a population reaches a maximum size and ceases to grow due to a limited availability of resources, the population is
    a. unstable.
    b. shrinking exponentially.
    c. at carrying capacity.
    d. moving towards extinction.

86. The following represents a simple food chain. What trophic level contains the greatest amount of energy?
                    Tree ? Caterpillar ? Frog ? Snake ? Hawk ? Worm
    a. Tree
    b. Caterpillar
    c. Hawk
    d. Worm

87. Which of the following sources of fresh water is unavailable for human use?
    a. Rivers
    b. Estuaries
    c. Aquifers
    d. Glaciers

88. Which of the following animals would most likely be found in the taiga?
    a. Antelope
    b. Snake
    c. Moose
    d. Polar Bear

89. Which of the following words is not connected to the process of mountain building?
    a. Folding
    b. Faulting
    c. Transform
    d. Convergent

90. The formation of sedimentary rock includes all of the following processes except
    a. layering.
    b. cementation.
    c. compaction.
    d. heat.

91. Which of the following is an example of chemical weathering?
    a. Rain freezing on the roadway.
    b. Ivy growing on the side of a wooden house.
    c. Vinegar fizzing when poured on a rock.
    d. A river carrying sediment downstream.

92. Which of the following situations would result in the generation of new crust?
    a. Two crustal plates converge.
    b. Two crustal plates move apart.
    c. Two crustal plates slide past one another.
    d. A crustal plate is pushed down into the mantle.

93. Which of the following terms describes an intrusion of magma injected between two layers of sedimentary rock, forcing the overlying strata upward to create a dome-like form?
    a. Sill
    b. Dike
    c. Laccolith
    d. Caldera

94. Which statement best describes the process of absolute dating?
    a. It compares the amount of radioactive material in a rock to the amount that has decayed into another element.
    b. It measures the age of a rock by comparing it to fossils found in the same stratigraphic layer as the rock.
    c. It measures the amount of daughter elements that have broken down by half.
    d. It measures the mass loss of a rock by estimating the amount of material that has eroded due to catastrophic events.

95. Fossils are least likely to be found in
    a. sedimentary rock.
    b. metamorphic rock.
    c. igneous rock.
    d. Fossils are commonly found in all types of rock.

96. Which of the following is an example of a trace fossil?
    a. A mouse jaw
    b. A footprint
    c. A shark tooth
    d. A cast of a skull

97. A time interval in which particular plants and animals were dominant or present in great abundance is defined as a(n)
    a. era.
    b. eon.
    c. epoch.
    d. period.

98. What is the major difference between the two paradigms of Earth's geologic past: catastrophism and uniformitarianism?
   a. The first implies that the Earth was shaped by destructive processes, while the second implies it was shaped by constructive processes.
   b. The first implies that the Earth has changed shape drastically several times, while the second implies it has not changed much over time.
   c. The first implies that the same natural catastrophes occur on Earth today that occurred in the past, while the second implies that catastrophes did not occur in the past like they do today.
   d. The first implies that the Earth was shaped by a series of quick, violent events, while the second implies that it changed slowly and incrementally.

99. Which of the following types of ocean currents would be the densest?
   a. Warm and high salinity
   b. Warm and low salinity
   c. Cold and high salinity
   d. Cold and low salinity

100. Which of the following does not control the movement of ocean currents?
   a. Wind
   b. Landmasses
   c. Earth's rotation
   d. Phase of the Moon

101. Compared to fresh water, the freezing point of sea water is
   a. higher.
   b. lower.
   c. about the same.
   d. Sea water does not freeze.

102. Which of the following statements best describes the mixed layer of the ocean?
   a. It is the layer between the warm, surface layer and the cold, deeper layer below.
   b. It is the transition zone where it becomes increasingly cold with depth due to loss of sunlight.
   c. It is the surface layer where wave action is present due to interaction with winds at the surface.
   d. It is the layer where upwelling and downwelling currents form due to density differences between the warm surface layer and the cold deeper layer.

103. Which of the following describes the physical or non-biological part of the carbon cycle?
   a. Phytoplankton use carbon dioxide and other nutrients to produce carbohydrates and oxygen.
   b. Cold water dissolves atmospheric carbon dioxide, stores it, and releases it back out to the atmosphere as needed.
   c. Carbon dioxide is dissolved in sea water, and is broken up to free carbon for use by marine life.
   d. Warm, surface water dissolves carbon dioxide where it is converted to nitrogen and phosphorus for use by marine life.

104. What drives weather systems to move west to east in the mid-latitudes?
   a. The prevailing westerlies
   b. The prevailing easterlies
   c. The trade winds
   d. The doldrums

105. If land cools off rapidly at night and the ocean water stays relatively warm, what type of wind is created?
   a. Sea breeze
   b. Land breeze
   c. Monsoon
   d. Trade wind

106. If the current air temperature is 65°F and the current dew point is 62°F, what is most likely the current relative humidity?
   a. 3%
   b. 10%
   c. 50%
   d. 90%

107. On a topographic map, an area where the contour lines are very close together indicates that
   a. a stream is present.
   b. the slope is very gentle.
   c. the slope is very steep.
   d. the area surrounds a depression.

108. What is the major driving force that controls Earth's heat budget?
   a. Advection
   b. Evaporation
   c. Solar radiation
   d. Tilt of the Earth

109. What other planet in the solar system experiences a greenhouse effect similar to that observed on Earth?
   a. Mercury
   b. Venus
   c. Neptune
   d. Saturn

110. Which of the following statements comparing the terrestrial planets and the Jovian planets is not true?
   a. The terrestrial planets are denser than the Jovian planets.
   b. The terrestrial planets are generally warmer than the Jovian planets.
   c. The terrestrial planets are smaller than the Jovian planets.
   d. The terrestrial planets have a longer orbit than the Jovian planets.

111. What is one astronomical unit (AU) equivalent to?
    a. One parsec
    b. One light year
    c. The distance between the Earth and Sun
    d. The distance across the entire width of the solar system

112. What instrument would be best to use to study the pressure and temperature change of a star?
    a. Reflecting telescope
    b. Refracting telescope
    c. Radio telescope
    d. Spectroscope

113. Which of the following is an example of a negative impact technology can have on the environment?
    a. Sewage treatment plants use microbes to break down organic compounds.
    b. Genes used in genetically modified foods may be released into natural plants and create new species that are pesticide-resistant.
    c. Genetically modified crops are given a viral gene that vaccinates the plant from a virus attack.
    d. Livestock are given growth hormones to optimize growth and production.

114. Which of the following practices would most likely reduce the chances of a human-induced natural disaster?
    a. Building new coal-fired power plants
    b. Clear-cutting an entire forested area
    c. Dumping hazardous waste into a river
    d. Building new systems of public transportation

115. Which of the following is considered a non-renewable resource?
    a. Glass
    b. Wood
    c. Cattle
    d. Soil

116. Which statement best explains the importance of recycling and using alternative sources of energy?
    a. It will lead to greater production of goods and consumer spending in the future.
    b. It will ensure the health and safety of populations and the long-term sustainability of the environment.
    c. It will get rid of human disease and end economic warfare in the future.
    d. It will allow fossil fuel supplies to be replenished for their continued use in the future.

117. Why would it be ethical for local and state governments to conduct a risk-benefit analysis in making decisions about city planning and development?
   a. Governments must know what the benefits of a new development are for people and the economy in order to persuade opponents and the public who are against it.
   b. Knowledge of the environmental risks and benefits to humans is required for gaining building permits.
   c. The benefits to people and the economy must outweigh the risks to determine whether their decision to build is fair.
   d. The benefits to people and the economy can be used to ignore the risks associated with any new development.

118. Which of the following ethical questions regarding biotechnology would be answered and regulated by the FDA (the Food and Drug Administration)?
   a. Should the packaging of meat products that come from cloned animals be labeled?
   b. Should nitrate or sulfate fertilizers be added to oil spills to assist the decomposition of crude oil by bacteria?
   c. Should parents be allowed to genetically alter an embryo by choosing its physical characteristics?
   d. Should cells or components of cells be used to create industrially useful products?

119. What is a potential drawback of medical advances on human life?
   a. Medical advances require humans to constantly re-examine their moral beliefs.
   b. Medical advances have drastically increased the human life span, placing stress on the environment and the economy.
   c. While medical advances have cured many diseases, new diseases may still arise and threaten lives.
   d. Medical advances have given people many more opportunities for treatments and drugs depending on what they can afford.

120. Which of the following results of increased health awareness is most likely to have negative effects on society if not regulated properly?
   a. Increased funding for medical research
   b. Greater health education in schools
   c. Wide availability and use of prescription drugs
   d. Increased knowledge of disease through world-wide awareness programs

Answer Explanations

1. C: Repeat the experiment. Repeating the experiment validates data. Each separate experiment is called a repetition. Results of experiments or tests should be able to be replicated. Similar data gathered from many experiments can also be used to quantify the validity of the hypothesis. Repeating the experiments allows the student to observe variation in the results. Variation in data can be caused by a variety of errors or may be disproving the hypothesis. Answer D, Create a hypothesis, comes before experiments. Answers A, Communicate the results, and B, Draw a conclusion, occur after testing.

2. A: Turn it into an "if/then" statement. A formalized hypothesis written in the form of an if/then statement can then be tested. A statement may make a prediction or imply a cause/effect relationship, but that does not necessarily make it a good hypothesis. In this example, having the student rewrite the statement in the form of an if/then statement could read: If the length of the string of the pendulum is varied, then the time it takes the ball to make one complete period changes. This hypothesis is testable, doesn't simple make a prediction, nor does it . e a conclusion. The validity of the hypothesis can then be supported or disproved by experimentation and observation.

3. C: The mass of the ball. The mass of the ball is appropriately called a control variable for the experiment. A control or controlled variable is a factor that could be varied, but for testing purposes should remain the same throughout all experiments, otherwise, it could affect the results. In this case, if the mass of the ball was changed, it could also affect the length of the period. The length of the string is meant to be an independent variable, one that is changed during experiments to observe the results upon the dependent variable, which is the variable (or variables) that are affected. In this case, the period would be the dependent variable.

4. D: theory. Once a hypothesis has been verified and accepted, it becomes a theory. A theory is a generally accepted explanation that has been highly developed and tested. A theory can explain data and be expected to predict outcomes of tests. Answer A, fact, is considered to be an objective and verifiable observation; whereas, a scientific theory is a greater body of accepted knowledge, principles, or relationships that might explain a fact. Answer B, law, is an explanation of events by which the outcome is always the same. Answer C, conclusion, is more of an opinion and could be based on observation, evidence, fact, laws or even beliefs.

5. B: A scatter plot with the width measurements on the y-axis and precipitation rates on the x-axis. Scatter plots are useful for illustrating two sets of numerical data on the two axes and their relationship. In this case, by plotting the width of the tree trunks along the x-axis and the corresponding average precipitation rates along the y-axis, any relationship between the two can be found. Scatter plots are also useful when there are many data points. Answer A, multi-line graph, is useful for showing sets of data that change over time. Answer C, bar graph, is a good choice for comparing individual data points. Answer D, pie chart, is useful for graphically illustrating the parts to a whole.

6. C: This is a systematic error and the student should take it into consideration when analyzing the results by increasing the temperatures 7/10 of a degree. Answer A, The student should recalibrate the instrument, is probably not realistic in that the student may not be qualified to recalibrate the instrument. Answer B, Since it is not a major error, the student can ignore it, is incorrect as the scientific process does not include ignoring errors and assuming they are minor. Answer D, This is a random error, is also incorrect as it is not random and does not take into account that the collected data will be off by 0.7 degrees.

7. B: 0.05. In the metric system, 5 decimeters is equal to 0.05 decameters. A meter is the standard measurement of length. Prefixes are defined in increments of 10 to increase or decrease quantity. The prefix "deci" is equivalent to 10-1 or a tenth (0.1). A decimeter would be equal to 0.1 meters. The prefix "deca" is equivalent to 10 or 101. A decameter would be equal to 10 meters. To convert a smaller unit to a larger one, move the decimal place to the left. Since 10 decimeters make up 1 meter, for 5 decimeters, move the decimal 1 place to the left to find meters, which would be 0.5 meters. Because a decameter is larger than 1 meter (10 meters in 1 decameter), move the decimal another place to the left to change from meters to decameters, which would be 0.05 decameters. An alternate method is to set up conversion factors. This method involves canceling units and is very helpful to learn for other scientific problems.

8. C: The distribution of weight among players of a football team. In this case, a pie chart can illustrate the whole number of players as well as the number (or percentage) of players at given weights. It would be easy to interpret the data that, for example, 75% of the team weigh 250 pounds or more, 20% weigh between 200 and 250 pounds, and a mere 5% weight less than 200 pounds. The other answers would be better served in bar or line charts to compare variables or amounts that do not vary greatly.

9. D: Electrophoresis. Electrophoresis, also known as gel electrophoresis, uses electrical charges to separate substances such as protein, DNA and RNA. Depending upon the electrical charge and size of the molecules, they will travel through a porous gel at different rates when a charge is applied. Answer A, Spectrophotometry, refers to the measurement of visible light, near-ultraviolet, and near-infrared wavelengths. Answer B, Chromatography, refers to a number of techniques that separate mixtures of chemicals based on the differences in the compound's affinity for a stationary phase, usually a porous solid, and a mobile phase, which can be either a liquid or a gas. Answer C, Centrifugation, separates mixtures by spinning to generate centripetal force, which causes heavier particles to separate from lighter particles.

10. A: By multiplying the ocular lens power times the objective being used. When using a light microscope, total magnification is determined by multiplying the ocular lens power times the objective being used. The ocular lens refers to the eyepiece, which has one magnification strength, typically 10x. The objective lens also has a magnification strength, often 4x, 10x, 40x or 100x. Using a 10x eyepiece with the 4x objective lens will give a magnification strength of 40x. Using a 10x eyepiece with the 100x objective lens will give a magnification strength of 1,000x. The shorter lens is the lesser magnification; the longer lens is the greater magnification.

11. C: Decaying specimens are never permitted but unknown specimens are sometimes permitted. When performing a dissection in class, decaying specimens can be permitted but

unknown specimens are never permitted. Answer A, Rinse the specimen before handling, can help wash away excess preservative, which may be irritating. Answer B, Dispose of harmful chemicals according to district regulations; this is always required. Answer D, Students with open sores on their hands that cannot be covered should be excused from the dissection, is a good precaution. Exposure to pathogens and toxic chemicals can occur through open breaks in the skin.

12. A: Dispose of the solutions according to local disposal procedures. Solutions and compounds used in labs may be hazardous according to state and local regulatory agencies and should be treated with such precaution. Answer B, Empty the solutions into the sink and rinse with warm water and soap, does not take into account the hazards associated with a specific solution in terms of vapors, or interactions with water, soap and waste piping systems. Answer C, Ensure the solutions are secured in closed containers and throw away, may allow toxic chemicals to get into landfills and subsequently into fresh water systems. Answer D, Store the solutions in a secured, dry place for later use, is incorrect as chemicals should not be re-used due to the possibility of contamination.

13. C: 20 g/L. One way to measure the density of an irregularly shaped object is to submerge it in water and measure the displacement. This is done by taking the mass (40 grams), then finding the volume by measuring how much water it displaces. Fill a graduated cylinder with water and record the amount. Put the object in the water and record the water level. Subtract the difference in water levels to get the amount of water displaced, which is also the volume of the object. In this case, 4.5 liters minus 2.5 liters equals 2 liters. Divide mass by volume (40 grams divided by 2 liters) to get 20 g/L (grams per liter).

14. B: A spoiling apple. A spoiling apple is an example of a chemical change. During a chemical change, one substance is changed into another. Oxidation, a chemical change, occurs when an apple spoils. Answer A, Sublimation of water, refers to the conversion between the solid and the gaseous phases of matter, with no intermediate liquid stage. This is a phase change, not a chemical reaction. Answer C, Dissolution of salt in water, refers to a physical change, since the salt and water can be separated again by evaporating the water, which is a physical change. Answer D, Pulverized rock, is an example of a physical change where the form has changed but not the substance itself.

15. D: temperature. The amount of potential energy an object has depends on mass, height above ground and gravitational attraction, but not temperature. The formula for potential energy is PE = mgh, or potential energy equals mass times gravity times height. Answers A, B, and C are all valid answers as they are all contained in the formula for potential energy. Potential energy is the amount of energy stored in a system particularly because of its position.

16. D: All of the above. Elements on the periodic table are arranged into periods, or rows, according to atomic number, which is the number of protons in the nucleus. The periodic table illustrates the recurrence of properties. Each column, or group, contains elements that share similar properties, such as reactivity.

17. A: It takes half the amount of energy to increase the temperature of a 1 kg sample of ice by 1°C than a 1 kg sample of water. Heat capacity refers to the amount of heat or thermal energy required to raise the temperature of a specific substance a given unit. A substance

with a higher heat capacity requires more heat to raise its temperature than a substance with a lower heat capacity. The comparison here is that the specific heat capacity of ice is half as much as that of liquid water, so it takes half the amount of energy to increase the same amount of ice one temperature unit than it would if it were liquid water.

18. D: Its temperature remains the same due to the latent heat of fusion. The temperature of a substance during the time of any phase change remains the same. In this case, the phase change was from liquid to solid, or freezing. Latent heat of fusion, in this case, is energy that is released from the substance as it reforms its solid form. This energy will be released and the liquid will turn to solid before the temperature of the substance will decrease further. If the substance were changing from solid to liquid, the heat of fusion would be the amount of heat required to break apart the attractions between the molecules in the solid form to change to the liquid form. The latent heat of fusion is exactly the same quantity of energy for a substance for either melting or freezing. Depending on the process, this amount of heat would either be absorbed by the substance (melting) or released (freezing).

19. B: Conduction. A long nail or other type of metal, substance or matter that is heated at one end and then the other end becomes equally hot is an example of conduction. Conduction is energy transfer by neighboring molecules from an area of hotter temperature to cooler temperature. Answer A, Radiation, or thermal radiation, refers to heat being transferred through empty space by electromagnetic radiation. An example is sunlight heating the earth. Answer C, Convection, refers to heat being transferred by molecules moving from one location in the substance to another creating a heat current, usually in a gas or a liquid. Answer D, Entropy, relates to the second law of thermodynamics and refers to how much heat or energy is no longer available to do work in a system. It can also be stated as the amount of disorder in a system.

20. C: Heat transfer can never occur from a cooler object to a warmer object. While the second law of thermodynamics implies that heat never spontaneously transfers from a cooler object to a warmer object, it is possible for heat to be transferred to a warmer object, given the proper input of work to the system. This is the principle by which a refrigerator operates. Work is done to the system to transfer heat from the objects inside the refrigerator to the air surrounding the refrigerator. All other answer choices are true.

21. B: heat. The measure of energy within a system is called heat. Answer A, temperature, is a measurement of the average kinetic energy of molecules in a substance. A higher temperature means greater kinetic energy or faster moving molecules. Answer C, entropy, is the amount of energy that is no longer available for work, related to the second law of thermodynamics. Answer D, thermodynamics, is the study of the conversion of energy into heat and work in a system.

22. D: It has a different number of neutrons than its element. An isotope is a variation of an element that has a different number of neutrons. The element and its various isotopes continue to have the same numbers of protons and electrons. For example, carbon has three naturally occurring isotopes, carbon-12, carbon-13 and carbon-14, which is radioactive. Isotopes of an element differ in mass number, which is the number of protons and neutrons added together, but have the same atomic number, or number of protons.

23. D: It is a stable atom. If an atom's outer shell is filled, it is a stable atom. The outer shell refers to one of many energy levels, or shells, that electrons occupy around a nucleus. An atom whose outer shell is not filled wants to become stable by filling the outer shell. It fills its outer shell by forming bonds. The atom can do this by gaining electrons or losing electrons in ionic compounds, or if the atom is a part of a molecule, by sharing electrons. If an atom has a full outer shell, such as the noble gases, it does not readily react with other atoms and does not exchange electrons to form bonds. These atoms are known as inert. Therefore, Answers A and B cannot be true. Answer C, It has 32 electrons in its outer shell, is not necessarily true because not all elements have the fourth shell that can hold 32 electrons. Some have fewer shells that hold fewer electrons.

24. A: Fission. Fission is a nuclear process where atomic nuclei split apart to form smaller nuclei. Nuclear fission can release large amounts of energy, emit gamma rays and form daughter products. It is used in nuclear power plants and bombs. Answer B, Fusion, refers to a nuclear process whereby atomic nuclei join to form a heavier nucleus, such as with stars. This can release or absorb energy depending upon the original elements. Answer C, Decay, refers to an atomic nucleus spontaneously losing energy and emitting ionizing particles and radiation. Answer D, Ionization, refers to a process by which atoms obtain a positive or negative charge because the number of electrons does not equal that of protons.

25. B: farther from. Electrons with greater amounts of energy are found farther from the nucleus than electrons with less energy. The principle quantum number describes the level or shell that an electron is in. The lower the number, the closer the electron is to the nucleus and the lower it is in energy.

26. D: decay. The process whereby a radioactive element releases energy slowly over a long period of time to lower its energy and become more stable is best described as decay. The nucleus undergoing decay, known as the parent nuclide, spontaneously releases energy most commonly through the emission of an alpha particle, a beta particle or a gamma ray. The changed nucleus, called the daughter nuclide, is now more stable than the parent nuclide, although the daughter nuclide may undergo another decay to an even more stable nucleus. A decay chain is a series of decays of a radioactive element into different more stable elements.

27. C: A screw. A screw is a type of simple machine. A screw is an inclined plane wrapped around a shaft. A wedge is also an inclined plane. A compound machine is a machine that employs two or more simple machines. Answer A, a bicycle, is a compound machine, consisting of a combination of the simple machines: wheels, levers, pulleys and wedges (used as stoppers). Answer B, a pair of scissors, is also a compound machine consisting of two wedges (the blades) that pivot on a lever. Answer D, a shovel, is a compound machine consisting of a lever (the handle) and a wedge (the head of the shovel).

28. D: Mario balances a book on his head and walks across the room. In this example, work is not applied to the book by Mario. Work is defined as a force acting on an object to cause displacement. In this case, the book was not displaced in the direction of the force applied to it. Mario's head applied a vertical force to the book. By moving horizontally across the room, the movement of the book was not in the direction of the force applied. Therefore, there was no work applied to the book by Mario. In Answer A, Mario moves a book from the floor to the top shelf. Mario lifted the book vertically, in the same direction as the force

applied. Therefore, work was done. In Answer B, A book drops off the shelf and falls to the floor, gravity has acted as the force and work was done. In Answer C, Mario pushes a box of books across the room, is also an example of work.

29. C: The ball will move forwards. Newton's first law of motion states that an object in motion tends to stay in motion until a force acts to change it. The ball is moving forward with the boat. When the front of the boat hits the dock, the ball's motion does not change. It continues to move forward because the force acting to stop the boat is not acting upon the ball. The forward motion of the boat is halted by the dock. The forward motion of the ball is not stopped. Since the ball is round there is little friction to provide an equal and opposite reaction to the forward motion.

30. A: Acceleration and centripetal force. Acceleration and centripetal force are required for circular motion to occur. Acceleration is defined as a change in direction of velocity. Centripetal force is toward the center, or inward force. Answer B, Acceleration and gravitational force, is incorrect because the force of gravity is not required for circular motion. Answer C, Constant speed and centripetal force, is also incorrect as constant speed is not required for circular motion to occur. Speed can vary and circular motion can still occur. Answer D, Constant speed and gravitational force is also incorrect as constant speed nor gravitational force are required for circular motion to occur.

31. B: Where the pipe is narrowest. A fluid, either a gas or a liquid, will flow faster through a narrow section of a pipe than a wider section of pipe. Bernoulli's Principle says that the faster a fluid flows, the less pressure the fluid exerts. Therefore, a fluid will exert a lower amount of pressure in the narrow section of pipe. A fluid moving through the pipe has the same flow throughout the wider and narrow portions. This means that the same volume and mass of fluid must go a specific distance in a certain amount of time. In a narrow portion of pipe, there is less area for the same volume and mass of fluid to flow, so the fluid must move faster to maintain the same flow as in the wider portion of pipe. A fluid moving faster through a narrow portion of pipe will exert less pressure and a fluid moving slower through a wide section of pipe will exert a greater pressure.

32. A: The charge on the glass rod is positive and the charge on the cloth is negative when the glass rod is rubbed with a cloth made of polyester. This is an example of static electricity — the collection of electrically charged particles on the surface of a material. A static charge can be quickly discharged, commonly called a "spark", or discharged more slowly by dissipating to the ground. A static charge occurs because different materials have a capacity for giving up electrons and becoming positive (+), or for attracting electrons and becoming negative (-). The triboelectric series is a list of materials and their propensities for either giving up electrons to become positive or to gain the electrons to become negative. Polyester has a tendency to gain electrons to become negative and glass has a tendency to lose electrons to become positive.

33. B: Voltage and current are directly proportional to one another. Ohm's Law states that voltage and current in an electrical circuit are directly proportional to one another. Ohm's Law can be expressed as V=IR, where V is voltage, I is current and R is resistance. Voltage is also known as electrical potential difference and is the force that moves electrons through a circuit. For a given amount of resistance, an increase in voltage will result in an increase in

current. Resistance and current are inversely proportional to each other. For a given voltage, an increase in resistance will result in a decrease in current.

34. C: spin unpaired. In an atom with paired electrons, the opposite spins of each electron in the pair cancel out the magnetic field of each electron. A material becomes magnetic when the individual electrons of an atom spin unpaired thus allowing their magnetic fields to add together. The spin of an unpaired electron generates its own magnetic field. This can be used to make a magnet. When an external magnetic field is applied, these spins are lined up and the combined forces make a magnet.

35. D: Voltage is the same for each path and current is greatest in path C. In a parallel circuit, the voltage is the same for all three paths. Because the resistance is different on each path but the voltage is the same, Ohm's law dictates that the current will also be different for each path. Ohm's law says that current is inversely related to resistance. Therefore, the current will be greatest in path C as it has the least resistance, 2 ohms.

36. B: High temperature and humidity. Sound travels the farthest with high temperature and humidity. Sound is a mechanical wave. The sound wave travels through matter by causing a molecule to vibrate which then collides with a neighboring molecule causing it to vibrate and so on. A solid whose molecules are closely packed together will transmit the wave faster than a liquid or a gas whose particles are further apart. This is because the solid particles are more rigid and will respond to the disturbance quicker than a liquid or a gas, whose molecules are fluid. For this reason, solids can also propagate a wave further than a liquid or a gas. The principles of how sound travels through a solid can be applied to sound traveling through the air, as in this question. Air that is high in humidity has a higher density than dry air and can propagate the sound wave faster and farther than dry air. Sound waves also travel faster and farther at high temperatures. This is because at higher temperatures molecules have more kinetic energy to transmit the sound wave. At higher temperatures, molecules will also have more collisions which will result in the sound wave traveling farther and faster.

37. A: A high angle of incidence of the wave. A high angle of incidence will cause a high angle of reflection of a light wave. The angle of incidence is the angle of the incoming light and the angle of reflection is the angle of the light after being reflected. They are equal. Answer B, A low angle of incidence of the wave, would cause an equally low angle of reflection. Answer C, A wave that travels through a medium of higher density, would cause an angle of refraction, not reflection. Answer D, A wave with a very short wavelength, is incorrect as wavelength is not changed by reflection.

38. D: Destructive interference. Destructive interference describes two waves that are out of phase as they come together to produce a new wave. Out of phase refers to the crest of one and the trough of another arriving together. Interference, when used to discuss wave phenomenon, is the interaction of two or more waves passing the same point, which could be either destructive or constructive. Answer A, Incomplete interference, and Answer B, Distorted interference, are not real terms. Answer C, Constructive interference, refers to wave interference that results in higher peaks than the waves singularly because the waves arrive in phase (the crests arrive together).

39. A: They will be refracted and converge. When light waves hit a convex lens they are refracted and converge. A convex lens curves or bulges with the middle being thicker and the edges thinner. A magnifying glass is an example. Light rays are refracted by different amounts as they pass through the lens. After light rays pass through, they converge at a point called the focus. An object viewed with a magnifying glass looks bigger because the lens bends the rays inwards. Answer B, would indicate a concave lens as it would cause the light to be refracted and diverge. Light is not reflected in this case so neither Answer C nor D would be applicable.

40. B: The star is moving closer or toward him. When an astronomer observing stars detects a blue shift, he can conclude the star is moving closer or toward him. This is an example of the practical application of the Doppler effect in astronomy as applied to electromagnetic waves. The Doppler effect explains the change of wavelength caused by motion of the source or the relative difference in velocity between the observer and the source. When observing stars, a red shift or blue shift can be used to measure the speed that stars and galaxies are approaching or receding. Blue light has a higher frequency than red light. A red shift indicates a receding source.

41. C: A cation from a base and an anion from an acid. A salt is a general term for the neutral ionic product of a neutralization reaction between an acid and a base. Often, table salt, or sodium chloride, is mistakenly characterized as "salt", indicating that all salts are this compound. Although it is very common for a salt to be composed of a metal and a nonmetal, this is not always true, as in the case of the salt ammonium chloride. The ammonium ion ($NH4+$) is a polyatomic ion composed of non-metals. Likewise, many salts are composed of an alkali or alkaline earth metal and a halogen, but this is not always the case.

42. B: Group 2. Group 2 makes up the alkaline earth metals on the periodic chart of elements. There are 18 groups, or vertical columns, on the periodic table. In general, Group 2, alkaline earth metals, are characterized by silver colored, soft metals that melt at high temperatures. They also combine well with halogens to form salts and have two electrons in their valence level. Answer A, Group 1, are called the alkali metals or lithium family. Answer C, Group 13, is the boron family. Answer D, Group 17, are known as the halogens or fluorine family.

43. C: Astatine. Astatine is not a noble gas (Group 18). Astatine is a halogen (Group 17). It is believed to be the rarest naturally occurring element. Its symbol is At and has an atomic number of 85. It is radioactive and has a short half life. Answers, A, B and D, Neon, Argon, and Krypton, are all noble gases. These gases have low reactivity as their valence levels are filled with 8 electrons, except for helium, whose valence level is filled with 2 electrons.

44. D: The atomic number is equal to the number of electrons. An atom has a neutral charge if its atomic number is equal to its number of electrons. The atomic number (Z) of an element refers to the number of protons in the nucleus. If an atom has fewer or more electrons than its atomic number, then it will be positively or negatively charged, respectively. Cations are positively charged ions; anions are negatively charged ones. Answer A, The nucleus contains only neutrons and no protons -- An element of this nature is referred to as neutronium, but is somewhat theoretical. Answer B, The atomic mass is equal to the number of neutrons, is incorrect.

45. A: high solubility in water. Most organic molecules have all of the following properties except high solubility in water. Answer B, a tendency to melt, Answer C, covalently bonded, and Answer D, high flammability, are all characteristics of organic molecules. Organic molecules are those that contain carbon molecules, with a few exceptions. Organic molecules tend to be less soluble in water than inorganic salts. They are good at forming unique structures and there are many organic compounds. Examples of organic compounds include hydrocarbons, carbohydrates, lipids and proteins.

46. C: Al2O3 + 2Fe. In a single replacement reaction equation, 2Al + Fe2O3 ----> could result in the products Al2O3 + 2Fe. The reactants of the original equation are aluminum and iron(III)oxide (rust). The products are aluminum oxide and elemental iron. Single replacement reactions occur when one uncombined element replaces another. In this reaction, the aluminum replaces the iron. This reaction is an example of a thermite reaction and generates a large amount of heat and light. It can be used in fireworks or welding.

47. C: Covalent. Covalent compounds are usually formed by the combination of two or more non-metallic elements with one another. In these compounds atoms share electrons. Ionic compounds are most often formed between a metal and a non-metal. Organic compounds are covalent compounds which contain carbon and hydrogen atoms. "Chemical compounds" is a general term that can mean any type of compound, either ionic or covalent.

48. B: They show all the electrons of each atom of a molecule. This is not correct. Lewis dot structures do not show all the electrons of each atom of a molecule. Lewis structures only show the valence electrons, or the outermost electrons, of all of the atoms in the molecule. The other answers are correct as Lewis dot structures show the bonding between atoms of a molecule and the lone pairs on an atom, and that the total number of electrons is equal to the sum of the number of valence electrons on each atom.

49. D: A carbon atom attached to a hydrogen atom by a double bond and to an oxygen atom by a double bond. This is not a correct description of the carboxyl group. Hydrogen can never have more than one bond since it only has a 1s level and can only accommodate two electrons. The other answers are correct, as a carboxyl group does have a carbon atom attached to an oxygen atom by a double bond and to a hydroxyl (-OH) group by a single bond and is a set of four atoms bonded together and abbreviated as CO2H.

50. C: The pressure decreases by one third. A gas in a closed container at constant temperature will decrease in pressure by one-third when the volume of the container is tripled. The ideal gas law is pV = nRT where p is pressure, V is volume, n is the moles of the gas, R is the gas constant and T is temperature. A variation to solve for pressure is: P = nRT/V. Boyle's Law infers that pressure and volume are inversely proportional. Answer A, The pressure is tripled, and Answer B, The pressure increases by one third, are incorrect because it would imply that that pressure and volume are directly proportional rather than inversely proportional.

51. A: Sample A. Sample A is the only one of the four that was heated enough to completely change its phase to gas, so it is exerting the most pressure on its container. Sample B is boiling, but it is still partially liquid, so it is not exerting the most pressure. Sample C is unchanged in phase, and we do not even know if it was heated or cooled. Sample D was

- 157 -

cooled to below the freezing temperature, so it is exerting very little if any pressure on its container.

52. B: Sample B would become a gas. Since each sample was given sufficient time to assume the temperature of its environment, we know from the description that sample B was first placed in an environment exactly at its boiling temperature. If this temperature were then increased by 10 degrees Celsius, it would be above the boiling point and sample B would have to vaporize completely in order to assume this temperature. None of the other events are guaranteed to occur. Answer C might occur, but we do not have enough information to determine this. Answer A is not possible as there would need to be a decrease in temperature for the gas to revert to a liquid.

53. A: The molecular arrangement is random in some directions and regular in others. This best describes the molecular arrangement of a liquid crystal. A liquid crystal may seem like a contradiction as it seems to refer to two different states of matter. Liquid crystals have properties of both liquids and solids. The molecules of a liquid crystal are loosely bound allowing them to flow, like a liquid, yet they arrange themselves in a repeating pattern, like the molecules of a solid which are rigidly fixed in a pattern. Liquid crystals can also organize into layers, but with randomness in the layers.

54. D: There may be a different number of atoms for the products and the reactants. This is not true of a chemical reaction. Chemical equations must be balanced on each side of the reaction. Balancing means the total number of atoms stays the same, but their arrangement within specific reactants and products can change. Answer A, Matter is never gained or lost, is a statement of the law of conservation of matter and is correct. Answer B, Heat may be absorbed or released, is also correct as reactions can be endothermic or exothermic. Answer C, The rate of the reaction increases with temperature, can be true as a higher temperature can increase the rate of reaction.

55. C: High concentration. A higher concentration could increase the reaction rate of a chemical reaction. The rate of reaction is affected by concentration, pressure and temperature. A higher concentration would allow for more potential collisions that set off the reaction. Low kinetic energy, Answer A, would lead to a lower rate of reaction, as does a lower temperature (usually), Answer B. The term activation energy refers to the specific threshold that must be overcome for a reaction to occur. If the activation energy is lowered, for example, by a catalyst or enzyme, then the reaction can occur quicker. This rules out Answer D, High activation energy.

56. C: Single Replacement. When copper is added to silver nitrate, copper nitrate and silver are formed in a single replacement reaction. In a single replacement reaction, one element replaces another. In this case, copper replaces the silver in the silver nitrate solution, forming copper nitrate and silver. The equation for this is 2 AgNO3 + Cu --> Cu(NO3)2 + 2 Ag. Answer A, Compound, does not refer to a type of chemical reaction. Answer B, Decomposition, refers to a type of reaction by which one reactant is broken down into two or more products. Answer D, Double Replacement, refers to a reaction whereby the cations and anions of two elements switch places.

57. B: A reaction that uses electricity to drive it. An electrolysis reaction is a chemical reaction that uses electricity to drive it. Electrolysis reactions take place in an electrolytic

cell where one substance will be oxidized and another will be reduced using electrical energy from a battery or other source. Usually, an electrolytic cell is made up of a battery connected to two metal electrodes which are placed in two separate ionic solutions. A salt bridge connects the two beakers of solution and allows positive or negative ions to flow into the solutions as needed to keep the charge balanced as the reaction takes place. The electrode where oxidation takes place is called the anode, which would be connected to the negative terminal on a battery. The electrode where reduction takes place is called the cathode and is connected to the positive terminal of a battery. These reactions are very important for electroplating metals.

58. C: A + BC. When the reactant ABC is decomposed, it will produce the products A + BC. The equation should read ABC ? A + BC. Answer A, 2AB+C would not be a balanced equation according to the law of conservation of mass since this would produce 2 A, 2 B and 1 C. Since the original reactant was ABC, this could not be balanced. Answer B, AB + CD, is incorrect as an element "D" was not an original reactant. This does not follow the law that matter cannot be created nor destroyed. Answer D, B + C, has a similar problem as element "A" drops out of the equation. Because A was a part of the reactant, it needs to be part of the product.

59. B: Cool the liquid. If a gas and a liquid are placed in a sealed container, cooling the liquid will help dissolve the gas into a liquid. Gases have higher solubility in liquids at lower temperatures. At higher temperatures, the gas molecules will have more kinetic energy and will have enough energy to overcome intermolecular interactions with the liquid solvent and leave the solution. This also explains why answer A, heat the liquid, is incorrect. Answer C, shake the container, is also incorrect as this would give the gas energy to escape. A common example of this is shaking a soda before opening. Answer D, decrease the pressure on the lid, will not affect the pressure inside the vessel. If the pressure were decreased on the inside of the container, it would allow less gas to dissolve in the liquid. Increasing the pressure would increase the solubility of the gas in the liquid.

60. D: Non-polar. A non-polar substance is least likely to be soluble in water. A rule of thumb for a substance's solubility is that like dissolves like. Polarity is affected by the types of bonds between atoms and the bonds are affected by the types of atoms. An unequal sharing of electrons leads to polar bonding and polar substances. Water is polar and can dissolve many other polar substances. Hydrophilic molecules are polar and this word means "water-loving". Water also dissolves many ionic substances since they are composed of charged ions and can interact with the polar water molecules. Many organic compounds are non-polar and do not dissolve well in water.

61. C: The vapor pressure decreases by an amount proportional to the amount of solute. Raoult's law states the the vapor pressure of a solution containing a non-volatile solute is equal to the vapor pressure of the volatile solvent multiplied by its mole fraction, which is basically the proportion of the solution that is made up by solvent. In a liquid, some of the surface particles have higher than average energy and can break away to become a gas, or evaporate. The pressure of this gas right above the surface of the liquid is called the vapor pressure. Increasing the amount of solute in a liquid decreases the number of solvent particles at the surface. Because of this, fewer solvent molecules are able to escape, thus lowering the vapor pressure.

62. B: Water plus salt. Water plus salt has the highest electrical conductivity. To conduct electricity, ions must be present to move electrons through the solution. Electrolytes are substances that break apart to become ions. Pure water is actually a very poor conductor, since it is a covalent molecule and not an electrolyte. A very small portion of water molecules may break apart to form H+ ions and OH- but not enough to make it a good conductor. Salt is an electrolyte and completely breaks apart into Na+ ions and Cl- ions upon dissolving. This solution is highly conductive. Sugar is a non-electrolyte because it is a covalent molecule and does not produce ions when it dissolves. Answer C, Water plus vinegar, would conduct electricity but would not be as conductive as the salt solution because vinegar is a weak electrolyte. This means that only a portion of the vinegar molecules break apart into ions. Answer D, Water plus carbonated soda would not be a good conductor since CO2 is a covalent molecule and is a non-electrolyte.

63. C: meiosis I. In humans, diploid cells are those that contain 46 chromosomes. There are 23 pairs of chromosomes each made up of one chromosome from the father and one from the mother. In meiosis I, each chromosome replicates itself and lines up, or synapses, with its homologous chromosome, and each of the daughter cells ends up with one copy of each of the chromosomes. The two daughter cells at the end of meiosis I are haploid because they contain half of the chromosomes of the parent cell. In humans, this would be 23 chromosomes. However, each of these chromosomes are made of two sister chromatids. In meiosis II, the sister chromatids in the daughter cells separate and result in the production of the gametes. These are also haploid cells because they contain one copy of half of the genetic material of the parent cell. Four haploid cells result from meiosis. Answer A, mitosis, can be eliminated as it refers to the process of cell division where each daughter cell contains exactly the same genetic material as the parent cell. Answer B, telophase, refers to phases of both mitosis and meiosis, during which chromosomes move toward the opposite ends of the cell.

64. A: Lysosomes. A lysosome is an organelle that contains digestive enzymes that break down food and unneeded substances and are thought to be linked to the aging process. Answer B, Chromatin, is the structure created by DNA and various proteins in the cell nucleus during interphase and condenses to form chromosomes. Plastids, Answer C, are found in plants and algae. They often contain pigments and usually help make chemical compounds for the plant. Answer D, Golgi apparatus, gets macromolecules, like proteins and lipids, ready for transport.

65. B: Anabolism undergoes condensation reactions, while catabolism undergoes hydrolysis. Anabolic processes are those that use energy to build larger molecules. In cells, adenosine triphosphate (ATP) is used as a source of energy. A condensation reaction joins two molecules together to make a larger molecule and in the process, produces a water molecule. Condensation reactions are important in protein synthesis. Anabolic processes are often reduction reactions. Catabolism breaks down molecules and usually generates energy. Catabolic reactions are often oxidation reactions. Hydrolysis is a catabolic process where water is added to a molecule and then split, resulting in the molecule breaking apart into two different molecules. Hydrolysis is the opposite of condensation.

66. B: Plant A lives in a very arid environment. Photosynthesis converts carbon dioxide into sugars that plants use. Three types are C3, C4 and CAM. C3 is used by most plants. C4 and CAM are used by desert plants. C4 first forms a four carbon sugar instead of the three

carbon sugar formed by C3. Also, the stomata of C4 plants are faster at absorbing carbon dioxide and do not have to open as long, so less water is lost by transpiration. A C4 plant, such as saltbush, corn or some grasses, would live in an arid environment rather than a moist, marine or dark environment. Plants that use the CAM (Crassulacean Acid Metabolism) type of photosynthesis also use water more efficiently as their stomata are closed during the day and open at night. Desert cacti are examples.

67. A: Cytoplasm. The type of RNA described by the question is transfer RNA (tRNA). tRNA is found in the cytoplasm and carries and positions amino acids at the ribosome for protein synthesis. There are two other types of RNA. Messenger RNA (mRNA) contains the coding for the amino acid sequence in the protein. mRNA is first made in the nucleus before traveling through the cytoplasm to a ribosome. Ribosomal RNA (rRNA) is the RNA that is found in the ribosome along with proteins and allow the mRNA and tRNA to bind for protein synthesis. All three types of RNA originate in the nucleus where they are transcribed from DNA. Mitochondria are organelles that harbor mitochondrial DNA (mtDNA).

68. C: U G C A U G C G A. Translation is the process of the tRNA bringing the correct amino acid to the ribosome according to the sequence of the mRNA. Since translation only involves RNA, the four bases are adenine (A), cytosine (C), guanine (G) and uracil (U). There is no thymine (T) used in RNA. Cytosine (C) and guanine (G) pair and adenine (A) and uracil (U) pair. A codon is the triplet sequence that represents a specific amino acid or a start/stop point. It is on the messenger RNA (mRNA). The anticodon is on tRNA and corresponds to the amino acid used by the ribosome during translation. They are complimentary. UGC becomes AUG; AUG becomes CGA. The original codon sequence is U G C A U G C G A if the anticodon sequence formed during translation is A C G U A C G C U.

69. C: 4/16. The fraction of offspring that that have the genotype BbSs is 4/16. A dihybrid cross considers two traits at a time, in this case, eye color and hair color. In the parent (P) generation, a parent with the genotype BBSS would be crossed with a parent with the genotype bbss. The offspring are considered the F1 generation and all would have the genotype BbSs. This question asks about the F2 generation, which is the offspring between a cross of the F1 generation. Therefore the parent genotypes in this question would be BbSs. To solve, develop a Punnet square of 16 cells. Each parent will produce the following gametes: BS, Bs, bS, bs. Place these across the top and the side. After completing the square, the resulting offspring show that four would have the genotype BbSs.

70. D: Inversion. This type of mutation is represented in the sequence 1 5 4 3 2 6. An inversion error is a type of mutation where an entire sequence of DNA is reversed. In this case, 2 3 4 5 has been reversed to 5 4 3 2. Breakage, Answer A, in a gene can mess up its function entirely or lead to a translocation of genetic information. Answer B, Deletion, is when a section of DNA is omitted or lost. Answer C, Insertion, is when an extra base pair is added to a DNA sequence. Deletions and insertions can lead to a frameshift effect where entire sequences are thrown off because one nucleotide is wrong. This could result in coding for the wrong amino acid and non-functioning proteins.

71. C: Vestigial structure. Wisdom teeth are an example of a vestigial structure. A vestigial structure is one that still exists in an organism, but through evolution has lost most of its original purpose. Wisdom teeth, or third molars, in humans were useful in grinding down

- 161 -

plant matter in larger jaws. Human diet has changed and jaws have become smaller, yet wisdom teeth still develop. Some vestigial organs may gain new function. Answer A, Analogous structure, is one that exists for the same purpose in two species but in different forms. Answer B, Homologous structure, is one that has the same basic structure but not purpose in two different species. Answer D, Divergent structure, is a made-up term and does not make sense.

72. B: It states that the status of species is based on the reproductive isolation of populations. Biological Species Concept (BSC) is an evolution concept that helps explains that species are distinct. A species is one that can interbreed and produce fertile offspring. Some species contain individuals whose appearance are drastically different yet are still within the same species, like two ants that play different roles in a colony. Other species may look very similar and have overlapping territories, like the Eastern and Western meadowlark, but because of their songs do not interbreed.

73. A: New species due to geographic isolation. Allopatric speciation refers to a new species brought about by geographic isolation. Speciation in general refers to the formation of a new species. Geographic isolation can be because of a great physical barrier or insurmountable distance between groups of individuals. This rules out Answer B, New species due to geographic overlap. Answer C, Hybrid species due to geographic overlap, is incorrect, as hybrid species has many definitions that do not necessarily relate to geography. Answer D, Loss of diversity of a species due to geographic divergence, is also incorrect as it does not refer to loss of diversity.

74. B: He proposed an alternate theory by stating that favorable traits developed due to environmental conditions and the desire and needs of the organisms. Jean Baptiste Lamarck's theory of acquired characteristics predated Darwin's book about theory of natural selection. Lamarck explained evolution as occurring when individual organisms of a species changed as a response to environmental conditions. Contrast this with Darwinism, which states that individuals with more successful characteristics are more likely to survive to breed and pass on those traits. Since Lamarck died in 1829 and Darwin published Origin of the Species in 1859 the other answers that Lamarck "expanded," "provided evidence for," or "opposed" Darwin's theories are not likely.

75. D: Reproductive habits. Reproductive habits would not be considered evidence for evolution. Usually how a species reproduces does not support nor add to the body of evidence for the theory of evolution. Reproduction habits might exemplify how any given organism can adapt to changes in its environment as a way to survive. This does not necessarily show evolution. Answer A, Fossil record, is evidence for evolution as it shows evolutionary change of organisms over time. Answer B, DNA sequences, shows that organisms that are related evolutionarily also have related gene sequences. Answer C, Anatomical structures, such as having an internal bony structure provides evidence of descent from a common ancestor.

76. B: Family. Organisms that belong to the same taxonomic group of family are most alike. In biological taxonomy, the ranks in descending order are Life, Domain, Kingdom, Phylum, Class, Order, Family, Genus and Species. The ranks become more exclusive and specific as the classification descends. Answer A, Phylum, Answer C, Class, and Answer D, Order, are all higher than the family group. The higher the rank, the fewer requirements it takes to be a

member. Two mnemonics for taxonomy are Kings Play Cards On Fat Green Snakes or King Philip Cuts Open Five Green Snakes.

77. A: Anthophyta. Anthophyta is a division of plants that produces seeds as part of reproduction. Anthophyta are also known as the group that contains flowering plants. It is the largest and most diverse grouping of plants and includes many food, clothing and medicinal uses for humans. Grains, beans, nuts, fruits, vegetables, spices, tea, coffee, chocolate, cotton, linen and aspirin are all derived from plants from anthophyta. Answer B, Lycophyta, is a small group of plants including club mosses and scale trees. Answer C, Sphenophyta, contains about 30 species including horsetails, foxtails, or scouring rushes. Answer D, Pterophyta, contains non-seed plants like ferns. Lycophyta, sphenophyta and pterophyta all use spores to reproduce sexually.

78. B: They use tube feet for locomotion and feeding. Animals belonging to the phylum Echinodermata have tube feet for locomotion and feeding. About 7,000 species are extant in this phylum including starfish and sand dollars. Tube feet are an organ system that provides locomotion, respiration, feeding and sensory functions. Answer A, They use multiple appendages for locomotion-- not all echinoderms have appendages. Answer C, They have an exoskeleton made of chitin, is the composition of the exoskeleton of Arthropods. Answer D, They must shed their outer layer of skin to grow, is also not a characteristic of Echinodermata, like sea urchins.

79. C: Flowers. Flowers are the reproductive organs of a plant. Flowering plants reproduce by sexual reproduction where the gametes join to form seeds. Pollen is sperm. Pollinators help transfer the sperm to the ovule, the egg. Answer A, Style, is the part of the female reproduction system that transports the sperm between the stigma and the ovary, all part of the pistil. Answer B, Stigma, the sticky tip of the style on which the pollen lands. Answer D, Sepals, are usually small leaves between or underneath the petals and are not as obvious or as large and colorful as the petals.

80. D: Carbon dioxide and water. Respiration produces carbon dioxide and water. The net equation of respiration is the reverse of the equation for photosynthesis. Respiration is a series of reactions that consume glucose and oxygen to release energy and produce carbon dioxide and water. Answer B, Oxygen and glucose, are what are broken down in respiration. Answer C, Carbon dioxide and sugar, is inaccurate as carbon dioxide is produced, but sugar is broken down.

81. D: Lower seed dispersal. Lower seed dispersal is not an advantage that angiosperms show over other types of plants. Gymnosperms, for example, have plentiful amounts of pollen, but it does not always hit its mark. Angiosperms are the most recently evolved plant division and contain at least 260,000 extant species. They are very diverse and occupy many habitats. Answer A, Larger leaves, many other species in other plant divisions do not have true leaves. Gymnosperms have modified leaves in the form of needles. Answer B, Double fertilization, refers to how one sperm cell fuses with an ovule. This makes the zygote. The second sperm forms into a triploid endosperm that provides energy for the embryo.

82. A: Through gills. Animals of the phylum Mollusca respire through gills. Respiration is the process of taking in oxygen and releasing carbon dioxide. Mollusks include five classes that include species as diverse as chitons, land and marine snails and squids. This

represents a diverse range of body structures. Many mollusks have a mantle that includes a cavity that is used for both breathing and excretion. Within the mantle are gills (ctenidia). Answer B, Through a trachea, is incorrect as mollusks do not have this structure. Answer C, Through lungs, is incorrect although some land snails have reduced gills which feature a respiratory cavity, but are not true lungs. Answer D, through muscle contraction, is not true for mollusks as muscle contraction is not required for ventilation of the gills. Other structures, such as cilia, work to pass water over the gills.

83. B: Stomata. A stoma is the part of a plant system that responds to stimuli by releasing water via transpiration. It can also close during adverse conditions like a drought to prevent the plant from dehydration. Stomata closure can also be triggered by the presence of bacteria. Answer A, Pith, refers to the central, spongy part of the stem in vascular plants. Answer C, Guard Cells, flank stomata and regulate the opening. Answer D, Sepals, are modified leaves that protect the flower bud before it opens.

84. D: Circulatory System – exchanges gases with the environment by delivering oxygen to the bloodstream and releasing carbon dioxide, is not paired correctly. It is the respiratory system that exchanges gases with the environment by delivering oxygen to the bloodstream and releasing carbon dioxide. The circulatory system transports nutrients, gases, hormones, and blood to and away from cells. Answer A, is correct as the muscle system controls movement through three types of muscle tissue. Answer B, is correct as the nervous system controls sensory responses by carrying impulses away from and toward the cell body. Answer C, digestive system breaks down food for absorption into the blood stream where it is delivered to cells for respiration.

85. C: at carrying capacity. A population that reaches maximum size and ceases to grow due to a limited availability of resources, is said to be at carrying capacity. The carrying capacity of a species is influenced by many factors such as the amount of land or water available, food supply and predators. Answer A, unstable, and Answer D, moving towards extinction, are not correct as carrying capacity does not necessarily mean it is unstable or becoming extinct. Answer B, shrinking exponentially, is incorrect as the question says it has stopped growing, not that it is reducing in size.

86. A: Tree. In the food chain of Tree ? Caterpillar ? Frog ? Snake ? Hawk ? Worm, the tree is at the trophic level with the the greatest amount of energy. Trophic level refers to the position of an organism in a food chain. Energy is lost according to the laws of thermodynamics as one moves up the food chain because it is converted to heat when consumers consume. Primary producers, such as autotrophs, are organisms who are at the base and capture solar energy. Primary consumers are herbivores that feed on the producers. Secondary consumers consume primary consumers and so on. Decomposers get their energy from the consumption of dead plants and animals.

87. D: Glaciers. Glaciers and ice caps are fresh water unavailable for human use as they are frozen. The hydrologic cycle refers to all the water on planet Earth. Some water is in forms that humans do not tend to use, such as oceans (too salty and expensive to desalinate) and glaciers. Water suitable for drinking can be found as surface water and in ground water, which is obtained through wells. Answers A, Rivers, B, Estuaries, and C, Aquifers, are all examples of surface water that are available to humans.

88. C: Moose. Moose are most likely be found in the taiga. Biomes are classifications of areas and communities of predominant plant and animal life that live within the area. The six major types of biomes are freshwater, marine, dessert, forest, grassland, and tundra. The taiga or boreal is one of the three major types of forests: tropical, temperate and taiga. They can be divided by latitude and the taiga runs through Canada, northern Europe and Russia, sandwiched between the tundra and deciduous forests. Taiga is a Russian word meaning swampy, moist forest.

89. C: Transform. Transform is not connected to the process of mountain building. Orogeny, or mountain building, occurs at the Earth's lithosphere or crust. Answer A, Folding, or deformation, is a process that occurs to make mountains where two portions of the lithosphere collide. One is subducted and the other is pushed upward forming a mountain. This action produces various types of folding. Answer B, Faulting, can be characterized by a brittle deformation where the rock breaks abruptly (compared with folding). Faulting and fault types are associated with earthquakes and relatively rapid deformation. D, Convergent, is a more general term used to describe plates converging.

90. D: heat. The formation of sedimentary rock does not include heat. Of the three types of rock igneous, sedimentary and metamorphic, heat is essential to two: igneous and metamorphic. Sedimentary rocks are formed by sediments that get deposited and then compacted or cemented together. Sedimentary rocks are classified into detrital, organic or chemical sediments. Answer A, layering, is correct since sediments can be deposited or otherwise formed in layers. Answer B, cementation, is also called lithification. Answer C, compaction, refers to the pressure forming sedimentary rock leading to cementation.

91. C: Vinegar fizzing when poured on a rock, is an example of chemical weathering. Mechanical and chemical weathering are processes that break down rocks. Mechanical weathering breaks down rocks physically, but does not change their chemical composition. Frost and abrasion are examples. Water, oxygen, carbon dioxide and living organisms can lead to the chemical weathering of rock. Vinegar is a weak acid and will undergo a chemical reaction, evidenced by fizzing, with the rock. Answer A, Rain freezing on the roadway, is an example of the phase change of water from a liquid to a solid and may lead to physical weathering. Answer B, Ivy growing on the side of a wooden house, is incorrect since the house is not a rock. Answer D, A river carrying sediment downstream, is an example of erosion.

92. B: Two crustal plates move apart. When two crustal plates move apart, magma welling up could result in the formation of new crust. This has been shown to be occurring on the ocean floor where places of the crust are weaker. The crust spreads apart at these trenches, pushing outward and erupting at the ridges. Answer A, When two crustal plates converge, sublimation occurs as one plate runs under another pushing it up. Answer C, Two crustal plates slide past one another, is an example of a transform fault, which does not create new crust. Answer D, A crustal plate is pushed down into the mantle, does not form new crust but perhaps recycles the old one.

93. C: Laccolith. A laccolith is formed when an intrusion of magma injected between two layers of sedimentary rock forces the overlying strata upward to create a dome-like form. Eventually, the magma cools, the sedimentary rock wears away and the formation is exposed. Answer A, Sill, and Answer B, Dike, are both examples of sheet intrusions: where

- 165 -

magma has inserted itself into other rock. Sills are horizontal and dikes are vertical. Answer D, Caldera, is a crater-like feature that was formed from the collapse of a volcano after erupting.

94. A: It compares the amount of radioactive material in a rock to the amount that has decayed into another element. This best describes the process of absolute dating. Answer B, It measures the age of a rock by comparing it to fossils found in the same stratigraphic layer as the rock, is not usually done. Usually the stratigraphic layer of rock is used to date the fossils, which is referred to as relative dating. Answer C, It measures the amount of daughter elements that have broken down by half, is incorrect as this would not lead to a correct date since the daughter elements may have a different half life than the parent material.

95. C: igneous rock. Fossils are least likely to be found in igneous rock. Igneous rock is formed by extreme heat as magma escapes through the Earth's crust and cools. The remains of plants and animals in fossil form are not usually preserved under these conditions. Answer A, sedimentary rock, is where the abundance of fossils are found. Sedimentary rock is formed more slowly and is very abundant. Since soft mud and silts compress into layers, organisms can be also be deposited. Answer B, metamorphic rock, is rock that has undergone change by heat and pressure. This usually destroys any fossils, but occasionally fossil remains are distorted and can be found in metamorphic rock.

96. B: A footprint. A trace fossil is that which shows evidence of existence, but is not an organism itself. A trace fossil can be contrasted with a body fossil, which has been formed from an organism. Other examples of trace fossils include eggs, nests, burrows, borings and coprolites (fossilized feces). Answer A, A mouse jaw, and Answer C, A shark tooth, are examples of body fossils. Answer D, A cast of a skull, is a replica and neither a body nor a trace fossil.

97. A: era. A time interval in which particular plants and animals were dominant or present in great abundance is defined as an era. On the geologic time scale, stratigraphy is used to provide approximate dates of events related to the Earth on a much grander time scale than our lives. Eons are divided into eras. Eras are separated by major events, such as the Cretaceous–Tertiary extinction event, which marked the end of the Mesozoic Era and the beginning of the Cenozoic Era. Eras are divided into periods, epochs and ages.

98. D: The first implies that the Earth was shaped by a series of quick, violent events, while the second implies that it changed slowly and incrementally. Catastrophism is the belief that the Earth was shaped by sudden, short-term catastrophic events. Uniformitarianism, also known as gradualism, is the belief among modern geologists that the forces, processes, and laws that we see in effect today have been in effect for a long period of time, that is, throughout geologic time. It involves the belief that the present is the key to the past, and that these relatively slow processes have shaped the Earth.

99. C: Cold and high salinity. Ocean currents that are cold and have high salinity are the densest. Sea water with a higher salinity is more dense that lower salinity sea water. The density of ocean water can also affect currents. Water from more dense areas flows to that of less dense areas. Denser ocean water sinks and becomes cooler. The deeper the water the greater the pressure, which also increases density. Answer B, Warm and low salinity, and Answer D, Cold and low salinity, can be ruled out because low salinity leads to lower

density. Answer A, Warm and high salinity, would also be less dense, warm fluid molecules are moving with more energy and are farther apart, resulting in a slightly larger volume.

100. D: Phase of the Moon. Ocean currents are not controlled by the phase of the Moon. The phases of the moon refer to our viewpoint from Earth of the Sun's illumination of the Moon. Half the moon is illuminated by the sun at any given time. For example, a new moon is one we do not see because the side being lit by the Sun is not facing us. The revolution of the Moon around the Earth affects the ocean tides, providing two highs and two lows at any given point during the day. Answer A, Wind, affects the surface currents of the ocean. Landmasses, Answer B, affect ocean currents as well. Answer C, Earth's rotation, affects the deep currents.

101. B: lower. The freezing point of sea water is lower than fresh water as sea water is more dense. It is more dense because it has more dissolved salts. The freezing point changes with salinity, pressure and density, but can be -2°C (28.4°F) compared with fresh water, 0°C (32°F). As sea water freezes, it forms pockets of high-salinity brine that do not freeze. The brine slowly leaches out of the sea water ice as it forms. When the ice eventually melts, it has a lesser degree of salinity.

102. C: It is the surface layer where wave action is present due to interaction with winds at the surface. The mixed layer of the ocean can be affected mainly by three processes: winds, cooling and an increase in density. The winds at the surface drive surface currents and therefore, mixing. The action of breaking waves imparts a large amount of energy to the surface mixed layer. Surface density can be changed by an increase in salinity, which can be caused both by the addition of brine from sea ice or net evaporation because of temperature and a lack of influx of more water.

103. B: Cold water dissolves atmospheric carbon dioxide, stores it, and releases it back out to the atmosphere as needed. This describes the physical or non-biological part of the carbon cycle. The carbon and nutrient cycles of the ocean are processed in part by the deep currents, mixing, and upwelling that occurs. Carbon dioxide (CO_2) from the atmosphere is dissolved into the ocean at the higher latitudes and distributed to the denser deep water. Where upwelling occurs, CO_2 is brought back to the surface and emitted into the tropical air.

104. A: The prevailing westerlies. The prevailing westerlies drive weather systems to move west to east in the mid-latitudes. The direction refers to that which the wind is coming from. Answer B, The prevailing easterlies, is incorrect. The polar easterlies that travel from the northeast occur between 90-60 degrees north latitude. The ones from the southeast are between 90-60 degrees south latitude. Answer C, The trade winds, refer to those occurring near the equator in the tropics moving east. Answer D, The doldrums, are also in the tropics, but refer to an area of low-pressure where frequently the winds are light and unpredictable.

105. B: Land breeze. When land cools off rapidly at night and the ocean water stays relatively warm, it creates a land breeze. Answer A, Sea breeze, or onshore breeze, occurs when the land heats the air above it. This heated, warmer air is less dense and rises. The cooler air from above the sea and higher sea level pressure creates a wind flow in the direction of the land. Coastal areas often have these cooler breezes. Answer C, Monsoon, is a seasonal wind in southern Asia that blows southwest in one season and northeast in

- 167 -

another. The southwest winds in the summer bring heavy rain. Answer D, Trade wind, is the steady easterlies about the equator.

106. D: 90%. If the current air temperature is 65°F and the current dew point is 62°F, the current relative humidity is 90%. Relative humidity is the ratio of water vapor that the air has compared with the amount possible for that temperature. Absolute humidity is the total moisture capable at a certain temperature. Warm air can hold more water vapor. Dew point refers to the temperature to which the air would have to be cooled for it to hold all the water it can hold (saturation). The ratio between current temperature and dew point indicates relative humidity. If the temperature is 65°F and the dew point is 65°F, then relative humidity is 100%. As a general approximation, relative humidity drops 10% for every 3oF difference between the temperature and the dew point. For Celsius, relative humidity drops 5% for each 1oC difference between the temperature and the dew point.

107. C: the slope is very steep. On a topographic map, an area where the contour lines are very close together indicates that the slope is very steep. Lines very far apart would indicate a more gradual change in elevation. Contour lines help represent the actual shape of the Earth's surface features and geographic landmarks like rivers, lakes and vegetation. Topographic maps also show man made features such as roads, dams and major buildings. They are based on aerial photography and the quadrangle maps are produced in various scales. The 7.5 minute quadrangle is very common and provides a 1:24,000 scale, where 1 inch represents 2,000 feet.

108. C: Solar radiation. Solar radiation is the major driving force that controls Earth's heat budget. The Earth's heat budget, or energy budget, refers to the total heat that moves through the Earth's system. Almost all of the energy is obtained by solar radiation and this heats the air, land and oceans. Insolation is a measure of the incident solar radiation and tells how much energy is absorbed on a given area in a given amount of time. Answer A, Advection, is the transportation of a substance or property, like silt in a river or heat in an atmosphere. Answer B, Evaporation, is a phase change from a liquid to a gas at the surface. Boiling is a type vaporization too, but one that occurs throughout the liquid. Answer D, Tilt of the Earth, does not affect the heat budget but is responsible for seasons.

109. B: Venus. Venus experiences a greenhouse effect similar to that observed on Earth as its dense atmosphere traps the solar radiation and creates a greenhouse effect. The greenhouse gases, including ozone, carbon dioxide, water vapor and methane, trap infrared radiation that is reflected back toward the atmosphere. Human activity generates more of the greenhouse gases than necessary. Some practices that increase the amount of greenhouse gases are burning natural gas and oil, farming, which leads to more methane and nitrous oxide, deforestation, which decreases the amount of offset oxygen, and population growth in general, which increases the volume of greenhouse gases. Increased gases mean more infrared radiation is trapped and the overall temperature at the Earth's surface rises.

110. D: The terrestrial planets have a longer orbit than the Jovian planets. This statement is false as the four Jovian planets, Jupiter, Saturn, Uranus and Neptune, are farther away from the sun than the four terrestrial planets, Mercury, Venus, Earth and Mars. The other statements are true as the terrestrial planets are denser, generally warmer and smaller than the Jovian planets. The four Jovian planets are also known as the gas giants.

111. C: The distance between the Earth and Sun. One astronomical unit (AU) is equivalent to the distance between the Earth and Sun, 93 million miles (150 million km). Scientists use astronomical units since cosmic distances are so great. Answer A, One parsec (pc), is the parallax of one arcsecond and is about 31 million million km (about 19 trillion miles), or about 3.26 light years. It is used to calculate distances by triangulation with the distance from the Earth to the Sun forming the side of a right triangle. Answer B, One light year, is the distance light travels in a vacuum in one year. It is equal to about 1013 km or 64,341 AU.

112. D: Spectroscope. A spectroscope would be the best instrument to use to study the pressure and temperature change of a star. A spectroscope measures properties of light and wavelengths. It can be used to make spectral lines and measure their subsequent wavelengths and intensities. Answer A, Reflecting telescope, does not make measurements. It reflects light and uses curved mirrors to form an image. Answer B, Refracting telescope, also does not make measurements. It bends light using a lens to form the image. Answer C, Radio telescope, is an antenna that collects radio wavelength frequencies, not light waves. These are typically large concave dishes.

113. B: Genes used in genetically modified foods may be released into natural plants and create new species that are pesticide-resistant. The possible negative impact is that the natural plants that become pesticide resistant are not beneficial, are considered weeds or poisonous. This acquired resistance to pesticides would make it more difficult to contain, which might be necessary, especially if they overrun another species. Answer A, Sewage treatment plants use microbes to break down organic compounds, is part of the process of sewage treatment. Answer C, Genetically modified crops are given a viral gene that vaccinates the plant from a virus attack, would be beneficial. Answer D, livestock are given growth hormones to optimize growth, is already a practice. The hormones are metabolized by the animal and are not a threat to the environment, however, their affect on the animal or food supply could be a subject of discussion.

114. D: Building new systems of public transportation. This would most likely reduce the chances of a human-induced natural disaster. All the rest are examples of humans harming their environment. Answer A, Building new coal-fired power plants, can be eliminated as coal-fired power plants release carbon dioxide, sulfur dioxide, particulates and mercury. Answer B, Clear-cutting an entire forested area, detracts from a healthy environment in that it reduces plants that help convert carbon dioxide into oxygen. Answer C, Dumping hazardous waste into a river, pollutes the food chain, harming and killing plants and animals, and toxins can enter the water table that humans drink.

115. A: Glass. Glass is considered a non-renewable resource. Glass is manufactured and can be recycled, but is considered a non-renewable resource. Answer B, Wood, is considered a renewable resource because with proper management, an equilibrium can be reached between harvesting trees and planting new ones. Cattle, Answer C, are managed in herds and a balance can be achieved between those consumed and those born. Answer D, Soil, is the result of long-term erosion and includes organic matter and minerals needed by plants. Soil found naturally in the environment is renewed. Crops can be rotated to help maintain a healthy soil composition for farming.

116. B: It will ensure the health and safety of populations and the long-term sustainability of the environment. Recycling and using alternative sources of energy reduce the amount of pollutants introduced into the ecosystem, reduce the potential for disease-related human maladies, and reduce the reliance on non-renewable resources. Answer A, It will lead to greater production of goods and consumer spending in the future, would probably be good for the economy, but not the environment. Answer C, It will get rid of human disease and end economic warfare in the future, is incorrect as recycling will not necessarily eliminate disease and economic warfare. Answer D is incorrect as fossil fuels are a non-renewable energy resource that cannot be replenished.

117. C: The benefits to people and the economy must outweigh the risks to determine whether their decision to build is fair. This is why governments would conduct a risk-benefit analysis in making decisions about city planning and development. Answer A, Governments must know what the benefits of a new development are for people and the economy in order to persuade opponents and the public who are against it, would be incorrect because the intention would be to build regardless of risk. Answer D, The benefits to people and the economy can be used to ignore the risks associated with any new development, would also be incorrect as it would be unethical to ignore the risks.

118. A: Should the packaging of meat products that come from cloned animals be labeled? This is an issue that would be regulated by the Food and Drug Administration (FDA) as it regulates the packaging of meat products, among many other types of food. Answer B, Should nitrate or sulfate fertilizers be added to oil spills to assist the decomposition of crude oil by bacteria, would not be an issue for the FDA. The Environmental Protection Agency (EPA) regulates issues regarding the environment as well as superfund clean ups. Neither Answer C, about genetic engineering of humans, nor Answer D, about cell use in industry, relate to food and drugs and would not fall under the jurisdiction of the FDA.

119. B: Medical advances have drastically increased the human life span, placing stress on the environment and the economy, could be considered a potential drawback of medical advances on human life. A longer life span does not necessarily lead to more productive years. It also leads to a larger aged population and increases the rate of population growth. Answer A, re-examining moral beliefs is not necessarily a drawback. Answer C, is not a drawback of medical advances. New diseases may arise but medical advances may aid in the cure of these diseases. Answer D, is an advantage of medical advances.

120. C: Wide availability and use of prescription drugs. If not regulated properly, the illicit use of prescription drugs could have a negative effect on society. It could lead to otherwise productive and healthy people becoming dependent upon prescription drugs either inadvertently through legitimate use or through experimentation. All other answer choices are not negative outcomes of increased health awareness.

Secret Key #1 - Time is Your Greatest Enemy

Pace Yourself

Wear a watch. At the beginning of the test, check the time (or start a chronometer on your watch to count the minutes), and check the time after every few questions to make sure you are "on schedule."

If you are forced to speed up, do it efficiently. Usually one or more answer choices can be eliminated without too much difficulty. Above all, don't panic. Don't speed up and just begin guessing at random choices. By pacing yourself, and continually monitoring your progress against your watch, you will always know exactly how far ahead or behind you are with your available time. If you find that you are one minute behind on the test, don't skip one question without spending any time on it, just to catch back up. Take 15 fewer seconds on the next four questions, and after four questions you'll have caught back up. Once you catch back up, you can continue working each problem at your normal pace.

Furthermore, don't dwell on the problems that you were rushed on. If a problem was taking up too much time and you made a hurried guess, it must be difficult. The difficult questions are the ones you are most likely to miss anyway, so it isn't a big loss. It is better to end with more time than you need than to run out of time.

Lastly, sometimes it is beneficial to slow down if you are constantly getting ahead of time. You are always more likely to catch a careless mistake by working more slowly than quickly, and among very high-scoring test takers (those who are likely to have lots of time left over), careless errors affect the score more than mastery of material.

Secret Key #2 - Guessing is not Guesswork

You probably know that guessing is a good idea - unlike other standardized tests, there is no penalty for getting a wrong answer. Even if you have no idea about a question, you still have a 20-25% chance of getting it right.

Most test takers do not understand the impact that proper guessing can have on their score. Unless you score extremely high, guessing will significantly contribute to your final score.

Monkeys Take the Test

What most test takers don't realize is that to insure that 20-25% chance, you have to guess randomly. If you put 20 monkeys in a room to take this test, assuming they answered once per question and behaved themselves, on average they would get 20-25% of the questions correct. Put 20 test takers in the room, and the average will be much lower among guessed questions. Why?

1. The test writers intentionally write deceptive answer choices that "look" right. A test taker has no idea about a question, so picks the "best looking" answer, which is often wrong. The monkey has no idea what looks good and what doesn't, so will consistently be lucky about 20-25% of the time.
2. Test takers will eliminate answer choices from the guessing pool based on a hunch or intuition. Simple but correct answers often get excluded, leaving a 0% chance of being correct. The monkey has no clue, and often gets lucky with the best choice.

This is why the process of elimination endorsed by most test courses is flawed and detrimental to your performance- test takers don't guess, they make an ignorant stab in the dark that is usually worse than random.

$5 Challenge

Let me introduce one of the most valuable ideas of this course- the $5 challenge:

You only mark your "best guess" if you are willing to bet $5 on it.
You only eliminate choices from guessing if you are willing to bet $5 on it.

Why $5? Five dollars is an amount of money that is small yet not insignificant, and can really add up fast (20 questions could cost you $100). Likewise, each answer choice on one question of the test will have a small impact on your overall score, but it can really add up to a lot of points in the end.

The process of elimination IS valuable. The following shows your chance of guessing it right:

If you eliminate wrong answer choices until only this many remain:	Chance of getting it correct:
1	100%
2	50%
3	33%

However, if you accidentally eliminate the right answer or go on a hunch for an incorrect answer, your chances drop dramatically: to 0%. By guessing among all the answer choices, you are GUARANTEED to have a shot at the right answer.
That's why the $5 test is so valuable- if you give up the advantage and safety of a pure guess, it had better be worth the risk.

What we still haven't covered is how to be sure that whatever guess you make is truly random. Here's the easiest way:

Always pick the first answer choice among those remaining.

Such a technique means that you have decided, **before you see a single test question**, exactly how you are going to guess- and since the order of choices tells you nothing about which one is correct, this guessing technique is perfectly random.

This section is not meant to scare you away from making educated guesses or eliminating choices- you just need to define when a choice is worth eliminating. The $5 test, along with a pre-defined random guessing strategy, is the best way to make sure you reap all of the benefits of guessing.

Secret Key #3 - Practice Smarter, Not Harder

Many test takers delay the test preparation process because they dread the awful amounts of practice time they think necessary to succeed on the test. We have refined an effective method that will take you only a fraction of the time.

There are a number of "obstacles" in your way to succeed. Among these are answering questions, finishing in time, and mastering test-taking strategies. All must be executed on the day of the test at peak performance, or your score will suffer. The test is a mental marathon that has a large impact on your future.

Just like a marathon runner, it is important to work your way up to the full challenge. So first you just worry about questions, and then time, and finally strategy:

Success Strategy

1. Find a good source for practice tests.
2. If you are willing to make a larger time investment, consider using more than one study guide- often the different approaches of multiple authors will help you "get" difficult concepts.
3. Take a practice test with no time constraints, with all study helps "open book." Take your time with questions and focus on applying strategies.
4. Take a practice test with time constraints, with all guides "open book."
5. Take a final practice test with no open material and time limits

If you have time to take more practice tests, just repeat step 5. By gradually exposing yourself to the full rigors of the test environment, you will condition your mind to the stress of test day and maximize your success.

Secret Key #4 - Prepare, Don't Procrastinate

Let me state an obvious fact: if you take the test three times, you will get three different scores. This is due to the way you feel on test day, the level of preparedness you have, and, despite the test writers' claims to the contrary, some tests WILL be easier for you than others.

Since your future depends so much on your score, you should maximize your chances of success. In order to maximize the likelihood of success, you've got to prepare in advance. This means taking practice tests and spending time learning the information and test taking strategies you will need to succeed.

Never take the test as a "practice" test, expecting that you can just take it again if you need to. Feel free to take sample tests on your own, but when you go to take the official test, be prepared, be focused, and do your best the first time!

Secret Key #5 - Test Yourself

Everyone knows that time is money. There is no need to spend too much of your time or too little of your time preparing for the test. You should only spend as much of your precious time preparing as is necessary for you to get the score you need.

Once you have taken a practice test under real conditions of time constraints, then you will know if you are ready for the test or not.

If you have scored extremely high the first time that you take the practice test, then there is not much point in spending countless hours studying. You are already there.

Benchmark your abilities by retaking practice tests and seeing how much you have improved. Once you score high enough to guarantee success, then you are ready.

If you have scored well below where you need, then knuckle down and begin studying in earnest. Check your improvement regularly through the use of practice tests under real conditions. Above all, don't worry, panic, or give up. The key is perseverance!

Then, when you go to take the test, remain confident and remember how well you did on the practice tests. If you can score high enough on a practice test, then you can do the same on the real thing.

General Strategies

The most important thing you can do is to ignore your fears and jump into the test immediately- do not be overwhelmed by any strange-sounding terms. You have to jump into the test like jumping into a pool- all at once is the easiest way.

Make Predictions
As you read and understand the question, try to guess what the answer will be. Remember that several of the answer choices are wrong, and once you begin reading them, your mind will immediately become cluttered with answer choices designed to throw you off. Your mind is typically the most focused immediately after you have read the question and digested its contents. If you can, try to predict what the correct answer will be. You may be surprised at what you can predict.

Quickly scan the choices and see if your prediction is in the listed answer choices. If it is, then you can be quite confident that you have the right answer. It still won't hurt to check the other answer choices, but most of the time, you've got it!

Answer the Question

It may seem obvious to only pick answer choices that answer the question, but the test writers can create some excellent answer choices that are wrong. Don't pick an answer just because it sounds right, or you believe it to be true. It MUST answer the question. Once you've made your selection, always go back and check it against the question and make sure that you didn't misread the question, and the answer choice does answer the question posed.

Benchmark

After you read the first answer choice, decide if you think it sounds correct or not. If it doesn't, move on to the next answer choice. If it does, mentally mark that answer choice. This doesn't mean that you've definitely selected it as your answer choice, it just means that it's the best you've seen thus far. Go ahead and read the next choice. If the next choice is worse than the one you've already selected, keep going to the next answer choice. If the next choice is better than the choice you've already selected, mentally mark the new answer choice as your best guess.

The first answer choice that you select becomes your standard. Every other answer choice must be benchmarked against that standard. That choice is correct until proven otherwise by another answer choice beating it out. Once you've decided that no other answer choice seems as good, do one final check to ensure that your answer choice answers the question posed.

Valid Information

Don't discount any of the information provided in the question. Every piece of information may be necessary to determine the correct answer. None of the information in the question is there to throw you off (while the answer choices will certainly have information to throw you off). If two seemingly unrelated topics are discussed, don't ignore either. You can be confident there is a relationship, or it wouldn't be included in the question, and you are probably going to have to determine what is that relationship to find the answer.

Avoid "Fact Traps"

Don't get distracted by a choice that is factually true. Your search is for the answer that answers the question. Stay focused and don't fall for an answer that is true but incorrect. Always go back to the question and make sure you're choosing an answer that actually answers the question and is not just a true statement. An answer can be factually correct, but it MUST answer the question asked. Additionally, two answers can both be seemingly correct, so be sure to read all of the answer choices, and make sure that you get the one that BEST answers the question.

Milk the Question

Some of the questions may throw you completely off. They might deal with a subject you have not been exposed to, or one that you haven't reviewed in years. While your lack of knowledge about the subject will be a hindrance, the question itself can give you many clues that will help you find the correct answer. Read the question carefully and look for clues. Watch particularly for adjectives and nouns describing difficult terms or words that you don't recognize. Regardless of if you completely understand a word or not, replacing it with a synonym either provided or one you more familiar with may help you to understand what the questions are asking. Rather than wracking your mind about specific detailed information concerning a difficult term or word, try to use mental substitutes that are easier to understand.

The Trap of Familiarity

Don't just choose a word because you recognize it. On difficult questions, you may not recognize a number of words in the answer choices. The test writers don't put "make-believe" words on the test; so don't think that just because you only recognize all the words in one answer choice means that answer choice must be correct. If you only recognize words in one answer choice, then focus on that one. Is it correct? Try your best to determine if it is correct. If it is, that is great, but if it doesn't, eliminate it. Each word and answer choice you eliminate increases your chances of getting the question correct, even if you then have to guess among the unfamiliar choices.

Eliminate Answers

Eliminate choices as soon as you realize they are wrong. But be careful! Make sure you consider all of the possible answer choices. Just because one appears right, doesn't mean that the next one won't be even better! The test writers will usually put more than one good answer choice for every question, so read all of them. Don't worry if you are stuck between two that seem right. By getting down to just two remaining possible choices, your odds are now 50/50. Rather than wasting too much time, play the odds. You are guessing, but guessing wisely, because you've been able to knock out some of the answer choices that you know are wrong. If you are eliminating choices and realize that the last answer choice you are left with is also obviously wrong, don't panic. Start over and consider each choice again. There may easily be something that you missed the first time and will realize on the second pass.

Tough Questions

If you are stumped on a problem or it appears too hard or too difficult, don't waste time. Move on! Remember though, if you can quickly check for obviously incorrect answer choices, your chances of guessing correctly are greatly improved. Before you completely give up, at least try to knock out a couple of possible answers. Eliminate what you can and then guess at the remaining answer choices before moving on.

Brainstorm

If you get stuck on a difficult question, spend a few seconds quickly brainstorming. Run through the complete list of possible answer choices. Look at each choice and ask yourself, "Could this answer the question satisfactorily?" Go through each answer choice and consider it independently of the other. By systematically going through all possibilities, you may find something that you would otherwise overlook. Remember that when you get stuck, it's important to try to keep moving.

Read Carefully

Understand the problem. Read the question and answer choices carefully. Don't miss the question because you misread the terms. You have plenty of time to read each question thoroughly and make sure you understand what is being asked. Yet a happy medium must be attained, so don't waste too much time. You must read carefully, but efficiently.

Face Value

When in doubt, use common sense. Always accept the situation in the problem at face value. Don't read too much into it. These problems will not require you to make huge leaps of logic. The test writers aren't trying to throw you off with a cheap trick. If you have to go beyond creativity and make a leap of logic in order to have an answer choice answer the question, then you should look at the other answer choices. Don't overcomplicate the problem by creating theoretical relationships or explanations that will warp time or space. These are normal problems rooted in reality. It's just that the applicable relationship or explanation may not be readily apparent and you have to figure things out. Use your common sense to interpret anything that isn't clear.

Prefixes
If you're having trouble with a word in the question or answer choices, try dissecting it. Take advantage of every clue that the word might include. Prefixes and suffixes can be a huge help. Usually they allow you to determine a basic meaning. Pre- means before, post- means after, pro - is positive, de- is negative. From these prefixes and suffixes, you can get an idea of the general meaning of the word and try to put it into context. Beware though of any traps. Just because con is the opposite of pro, doesn't necessarily mean congress is the opposite of progress!

Hedge Phrases
Watch out for critical "hedge" phrases, such as likely, may, can, will often, sometimes, often, almost, mostly, usually, generally, rarely, sometimes. Question writers insert these hedge phrases to cover every possibility. Often an answer choice will be wrong simply because it leaves no room for exception. Avoid answer choices that have definitive words like "exactly," and "always".

Switchback Words
Stay alert for "switchbacks". These are the words and phrases frequently used to alert you to shifts in thought. The most common switchback word is "but". Others include although, however, nevertheless, on the other hand, even though, while, in spite of, despite, regardless of.

New Information
Correct answer choices will rarely have completely new information included. Answer choices typically are straightforward reflections of the material asked about and will directly relate to the question. If a new piece of information is included in an answer choice that doesn't even seem to relate to the topic being asked about, then that answer choice is likely incorrect. All of the information needed to answer the question is usually provided for you, and so you should not have to make guesses that are unsupported or choose answer choices that require unknown information that cannot be reasoned on its own.

Time Management
On technical questions, don't get lost on the technical terms. Don't spend too much time on any one question. If you don't know what a term means, then since you don't have a dictionary, odds are you aren't going to get much further. You should immediately recognize terms as whether or not you know them. If you don't, work with the other clues that you have, the other answer choices and terms provided, but don't waste too much time trying to figure out a difficult term.

Contextual Clues
Look for contextual clues. An answer can be right but not correct. The contextual clues will help you find the answer that is most right and is correct. Understand the context in which

a phrase or statement is made. This will help you make important distinctions.

Don't Panic
Panicking will not answer any questions for you. Therefore, it isn't helpful. When you first see the question, if your mind goes blank, take a deep breath. Force yourself to mechanically go through the steps of solving the problem and using the strategies you've learned.

Pace Yourself
Don't get clock fever. It's easy to be overwhelmed when you're looking at a page full of questions, your mind is full of random thoughts and feeling confused, and the clock is ticking down faster than you would like. Calm down and maintain the pace that you have set for yourself. As long as you are on track by monitoring your pace, you are guaranteed to have enough time for yourself. When you get to the last few minutes of the test, it may seem like you won't have enough time left, but if you only have as many questions as you should have left at that point, then you're right on track!

Answer Selection
The best way to pick an answer choice is to eliminate all of those that are wrong, until only one is left and confirm that is the correct answer. Sometimes though, an answer choice may immediately look right. Be careful! Take a second to make sure that the other choices are not equally obvious. Don't make a hasty mistake. There are only two times that you should stop before checking other answers. First is when you are positive that the answer choice you have selected is correct. Second is when time is almost out and you have to make a quick guess!

Check Your Work
Since you will probably not know every term listed and the answer to every question, it is important that you get credit for the ones that you do know. Don't miss any questions through careless mistakes. If at all possible, try to take a second to look back over your answer selection and make sure you've selected the correct answer choice and haven't made a costly careless mistake (such as marking an answer choice that you didn't mean to mark). This quick double check should more than pay for itself in caught mistakes for the time it costs.

Beware of Directly Quoted Answers
Sometimes an answer choice will repeat word for word a portion of the question or reference section. However, beware of such exact duplication – it may be a trap! More than likely, the correct choice will paraphrase or summarize a point, rather than being exactly the same wording.

Slang
Scientific sounding answers are better than slang ones. An answer choice that begins "To compare the outcomes…" is much more likely to be correct than one that begins "Because some people insisted…"

Extreme Statements
Avoid wild answers that throw out highly controversial ideas that are proclaimed as established fact. An answer choice that states the "process should be used in certain situations, if…" is much more likely to be correct than one that states the "process should be discontinued completely." The first is a calm rational statement and doesn't even make a

definitive, uncompromising stance, using a hedge word "if" to provide wiggle room, whereas the second choice is a radical idea and far more extreme.

Answer Choice Families

When you have two or more answer choices that are direct opposites or parallels, one of them is usually the correct answer. For instance, if one answer choice states "x increases" and another answer choice states "x decreases" or "y increases," then those two or three answer choices are very similar in construction and fall into the same family of answer choices. A family of answer choices is when two or three answer choices are very similar in construction, and yet often have a directly opposite meaning. Usually the correct answer choice will be in that family of answer choices. The "odd man out" or answer choice that doesn't seem to fit the parallel construction of the other answer choices is more likely to be incorrect.

Special Report: Additional Bonus Material

Due to our efforts to try to keep this book to a manageable length, we've created a link that will give you access to all of your additional bonus material.

Please visit http://www.mometrix.com/bonus948/clepnaturalsci to access the information.